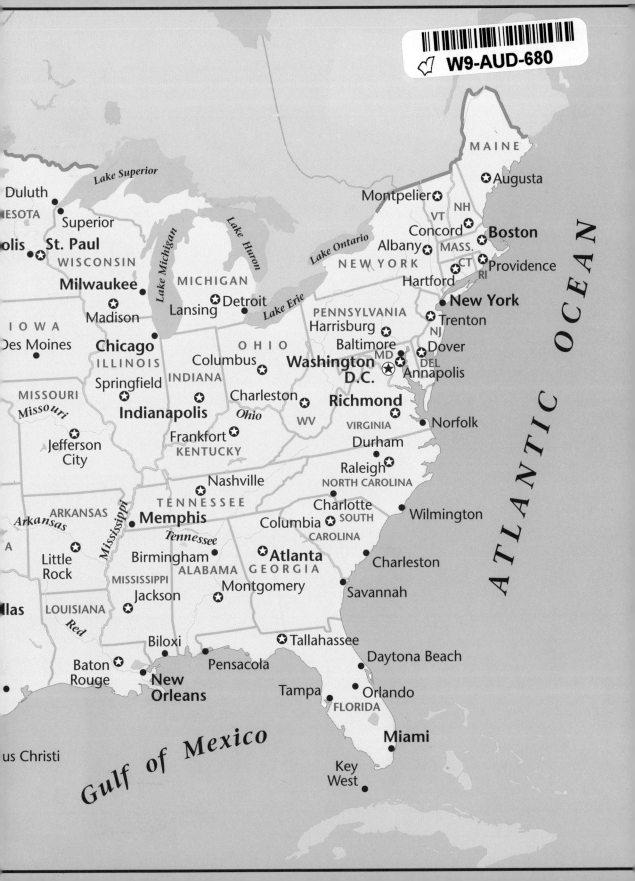

135.00

Junior Worldmark Encyclopedia of the States

DATE DUE			

Junior Worldmark Encyclopedia of the

States

Third Edition

VOLUME

Indiana to Nebraska

GALE GROUP

THOMSON LEARNING

Detroit • New York • San Diego • San Francisco
Boston • New Haven, Conn. • Waterville, Maine
London • Munich

JUNIOR WORLDMARK ENCYCLOPEDIA OF THE STATES, THIRD EDITION

Timothy L. Gall and Susan Bevan Gall, *Editors*
Karen Hanson, *Associate Editor*
Barbara Dickinson, Jennifer Jackson, Sarah Kunz, and Jennifer Wallace, *Assistant Editors*
Brian Rajewski, Deborah Rutti, and Bram Lambrecht, *Graphics and Layout*
Janet Fenn and Matthew Markovich, *Proofreaders*
University of Akron Laboratory for Cartographic and
    Spatial Analysis, Joseph W. Stoll, Supervisor;
    Scott Raypholtz, Mike Meger, *Cartographers*

U•X•L Staff

Allison McNeill, *U•X•L Senior Editor*
Carol DeKane Nagel, *U•X•L Managing Editor*
Thomas L. Romig, *U•X•L Publisher*
Evi Seoud, *Assistant Manager, Composition Purchasing and Electronic Prepress*
Rita Wimberley, *Senior Buyer*
Mary Krzewinski, *Art Director*
Mike Logusz, *Graphic Artist*

Library of Congress Cataloging-in-Publication Data

Junior Worldmark encyclopedia of the states / [Timothy L. Gall and Susan Bevan Gall, editors]. -- 3rd ed.
        p. cm.
    Includes bibliographical references and index.
    Contents : v. 1. Alabama to Illinois -- v. 2. Indiana to Nebraska -- v. 3. Nevada to South Dakota -- v. 4. Tennessee to Wyoming
    ISBN 0-7876-5376-4 (set) -- ISBN 0-7876-5377-2 (v. l) -- ISBN 0-7876-5378-0 (v. 2) -- ISBN 0-7876-5379-9 (v. 3) -- ISBN 0-7876-5380-2 (v. 4)
    1. United States--Encyclopedias, Juvenile. 2. U.S. states--Encyclopedias, Juvenile.
    [1. United States--Encyclopedias.] I. Gall, Timothy L. II. Gall, Susan B.

E156.J86 2001
973'.03--dc21
                                                                    2010041056

CONTENTS

READER'S GUIDE

Junior Worldmark Encyclopedia of the States, Third Edition, presents profiles of the 50 states of the nation, the District of Columbia, Puerto Rico, and the U.S. dependencies, arranged alphabetically in four volumes. *Junior Worldmark* is based on the fifth edition of the reference work, *Worldmark Encyclopedia of the States.* The *Worldmark* design organizes facts and data about every state in a common structure. Every profile contains a map, showing the state and its location in the nation.

For this third edition of *Junior Worldmark,* facts were updated and many new photographs were added. While the second edition photographs were chosen to illustrate economic activity in the state, new photographs for this edition were selected to feature notable citizens. In addition, a Population Profile was added to each state entry giving the breakdown of the state's population by race as enumerated by Census 2000. For the first time in history, respondents to Census 2000 were given the opportunity to select one or more race categories to indicate their racial identity. The U.S. Census Bureau reported data for each state in seven race categories: White *alone;* Black or African American *alone;* American Indian and Alaska Native *alone;* Asian *alone;* Native Hawaiian and Other Pacific Islander *alone;* Some other race *alone;* and Two or more races. About 98% of all respondents reported only one race. The population profile gives users of *Junior Worldmark* access to the latest population data for the states.

Each state's political history is documented in the updated table listing the governors who have served the state since the founding of the nation. As with the first and second editions, recognition is due to the many professional photographers, tourist bureaus, convention centers, press offices, and state agencies that contributed the photographs that illustrate this encyclopedia.

Web sites listed at the end of the Bibliography for each state article have been verified and updated. An extensive survey of available sites was undertaken in May 2001 and only those with information relevant to the needs of students were chosen for inclusion.

Attention is also drawn to the many article reviewers listed at the end of this Reader's Guide. The reviewers contributed insights, updates, and substantive additions that were instrumental to the creation of this work. The editors are extremely grateful for the time and effort these distinguished reviewers devoted to improving the quality of this encyclopedia.

Sources

Due to the broad scope of this encyclopedia many sources were consulted in compiling the information and statistics presented in these volumes. Of primary importance were the publications of the U.S. Bureau of the Census. The most recent agricultural statistics on crops and livestock were obtained from files posted by the U.S. Department of Agriculture on its gopher server and its world-wide web site at http://www.econ.ag.gov. Finally, many fact sheets, booklets, and state statistical abstracts were used to update data not collected by the federal government.

Profile Features

The *Junior Worldmark* structure—40 numbered headings—allows student researchers to compare two or more states in a variety of ways.

Each state profile begins by listing the origin of the state name, its nickname, the capital, the date it entered the union, the state song and motto, and a description of the state coat of arms. The profile also presents a picture and textual description of both the state seal and the state flag (a key to the flag color symbols appears on page xii of each volume). Next, a listing of the official state animal, bird, fish, flower, tree, gem, etc. is given. The introductory information ends with the standard time given by time zone in relation to Greenwich mean time (GMT). The world is divided into 24 time zones, each one hour apart. The Greenwich meridian, which is 0 degrees, passes through Greenwich, England, a suburb of London. Greenwich is at the center of the initial time zone, known as Greenwich mean time (GMT). All times given are converted from noon in this zone. The time reported for the state is the official time zone.

The body of each country's profile is arranged in 40 numbered headings as follows:

[1] LOCATION AND SIZE. The state is located on the North American continent. Statistics are given on area and boundary length. Size comparisons are made to the other 50 states of the United States.

[2] TOPOGRAPHY. Dominant geographic features including terrain and major rivers and lakes are described.

[3] CLIMATE. Temperature and rainfall are given for the various regions of the state in both English and metric units.

[4] PLANTS AND ANIMALS. Described here are the plants and animals native to the state.

[5] ENVIRONMENTAL PROTECTION. Destruction of natural resources—forests, water supply, air—is described here. Statistics on solid waste production, hazardous waste sites, and endangered and extinct species are also included.

[6] POPULATION. Census 2000 statistics, including the seven categories identifying race introduced with the 2000 census of population, are provided. Population density and major urban populations are summarized.

[7] ETHNIC GROUPS. The major ethnic groups are ranked in percentages. Where appropriate, some description of the influence or history of ethnicity is provided.

[8] LANGUAGES. The regional dialects of the state are summarized as well as the number of people speaking languages other than English at home.

[9] **RELIGIONS.** The population is broken down according to religion and/or denominations.

[10] **TRANSPORTATION.** Statistics on roads, railways, waterways, and air traffic, along with a listing of key ports for trade and travel, are provided.

[11] **HISTORY.** Includes a concise summary of the state's history from ancient times (where appropriate) to the present.

[12] **STATE GOVERNMENT.** The form of government is described, and the process of governing is summarized. A table listing the state governors, updated to 2000, accompanies each entry.

[13] **POLITICAL PARTIES.** Describes the significant political parties through history, where appropriate, and the influential parties in the mid-1990s.

[14] **LOCAL GOVERNMENT.** The system of local government structure is summarized.

[15] **JUDICIAL SYSTEM.** Structure of the court system and the jurisdiction of courts in each category is provided. Crime rates as reported by the Federal Bureau of Investigation (FBI) are also included.

[16] **MIGRATION.** Population shifts since the end of World War II are summarized.

[17] **ECONOMY.** This section presents the key elements of the economy. Major industries and employment figures are also summarized.

[18] **INCOME.** Personal income and the poverty level are given as is the state's ranking among the 50 states in per person income.

[19] **INDUSTRY.** Key industries are listed, and important aspects of industrial development are described.

[20] **LABOR.** Statistics are given on the civilian labor force, including numbers of workers, leading areas of employment, and unemployment figures.

[21] **AGRICULTURE.** Statistics on key agricultural crops, market share, and total farm income are provided.

[22] **DOMESTICATED ANIMALS.** Statistics on livestock—cattle, hogs, sheep, etc.—and the land area devoted to raising them are given.

[23] **FISHING.** The relative significance of fishing to the state is provided, with statistics on fish and seafood products.

[24] **FORESTRY.** Land area classified as forest is given, along with a listing of key forest products and a description of government policy toward forest land.

[25] **MINING.** Description of mineral deposits and statistics on related mining activity and export are provided.

[26] **ENERGY AND POWER.** Description of the state's power resources, including electricity produced and oil reserves and production, are provided.

[27] **COMMERCE.** A summary of the amount of wholesale trade, retail trade, and receipts of service establishments is given.

[28] PUBLIC FINANCE. Revenues, expenditures, and total and per person debt are provided.

[29] TAXATION. The state's tax system is explained.

[30] HEALTH. Statistics on and description of such public health factors as disease and suicide rates, principal causes of death, numbers of hospitals and medical facilities appear here. Information is also provided on the percentage of citizens without health insurance within each state.

[31] HOUSING. Housing shortages and government programs to build housing are described. Statistics on numbers of dwellings and median home values are provided.

[32] EDUCATION. Statistical data on educational achievement and primary and secondary schools is given. Per person state spending on primary and secondary education is also given. Major universities are listed, and government programs to foster education are described.

[33] ARTS. A summary of the state's major cultural institutions is provided together with the amount of federal and state funds designated to the arts.

[34] LIBRARIES AND MUSEUMS. The number of libraries, their holdings, and their yearly circulation is provided. Major museums are listed.

[35] COMMUNICATIONS. The state of telecommunications (television, radio, and telephone) is summarized. Activity related to the Internet is reported where available.

[36] PRESS. Major daily and Sunday newspapers are listed together with data on their circulations.

[37] TOURISM, TRAVEL, AND RECREATION. Under this heading, the student will find a summary of the importance of tourism to the state, and factors affecting the tourism industry. Key tourist attractions are listed.

[38] SPORTS. The major sports teams in the state, both professional and collegiate, are summarized.

[39] FAMOUS PEOPLE. In this section, some of the best-known citizens of the state are listed. When a person is noted in a state that is not the state of his of her birth, the birthplace is given.

[40] BIBLIOGRAPHY. The bibliographic and web site listings at the end of each profile are provided as a guide for further reading.

Because many terms used in this encyclopedia will be new to students, each volume includes a glossary and a list of abbreviations and acronyms. A keyword index to all four volumes appears in Volume 4.

Acknowledgments

Junior Worldmark Encyclopedia of the States, Third Edition, draws on the fifth edition of the *Worldmark Encyclopedia of the States.* Readers are directed to that work for a complete list of contributors, too numerous to list here. Special acknowledgment goes to the government officials throughout the nation who gave their cooperation to this project.

Reviewers

The following individuals reviewed state articles for this or previous editions. In all cases the reviewers added important information and updated facts that might have gone unnoticed. The reviewers were also instrumental in suggesting changes and improvements.

Patricia L. Harris, Executive Director, Alabama Public Library Service

Patience Frederiksen, Head, Government Publications, Alaska State Library

Jacqueline L. Miller, Curator of Education, Arizona State Capitol Museum

John A. Murphey, Jr., State Librarian, Arkansas State Library

Eugene Hainer, School Library Media Consultant, Colorado State Library

Susan Cormier, Connecticut State Library

Dr. Annette Woolard, Director of Development, Historical Society of Delaware

Reference Staff, State Library of Florida

Cheryl Rogers, Consultant, Georgia Department of Education, Public Library Services

Lorna J. T. Peck, School Library Services, Specialist, State of Hawaii Department of Education

Marcia J. Beckwith, Director, Information Services/Library, Centennial High School, Boise, Idaho

Karen McIlrath-Muskopf, Youth Services Consultant, Illinois State Library

Cordell Svengalis, Social Science Consultant, Iowa Department of Education

Marc Galbraith, Director of Reference Services, Kansas State Library

James C. Klotter, State Historian, Kentucky Historical Society

Virginia R. Smith, Head, Louisiana Section, State Library of Louisiana

Ben Keating, Division Director, Maine State Library

Patricia V. Melville, Director of Reference Services, Maryland State Archives

Brian Donoghue, Reference Librarian, Massachusetts Board of Library Commissioners

Denise E. Carlson, Head of Reference, Minnesota Historical Society

Ronnie Smith, Reference Specialist, Mississippi Library Commission

Darlene Staffeldt, Director, Statewide Library Resources, Montana State Library

Rod Wagner, Director, Nebraska Library Commission

Reference Services and Archives Staff, Nevada State Library & Archives

Kendall F. Wiggin, State Librarian, New Hampshire State Library

John H. Livingstone, Acting Assistant Commissioner and State Librarian, New Jersey State Library

Robert J. Torrez, State Historian, New Mexico State Records and Archives

R. Allan Carter, Senior Librarian, New York State Library

Staff, Information Services and State Archives Research, State Library of North Carolina

Doris Daugherty, Assistant State Librarian, North Dakota State Library

Carol Brieck and Audrey Hall, Reference Librarians, State Library of Ohio

Audrey Wolfe-Clark, Edmond, Oklahoma

Paul Gregorio, Assistant Professor of Education, Portland State University, Portland, Oregon

Alice L. Lubrecht, Acting Bureau Director, State Library of Pennsylvania

Barbara Weaver, Director, Department of State Library Services, Rhode Island

Michele M. Reid, Director of Public Services, South Dakota State Library

Dr. Wayne C. Moore, Archivist, Tennessee State Library and Archives

Douglas E. Barnett, Managing Editor, New Handbook of Texas, Texas State Historical Association

Lou Reinwand, Director of Information Services, Utah State Library

Paul J. Donovan, Senior Reference Librarian, Vermont Department of Libraries

Catherine Mishler, Head, Reference, Library of Virginia

Gayle Palmer, Senior Library Information Specialist, Washington/Northwest Collections, Washington State Library

Karen Goff, Head of Reference, West Virginia Library Commission

Richard L. Roe, Research Analyst, Wisconsin Legislative Reference Bureau

Priscilla Golden, Principal Librarian, Wyoming State Library

Staff, Washingtoniana Division, Martin Luther King Memorial Library, Washington, D.C.

Jean Hanson, MLS, Consultant, web sites.

Advisors

The following persons were consulted on the content and structure of this encyclopedia. Their insights, opinions, and suggestions led to many enhancements and improvements in the presentation of the material.

Mary Alice Anderson, Media Specialist, Winona Middle School, Winona, Minnesota

Pat Baird, Library Media Specialist and Department Chair, Shaker Heights Middle School, Shaker Heights, Ohio

Pat Fagel, Library Media Specialist, Shaker Heights Middle School, Shaker Heights, Ohio

Nancy Guidry, Young Adult Librarian, Santa Monica Public Library, Santa Monica, California

Ann West LaPrise, Children's Librarian, Redford Branch, Detroit Public Library, Detroit, Michigan

Nancy C. Nieman, Teacher, U.S. History, Social Studies, Journalism, Delta Middle School, Muncie, Indiana

Madeleine Obrock, Library Media Specialist, Woodbury Elementary School, Shaker Heights, Ohio

Ernest L. O'Roark, Teacher, Social Studies, Martin Luther King Middle School, Germantown, Maryland

Ellen Stepanian, Director of Library Services, Shaker Heights Board of Education, Shaker Heights, Ohio

Mary Strouse, Library Media Specialist, Woodbury Elementary School, Shaker Heights, Ohio

Comments and Suggestions

We welcome your comments on the *Junior Worldmark Encyclopedia of the States, Third Edition,* as well as your suggestions for features to be included in future editions. Please write to: Editors, *Junior Worldmark Encyclopedia of the States,* U•X•L, 27500 Drake Road, Farmington Hills, Michigan 48331-3535; or call toll-free: 1-800-877-4253.

Guide to State Articles

All information contained within a state article is uniformly keyed by means of a boxed number to the left of the subject headings. A heading such as "Population," for example, carries the same key numeral (6) in every article. Therefore, to find information about the population of Alabama, consult the table of contents for the page number where the Alabama article begins and look for section 6.

Introductory matter for each state includes: Origin of state name
Nickname
Capital
Date and order of statehood
Song
Motto
Flag
Official seal
Symbols (animal, tree, flower, etc.)
Time zone.

Flag color symbols

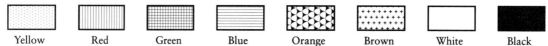

| Yellow | Red | Green | Blue | Orange | Brown | White | Black |

Sections listed numerically

Alphabetical listing of sections

Explanation of symbols

A fiscal split year is indicated by a stroke (e.g. 1999/00).
Note that 1 billion = 1,000 million = 10^9.
The use of a small dash (e.g., 1998–99) normally signifies the
    full period of calendar years covered (including the end year indicated).

INDIANA

State of Indiana

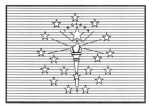

ORIGIN OF STATE NAME: Named "land of Indians" for the many Indian tribes that formerly lived in the state.

NICKNAME: The Hoosier State.

CAPITAL: Indianapolis.

ENTERED UNION: 11 December 1816 (19th).

SONG: "On the Banks of the Wabash, Far Away."

MOTTO: The Crossroads of America.

FLAG: A flaming torch representing liberty is surrounded by 19 gold stars against a blue background. The word "Indiana" is above the flame.

OFFICIAL SEAL: In a pioneer setting, a farmer fells a tree while a buffalo flees from the forest and across the prairie; in the background, the sun sets over distant hills. The words "Seal of the State of Indiana 1816" surround the scene.

BIRD: Cardinal.

FLOWER: Peony.

TREE: Tulip tree (yellow poplar).

STONE: Indiana limestone.

POEM: "Indiana."

TIME: 7 AM EST = noon GMT; 6 AM CST = noon GMT.

1 LOCATION AND SIZE

Situated in the eastern north-central US, Indiana is the smallest of the 12 midwestern states and ranks 38th in size among the 50 states. Indiana's total area is 36,185 square miles (93,720 square kilometers). The state extends about 160 miles (257 kilometers) east-west and about 280 miles (451 kilometers) north-south. The total boundary length of Indiana is 1,696 miles (2,729 kilometers).

2 TOPOGRAPHY

Indiana has two principal types of terrain: slightly rolling land in the northern half of the state, and rugged hills in the southern, extending to the Ohio River. The highest point in the state is 1,257 feet (383 meters) above sea level. The lowest point, on the Ohio River, is 320 feet (98 meters).

Four-fifths of the state's land is drained by the Wabash River and by its tributaries, the White, Eel, Mississinewa, and Tippecanoe rivers. The northern region is drained by the Maumee, Calumet, and Kankakee rivers. In the southwest, the two White River forks empty into the Wabash, and in the southeast, the Whitewater River flows into the Ohio.

In addition to Lake Michigan on the northwestern border, there are more than 400 lakes in the northern part of the state. The largest lakes include Wawasee, Maxinkuckee, Freeman, and Shafer. There are mineral springs at French Lick and West Baden in Orange County.

3 CLIMATE

Temperatures vary from the extreme north to the extreme south of the state. The annual mean temperature is 49°F–58°F (9°C–12°C) in the north and 57°F (14°C) in the south. The average temperatures in January range between 17°F (–8°C) and 35°F (2°C). Average temperatures during July vary from 63°F (17°C) to 88°F (31°C). Rainfall is distributed fairly evenly throughout the year, although drought sometimes occurs in the southern region. The average annual precipitation in the state is 40 inches (102 centimeters), ranging from about 35 inches (89 centimeters) near Lake Michigan to 45 inches (114 centimeters) along the Ohio River. The annual snowfall in Indiana averages less than 22 inches (56 centimeters).

4 PLANTS AND ANIMALS

There are 124 native tree species, including 17 varieties of oak, as well as black walnut, sycamore, and the tulip tree (yellow poplar), the state tree. Fruit trees— apple, cherry, peach, and pear—are common. American elderberry and bittersweet are common shrubs, while various jack-in-the-pulpits and spring beauties are among the indigenous wildflowers. The peony is the state flower. Mountain laurel

Indiana Population Profile

Total population in 2000:	6,080,485
Population change, 1990–2000:	9.7%
Hispanic or Latino†:	3.5%
Population by race	
One race:	98.8%
White:	87.5%
Black or African American:	8.4%%
American Indian/Alaska Native:	0.3%
Asian:	1.0%
Native Hawaiian/Pacific Islander:	—
Some other race:	1.6%
Two or more races:	1.2%

Population by Age Group

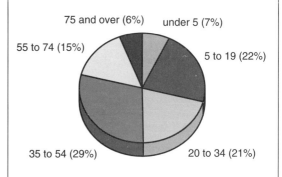

75 and over (6%)   under 5 (7%)
55 to 74 (15%)
5 to 19 (22%)
35 to 54 (29%)
20 to 34 (21%)

Top Cities by Population

City	Population	% change 1990–2000
Indianapolis	791,926	6.7
Fort Wayne	205,727	18.9
Evansville	121,582	–3.7
South Bend	107,789	2.2
Gary	102,746	–11.9
Hammond	83,048	–1.4
Bloomington	69,291	14.3
Muncie	67,430	–5.1
Anderson	59,734	.5
Terre Haute	59,614	3.7

Notes: †A person of Hispanic or Latino origin may be of any race. NA indicates that data are not available.
Sources: U.S. Census Bureau. Public Information Office. *Demographic Profiles.* [Online] Available http://www.census.gov/Press-Release/www/2001/demoprofile.html. Accessed June 1, 2001. U.S. Census Bureau. *Census 2000: Redistricting Data.* Press release issued by the Redistricting Data Office. Washington, D.C., March, 2001.

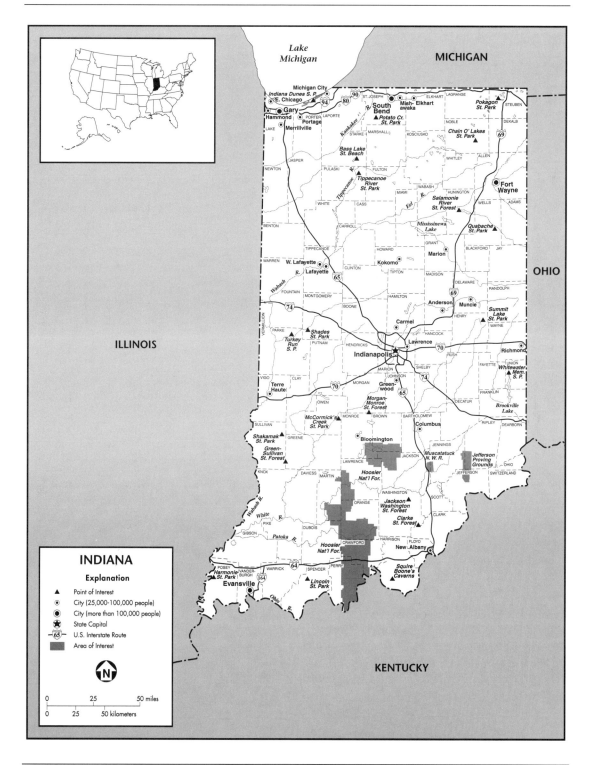

is considered threatened, and the prairie white-fringed orchid is endangered.

Although the presence of wolves and coyotes has been reported occasionally, the red fox is Indiana's only common carnivorous mammal. Other native mammals include the common cottontail, muskrat, and raccoon. Many waterfowl and marsh birds, including the black duck and great blue heron, inhabit northern Indiana, while the field sparrow, yellow warbler, and red-headed woodpecker nest in central Indiana. Catfish, pike, bass, and sunfish are native to state waters. Among endangered species for which the state provides protection are the bobcat, badger, otter, and big-eared bat.

5 ENVIRONMENTAL PROTECTION

The Indiana Department of Environmental Management (IDEM) was established in 1986, with a legislative order to protect public health through various environmental programs.

In 1990, IDEM spearheaded landmark legislation requiring counties to form solid waste management districts to develop plans for meeting statewide waste reduction goals.

Indiana's Water Pollution Control Board has adopted some of the strictest water quality standards in the nation for more than 90 chemicals, and included almost all water bodies for protection of aquatic life and recreational use. Indiana is the tenth largest producer of hazardous waste in the country. IDEM devotes much attention to identifying, cleaning up, and lessening all forms of toxic contamination.

Some of the state's most serious environmental challenges lie in Lake and Porter counties in northwest Indiana. A century of spills, emissions, and discharges to the environment there require comprehensive, regionally coordinated programs. The Northwest Indiana Remedial Action Plan (RAP) is a three-phased program designed especially for the Grand Calumet River and the Indiana Harbor Ship Canal. Both waterways are heavily contaminated and, if left at their current state, would degrade the waters of Lake Michigan, the primary source of drinking water for the Northwest Indiana area.

6 POPULATION

In 2000, Indiana had a population of over 6 million and ranked 14th in population among the 50 states. The population density was 169.5 persons per square mile (65.4 persons per square kilometer). Of the 1990 census population, 64.9% lived in urban areas and 35.1% resided in rural areas. Indianapolis, the capital and largest city, had a population of 791,926 in 2000. Other cities with their 2000 populations were Fort Wayne, 205,727; Evansville, 121,582; South Bend, 107,789; and Gary, 102,746. Like that of Illinois, 29% of Indiana's population is 19 years of age and younger. The state's median age is nearly identical to the national average of 35.3.

7 ETHNIC GROUPS

Restrictions on foreign immigration and the availability of jobs spurred the migra-

Indiana Population by Race

Census 2000 was the first national census in which the instructions to respondents said, "Mark one or more races." This table shows the number of people who are of one, two, or three or more races. For those claiming two races, the number of people belonging to the various categories is listed. The U.S. government conducts a census of the population every ten years.

	Number	Percent
Total population	6,080,485	100.0
One race	6,004,813	98.8
Two races	71,132	1.2
White *and* Black or African American	19,187	0.3
White *and* American Indian/Alaska Native	18,053	0.3
White *and* Asian	9,131	0.2
White *and* Native Hawaiian/Pacific Islander	843	—
White *and* some other race	15,756	0.3
Black or African American *and* American Indian/Alaska Native	1,883	—
Black or African American *and* Asian	959	—
Black or African American *and* Native Hawaiian/Pacific Islander	156	—
Black or African American *and* some other race	2,432	—
American Indian/Alaska Native *and* Asian	298	—
American Indian/Alaska Native *and* Native Hawaiian/Pacific Islander	30	—
American Indian/Alaska Native *and* some other race	458	—
Asian *and* Native Hawaiian/Pacific Islander	512	—
Asian *and* some other race	1,291	—
Native Hawaiian/Pacific Islander *and* some other race	143	—
Three or more races	4,540	0.1

Source: U.S. Census Bureau. *Census 2000: Redistricting Data.* Press release issued by the Redistricting Data Office. Washington, D.C., March, 2001. A dash (—) indicates that the percent is less than 0.1.

tion of black Americans to Indiana after World War I. By 1997, the state had an estimated 483,500 blacks, representing about 8.2% of the total population. In 1997, approximately 2.3% (136,600) of Indiana's population was of Hispanic origin. That year, Indiana's Asian residents were estimated at 53,400 (0.9%), consisting primarily of Japanese, Koreans, Chinese, Indians, and Vietnamese. In 1997, there were an estimated 14,300 Native Americans (0.2%).

8 LANGUAGES

Most Indiana speech is basically that of the South Midland pioneers from south of the Ohio River, with a transition to North Midland north of Indianapolis.

In 1990, 95.2% of all Hoosiers five years old and older spoke only English at home. Other languages spoken at home (and number of speakers) include Spanish (90,146), German (46,034), French (20,578), and Polish (11,552). Chinese, Indic, Greek, Italian, and Korean were also reported.

9 RELIGIONS

In addition to a sizable Roman Catholic population, the largest Protestant denominations were United Methodist Church, Churches of Christ, American Baptist

The Interstate Exchange encircles the city of Indianapolis.

Churches in USA, Lutheran Church–Missouri Synod, and Presbyterian Church (USA). The estimated Jewish population of the state was 18,000 as of 1994. A group of religious dissidents founded the Pentecostal Church of God at Beaver Dam in 1881. The world headquarters of the church, which had 22,569 adherents in 1990, is now at Anderson.

10 TRANSPORTATION

Indiana's central location in the US and its position between Lake Michigan to the north and the Ohio River to the south gave the state its motto, "The Crossroads of America." Historically, the state took advantage of its strategic location by digging canals to connect Indiana rivers and by building roads and railroads to provide farmers access to national markets. In 1998, there were 37 railroads operating on 4,256 rail miles (6,848 kilometers) of track. Regularly scheduled Amtrak passenger trains served Indianapolis and 13 other stations in the state, with a total of nearly 90,000 riders in Indiana in 1996. The South Shore commuter railroad connects South Bend, Gary, and East Chicago with Chicago, Illinois.

In 1996, Indiana had 1,172 miles (1,886 kilometers) of interstate highways—more than other states of comparable size. In that year, there were 11,293 miles (18,170 kilometers) of state highways and 80,505 miles (129,533 kilometers) of country and municipal roads. In 1997, motor vehicle registrations totaled 5.3 million, including more than 3.2 million passenger cars and over 2 million trucks.

The transport of freight via Lake Michigan and the Ohio River helped to spark Indiana's industrial development. The deepwater port of Burns Harbor on Lake Michigan, which became operational in 1970, provided access to world markets via the St. Lawrence Seaway. Indiana Harbor handled 14.9 million tons of goods in 1998, and the tonnage at the port of Gary was nearly 9.1 million tons. In 1997, there were 675 public and private air facilities in the state. The number of active general aviation aircraft in Indiana was 4,194 in 1996.

11 HISTORY

The first Native Americans to be seen by Europeans in present-day Indiana were probably the Miami and Potawatomi tribes. The first European penetration was made in the 1670s by the French explorers Father Jacques Marquette and Robert Cavelier, Sieur de la Salle. After the founding of Detroit, Michigan, in 1701, the Maumee-Wabash river route to the lower Ohio was discovered. The first French fort was built farther down the Wabash among the Wea tribe, near present-day Lafayette, in 1717.

By 1765, Indiana had fallen to the English. The pre-Revolutionary turmoil in the colonies on the Atlantic was hardly felt in Indiana. However, the region did not escape the Revolutionary War itself. Colonel George Rogers Clark, acting for Virginia, captured Vincennes from a British garrison early in 1779. Following the war, the area northwest of the Ohio River was granted to the new nation by treaty in 1783.

The first US town plotted in Indiana was Clarksville, established in 1784. A government for the region was established by the Continental Congress under the Northwest Ordinance of 1787. Known as the Northwest Territory, it included present-day Indiana, Ohio, Illinois, Michigan, Wisconsin, and part of Minnesota. After continued Native American unrest, General Anthony Wayne was put in command of an enlarged army, which ended the disturbance in 1794 at Fallen Timbers (near Toledo, Ohio).

Statehood

In 1800, as Ohio prepared to enter the Union, the rest of the Northwest Territory was set off and called Indiana Territory, with its capital at Vincennes. After Michigan Territory was detached in 1805, and Illinois Territory in 1809, Indiana assumed its present boundaries (having added about 10 miles to its northern border in 1816). William Henry Harrison was appointed first governor and, with a secretary and three appointed judges, constituted the government of Indiana Territory. When the population totaled 60,000—as it did in 1815—the voters were allowed to elect delegates to write a state constitution and to apply for admission to the Union. Indiana became the 19th state on 11 December 1816.

Photo credit: Northern Indiana Historical Society.

The Oliver chilled plow was developed by James Oliver, an industrialist who came to South Bend, Indiana, in the 1850s. A superior farm plow made of chilled and hardened steel, it revolutionized farming in the later half of the 19th century.

After the War of 1812, new settlers began pouring into the state from the upper South and in fewer numbers from Ohio, Pennsylvania, New York, and New England. In 1816, Thomas Lincoln brought his family from Kentucky, and his son Abe grew up in southern Indiana from age 7 to 21. Unlike most other frontier states, Indiana was settled from south to north. Central and northern Indiana were opened up as land was purchased from the Native Americans. Railroads began to tie Indiana commercially with the East. Irish immigrants dug canals and laid the rails, and German immigrants took up woodworking and farming. Levi Coffin, a Quaker who moved to Fountain City in 1826, operated the Underground Railroad, a network of people dedicated to help escaping slaves from the South.

Civil War

Hoosiers (as Indianans are called) showed considerable sympathy with the South in the 1850s. However, Indiana remained staunchly in the Union under Governor Oliver P. Morton, sending some 200,000 soldiers to the Civil War. The state suffered no battles, but General John Hunt Morgan's Confederate cavalry raided the southeastern sector of Indiana in July 1863.

After the Civil War, small local industries expanded rapidly. Discovery of natural gas in several northeastern counties in 1886, and the resultant low fuel prices, spurred the growth of energy-intensive glass factories. As America became captivated by the automobile, a racetrack for testing cars was built outside Indianapolis in 1908, and the famous 500-mile (805-kilometer) race on Memorial Day weekend began in 1911. Five years earlier, US Steel had constructed a steel plant at the south end of Lake Michigan. The town built by the company to house the workers was called Gary, and it grew rapidly with the help of the company and the onset of World War I.

World Wars

Although many Hoosiers of German and Irish descent favored neutrality when

Indiana Governors: 1816–2001

1816–1822	Johathan Jennings	Dem-Rep	1905–1909	James Franklin Hanly	Republican
1822	Ratliff Boone	Jackson Democrat	1909–1913	Thomas Riley Marshall	Democrat
1822–1825	William Hendricks	Dem-Rep	1913–1917	Samuel Moffett Ralston	Democrat
1825–1831	James Brown Ray	Anti–Jacksonian/Indep	1917–1921	James Putnam Goodrich	Republican
1831–1837	Noah Noble	Nat-Rep/Whig	1921–1924	Warren Terry McCray	Republican
1837–1840	David Wallace	Whig	1924–1925	Emmett Forest Branch	Republican
1840–1843	Samuel Bigger	Whig	1925–1929	Edward L. Jackson	Republican
1843–1848	James Whitcomb	Democrat	1929–1933	Harry Guyer Leslie	Republican
1848–1849	Paris Chipman Dunning	Democrat	1933–1937	Paul Vories McNutt	Democrat
1849–1857	Joseph Albert Wright	Unionist	1937–1941	Mourice Clifford Townsend	Democrat
1857–1860	Ashbel Parsons Willard	Democrat	1941–1945	Henry Frederick Schricker	Democrat
1860–1861	Abram Adams Hammond	Democrat	1945–1949	Ralph Fesler Gates	Republican
1861	Henry Smith Lane	Republican	1949–1953	Henry Frederick Schricker	Democrat
1861–1867	Oliver Hazzard Perry Morton	Republican	1953–1957	George North Craig	Republican
1867–1873	Conrad Baker	Republican	1957–1961	Harold Willis Handley	Republican
1873–1877	Thomas Andrews Hendricks	Democrat	1961–1965	Matthew Empson Welsh	Democrat
1877–1880	James Douglas Williams	Democrat	1965–1969	Roger Douglas Branigin	Democrat
1880–1881	Isaac Pusey Gray	Democrat	1969–1973	Edgar Doud Whitcomb	Republican
1881–1885	Albert Gallatin Porter	Republican	1973–1981	Otis Ray Bowen	Republican
1885–1889	Isaac Pusey Gray	Democrat	1981–1989	Robert Dunkerson Orr	Republican
1889–1891	Alvin Peterson Hovey	Republican	1989–1997	Evan Bayh	Democrat
1891–1893	Ira Joy Chase	Republican	1997–	Frank O'Bannon	Democrat
1893–1897	Claude Matthews	Democrat			
1897–1901	James Atwell Mount	Republican		Democratic Republican – Dem-Rep	
1901–1905	Winfield Taylor Durbin	Republican		Independent – Indep	
				National Republican – Nat-Rep	

World War I began, Indiana industries boomed with war orders, and public sympathy swung heavily toward the Allies. Indiana furnished 118,000 men and women to the armed forces and suffered the loss of 3,370.

After 1920, only about a dozen makes of cars were still being manufactured in Indiana, and those factories steadily lost out to the three largest car makers in Detroit. Auto parts continued to be a big business, however, along with steelmaking and oil-refining in the Calumet region. Elsewhere there was manufacturing of machinery, farm implements, railway cars, furniture, and pharmaceuticals. Meatpacking, coal-mining, and limestone-quarrying continued to be important. With increasing industrialization, cities grew, particularly in the northern half of the state, and the number of farms diminished. The balance of rural and urban population, about even in 1920, tilted in favor of urban dwellers.

World War II had a greater impact on Indiana than did World War I. Most factories converted to production of war materials, and 300 of them held defense orders in 1942. Military training facilities were created. Camp Atterbury covered 100 square miles (259 square kilometers) in Bartholomew County, and two air stations trained aviators. Two large ammunition depots loaded and stored shells, and the enormous Jefferson Proving Grounds tested ammunition and parachutes.

Post-War Period

After the war, many small local industries were taken over by national corporations, and their plants were expanded. By 1984, the largest employer in Indiana was General Motors, with 47,800 employees in six cities. Inland Steel, with 18,500 workers, was second, followed by US Steel with 13,800 workers.

Nostalgia for an older, simpler, rural way of life pervades much Hoosier thinking. The state's conservation efforts were guided by Richard Lieber, a state official during 1915–33. During the 1930s and 1940s, Lieber nationally promoted the preservation of land for state parks and recreational areas as well as for state and federal forests.

Hoosiers enjoy politics and participate intensively in conventions and elections. The percentage of registered voters who vote has generally exceeded the national average by a wide margin. The state legislature was dominated by rural interests until a 1966 reorganization gave urban counties more representation.

12 STATE GOVERNMENT

The Indiana general assembly consists of a 50-member senate elected to four-year terms, with half the senators elected every two years, and a 100-member house of representatives elected to two-year terms. The state's chief executive is the governor, elected to a four-year term. The governor may call special sessions of the legislature and may veto bills passed by the legislature, but his veto can be overridden by a majority vote in each house.

Indiana's other top elected officials are the lieutenant governor, secretary of

Indiana Presidential Vote by Political Parties, 1948–2000

YEAR	INDIANA WINNER	DEMOCRAT	REPUBLICAN	PROGRESSIVE	PROHIBITION
1948	Dewey (R)	807,833	821,079	9,649	14,711
1952	*Eisenhower (R)	801,530	1,136,259	1,222	15,335
1956	*Eisenhower (R)	783,908	1,182,811	—	6,554
1960	*Nixon (R)	952,358	1,175,120	—	6,746
1964	*Johnson (D)	1,170,848	911,118	—	8,266
				AMERICAN IND.	
1968	*Nixon (R)	806,659	1,067,885	243,108	4,616
				PEOPLE'S	SOC. WORKERS
1972	*Nixon (R)	708,568	1,405,154	4,544	5,575
				AMERICAN	
1976	Ford (R)	1,014,714	1,185,958	14,048	5,695
				CITIZENS	LIBERTARIAN
1980	*Reagan (R)	844,197	1,255,656	4,852	19,627
1984	*Reagan (R)	841,481	1,377,230	—	6,741
				NEW ALLIANCE	
1988	*Bush (R)	860,643	1,297,763	10,215	—
				IND. (Perot)	
1992	Bush (R)	848,420	989,375	455,934	7,936
1996	Dole (R)	887,424	1,006,693	224,299	15,632
					REFORM
2000	*Bush (R)	901,980	1,245,836	18,531	16,959

* Won US presidential election.

state, treasurer, auditor, attorney general, and superintendent of public instruction. Each is elected to a four-year term. The lieutenant governor is constitutionally empowered to preside over the state senate and to act as governor if that office should become vacant or the governor is unable to discharge his duties. Legislation may be introduced in either house of the general assembly, although bills for raising revenue must originate in the house of representatives.

13 POLITICAL PARTIES

After voting Republican in four successive presidential elections, Indiana voted Democratic in 1876 and became a swing state. More recently, a Republican trend has been evident: the state voted Republican in 15 out of 16 presidential elections between 1940 and 2000.

In 2000, Indiana gave 57% of the vote to Republican George W. Bush and 41% to Democrat Al Gore. That same year, Governor Frank O'Bannon was reelected. Richard Lugar, a Republican, also won reelection in the Senate in 2000, and Democrat Evan Bayh was elected to the Senate in 1998. Indiana's 2001 delegation to the US House of Representatives included four Democrats and six Republicans. In the state senate, Republicans numbered 32; Democrats, 18. In the state house, there were 53 Democrats and 47 Republicans.

14 LOCAL GOVERNMENT

Indiana's 91 counties have traditionally provided law enforcement in rural areas, operated county courts and institutions,

maintained county roads, administered public welfare programs, and collected taxes. In 1984, counties were given the power to impose local income taxes. The county's business is conducted by a Board of County Commissioners, consisting of three members elected to four-year terms.

Townships provide assistance for the poor and assess taxable property. Each of the 1,007 townships is administered by a trustee elected to a four-year term. Indiana had 568 municipal governments in 1997. They are governed by elected city councils varying in membership from five to 25 persons.

15 JUDICIAL SYSTEM

The Indiana supreme court consists of five justices who are appointed by the governor. The state court of appeals consists of 15 justices. The court exercises appeals jurisdiction under rules set by the state supreme court. Superior courts, probate courts, and circuit courts all function as general trial courts and are presided over by 279 judges who serve a term of six years. Indiana had 19,631 prisoners in state and federal correctional facilities as of June 1999. For 1996, the FBI Crime Index reported a total crime rate of 4,169.4 per 100,000 people statewide.

16 MIGRATION

The principal migratory pattern since 1920 has been within the state, from the farms to the cities. Since World War II, Indiana has lost population through a growing migratory movement to other states, mostly to Florida and the Southwest. From 1985 to 1990, however, there

Insulin is produced at the Eli Lilly Company in Indianapolis.

was a net gain in migration of over 35,000, 90% of whom came from abroad. During 1990–98, Indiana had a net gain of 76,000 from interstate migration and 25,000 from international migration. In 1998, 3,981 foreign immigrants arrived in Indiana.

17 ECONOMY

Indiana is both a leading agricultural and industrial state. The state's industrial development in Indianapolis, Gary, and other cities was based on its plentiful natural resources—coal, natural gas, timber, stone, and clay—and on good transportation facilities. The northwestern corner of the state is the site of one of the world's greatest concentrations of heavy industry, especially steel.

In 1999, the gross state product was $162 billion, of which manufacturing industries contributed $50 billion; private services-producing industries, $26 billion; financial industries, $21 billion; and government, $16 billion.

18 INCOME

In 1998, Indiana ranked 30th among the 50 states in individual personal income, with an average of $25,163 per capita (per person). Total personal income amounted to $148.7 billion. About 8.6% of the population lived below the federal poverty level in 1998.

19 INDUSTRY

The industrialization of Indiana that began in the Civil War era was spurred by technological advances in processing agricultural products, manufacturing farm equipment, and improving transportation facilities. Meat-packing plants, textile mills, furniture factories, and wagon works—including Studebaker wagons—were soon followed by metal foundries, machine shops, farm implement plants, and various other durable-goods plants.

In 1997, the estimated total value of shipments by manufacturers in Indiana was $143 billion. Among the leading industry groups were transportation equipment, primary metal products, chemicals, food products, and electrical equipment. Indiana is a leading producer of storage batteries, small motors and generators, mobile homes, household furniture, burial caskets, and musical instruments. Most manufacturing plants are located in and around Indianapolis and in the Calumet region.

20 LABOR

In mid-1998, the state's civilian labor force totaled 3.08 million persons, with an unemployment rate of 3.1%. Unemployment rates are usually higher than the state average around Terre Haute and Gary, and lower in the Bloomington area.

In 1998, 16.2% of all workers were members of unions.

21 AGRICULTURE

Agriculture remains vital to the state's economy, and nearly 69% of its total area is farmland. There were 66,000 farms being worked in 1999, when farmland totaled 15.6 million acres (6.3 million hectares). In 1995, Indiana ranked 15th among the 50 states in cash farm receipts. The state's total crop marketings that year were valued at $2.8 billion. The leading crops were corn and soybeans.

In 1998, Indiana ranked fourth in the production of peppermint and cantaloupes, and fifth in production of spearmint and corn for grain. Indiana's principal field crops were as follows:

CROPS	% OF U.S.	QUANTITY
Corn for grain	7.7	760.3 million bushels
Spearmint	3.7	110,000 pounds
Peppermint	11.3	1,104,000 pounds
Cantaloupes	2.8	624,000 cwt.

22 DOMESTICATED ANIMALS

In 1999, the sale of livestock and livestock products amounted to $1.58 billion.

Dairy farms contribute about 6% to total agricultural receipts. The numbers of livestock on Indiana farms at the end of 1996 were hogs, 3,750,000; cattle, 1,150,000; milk cows, 145,000; and sheep, 57,000. The state's poultry farmers sold an estimated 39.5 million pounds of chicken and 359.6 million pounds of turkey in 1997. Other animal products are honey, beeswax, and wool.

23 FISHING

Fishing is not of commercial importance in Indiana. In 1997, only 158,000 pounds of fish valued at $327,000 were landed. Fishing for bass, pike, perch, catfish, and trout is a popular sport with Indiana anglers. In 1998, there were 643,741 sport fishing license holders.

24 FORESTRY

About 20% of Indiana land is forested. Indiana has 4.5 million acres (1.82 million hectares) of forestland. Indiana has always been noted for the quality of its hardwood forests and the trees it produces. It presently is the third leading producer of hardwood lumber, following Pennsylvania and North Carolina. In the southern half of Indiana, oak, hickory, beech, maple, yellow poplar, and ash predominate in the uplands. Soft maple, sweetgum, pin oak, cottonwood, sycamore, and river birch are the most common species found in wetlands and drainage corridors.

Approximately 25,400 people are employed in Indiana's wood-using industry. Indiana's wood-using industries manufacture everything from the "crinkle" center lining in cardboard boxes to the finest furniture in the world. Products such as pallets, desks, fancy face veneer, millwork, flooring, mobile homes and even recreational vehicles use about 500 million board feet (42 million cubic feet/1.2 million cubic meters) of lumber each year.

25 MINING

The value of nonfuel mineral production in Indiana in 1998 was about $700 million. The state's top two mineral commodities, crushed stone and cement, together accounted for approximately 66% of Indiana's total nonfuel value. Indiana was among the nation's top twelve states in output of both of these commodities, and seventh in production of crude gypsum. In 1998, Indiana was the leading producer of dimension stone in the United States.

26 ENERGY AND POWER

In 1997, Indiana's gross energy consumption totaled 2.6 trillion Btu, of which 51% was provided by coal, 35% by petroleum products, 10% by dry natural gas, and 4% by other sources. The state has no nuclear power plants. Per capita (per person) energy consumption in the state in 1997 was 457.5 million Btu, the seventh highest in the United States. Indiana ranks high in energy expenditures per capita—$2,405 in 1997.

Electric power produced in Indiana in 1998 totaled 110.7 billion kilowatt hours.

Indiana's 1999 estimated proved reserves of petroleum totaled 13 million barrels; production of crude petroleum totaled 1.96 million barrels. In 1998, Indiana's coal production was estimated at 36.8 million short tons of coal, eighth in the US. Recoverable reserves totaled 313 million short tons.

27 COMMERCE

Wholesale sales in 1997 totaled $70 billion; retail sales that year totaled $59 billion (16th among the states). Indiana ranked 16th among the 50 states in exports during 1998, when its goods shipped abroad were valued at $12 billion.

28 PUBLIC FINANCE

The State Budget Agency acts as a watchdog over state financial affairs.

The total revenues for fiscal year 1997 were $17.536 billion; expenditures were $16.37 billion.

The total indebtedness of the state government was nearly $6.14 billion in 1997. This debt amounted to $1,047 per capita (per person). Indiana has a constitutional prohibition against the state government directly carrying debt. Therefore, the state uses entities tied with the private sector to issue bonds.

29 TAXATION

Indiana imposes property, gasoline, income, and sales taxes, as well as taxes on the manufacture and sale of alcoholic beverages. In 1996, the state sales tax was 5%, and the state tax on cigarettes was 15.5¢ per pack. The state's personal income tax was 3.4% of adjusted gross income. In the 1999 fiscal year, Indiana's state tax revenue totaled $10.6 billion, 27th among the states. The total federal income tax burden in Indiana amounted to $26.1 billion in 1995, or $4,501 per person.

30 HEALTH

In 1998, the principal causes of death were heart disease, cerebrovascular diseases, accidents, and suicide. Indiana had 111 community hospitals in 1998, with 19,401 beds. The state had over 10,000 active non-federal physicians in that year. The average expense for care per patient per day came to $1,046.10, or $5,976.20

Photo credit: South Bend/Mishawaka Convention and Visitors Bureau.

A kayaker looking at Century Center, South Bend.

per hospital admission. About 14.4% of Indianans did not have health insurance coverage in 1998.

31 HOUSING

The great majority of Indiana families enjoy adequate housing, particularly in newly built suburbs, but inadequate housing exists in the deteriorating central cores of large cities. In 1999, the state had an estimated 2.5 million housing units. The median monthly payment for mortgage and other selected costs was $561, and the median monthly cost for owners without a mortgage was $188. Median monthly rent was $374. In 1998, 40,700 new housing

University of Notre Dame, Hesburgh Library.

As of fall 1997, there were 295,517 students attending colleges and universities in the state. Indiana University, the state's largest institution of higher education, is one of the largest state universities in the US, with eight campuses. The Bloomington campus has the largest enrollment with 35,600 students. Other major state universities are Purdue University (Lafayette), Ball State University (Muncie), and Indiana State University (Terre Haute). Well-known private universities in the state include Notre Dame University (South Bend) and Butler University (Indianapolis). Small private schools include DePauw University (Greencastle) and Earlham College (Richmond).

33 ARTS

Indianapolis remains the state's cultural center, especially after the opening in the late 1960s of the Lilly Pavilion of the Decorative Arts; the Krannert Pavilion; the Clowes Art Pavilion; and the Grace Showalter Pavilion of the Performing Arts. Since 1969, the Indiana Arts Commission has taken art—and artists—into many Indiana communities; the commission also sponsors biennial awards to artists in the state.

Amateur theater has been popular since the founding in 1915 of the nation's oldest amateur drama group, the Little Theater Society, which later became the Civic Theater of Indianapolis. The Indiana Symphony Orchestra was founded in 1930. There are 23 symphony orchestras in the state. The Arthur Jordan College of Music of Butler University in Indianapolis and Indiana University's School of Music in Bloomington are major music schools.

units were authorized for construction, at an estimated value of $4.3 billion.

32 EDUCATION

In 1998, 83.5% of those aged 25 years and over were high school graduates, and 17.7% had completed four years of college. In the fall of 1997, Indiana had about 987,483 pupils enrolled in public elementary and secondary schools, and 105,358 in private schools. Expenditures for public elementary and secondary schools amounted to $6,658 per student in 1999/00.

34 LIBRARIES AND MUSEUMS

In 1998, there were 24 public library systems, and every county received some form of library service. The largest book collections are at public libraries in Indianapolis, Fort Wayne, Gary, Evansville, South Bend, and Hammond. The total book stock of all Indiana public libraries was 22.2 million volumes in 1996. The Indiana State Library maintains a major collection of documents about Indiana's history and a large genealogical collection.

Private libraries and museums include those maintained by historical societies in Indianapolis, Fort Wayne, and South Bend. Also of note are the General Lew Wallace Study museum in Crawfordsville and the Elwood Haynes Museum of early technology in Kokomo. In all, Indiana had 179 museums in 2000. Indiana's historic sites of most interest to visitors are the Lincoln Boyhood National Memorial near Gentryville, and the Benjamin Harrison Memorial Home and the James Whitcomb Riley Home, both in Indianapolis.

35 COMMUNICATIONS

About 93.8% of all households had telephone service in 1999. The state's first radio station was licensed in 1922 at Purdue University, Lafayette. Indiana had 88 AM and 228 FM radio stations and 44 television stations as of 2000. Powerful radio and television transmissions from Chicago and Cincinnati also blanket the state. In 1996, 15 large cable systems served the state. About 65% received cable in 2000.

36 PRESS

In 1998, the state had 21 morning dailies and 48 evening dailies; Sunday papers numbered 21. In 1998, the Indianapolis morning *Star* had a daily circulation of 230,223 (Sunday circulation, 391,496); the Indianapolis evening *News* had a daily circulation of 35,602; and the Gary evening *Post-Tribune's* circulation averaged 60,675 daily and 60,016 on Sundays.

A number of national magazines are published in Indiana, including *Children's Digest* and *The Saturday Evening Post*. Indiana University Press is an important publisher of scholarly books.

37 TOURISM, TRAVEL, AND RECREATION

Tourism is of moderate economic importance to Indiana. The state's three national parks had 1.8 million visitors in 1996. Summer resorts are located in the north, along Lake Michigan and in Steuben and Kosciusko counties, where there are nearly 200 lakes. Popular tourist sites include the reconstructed village of New Harmony, site of famous communal living experiments in the early 19th century; the Indianapolis Motor Speedway and Museum; and the George Rogers Clark National Historic Park at Vincennes.

Among the natural attractions are the Indiana Dunes National Lakeshore on Lake Michigan; the state's largest waterfall, Cataract Falls, near Cloverdale; and the largest underground cavern, at Wyandotte. Indiana has 23 state parks, comprising 59,292 acres (21,800 hectares). The largest state park is Brown County

Photo credit: Rob Banayote.

The Indianapolis skyline featuring the Indiana Convention Center & RCA Dome. The RCA Dome is the home of the Indianapolis Colts professional football team.

(15,543 acres—6,290 hectares), near Nashville.

38 SPORTS

Indiana is represented in professional sports by the Indiana Pacers of the National Basketball Association and by the National Football League's Colts, who moved to Indianapolis from Baltimore in 1984. Indianapolis is also represented in baseball's Class AAA American Association. The state's biggest annual sport event is the Indianapolis 500, which has been held at the Indianapolis Motor Speedway on Memorial Day weekend almost every year since 1911. The state's most popular amateur sport is basketball.

Collegiate football in Indiana has a colorful tradition stretching back to at least 1913, when Knute Rockne of Notre Dame unleashed the forward pass as a potent football weapon. Notre Dame won the Orange Bowl in 1975 and 1990, and the Cotton Bowl in 1971, 1978, 1979, 1993, and 1994. Indiana and Purdue Universities compete in the Big Ten.

39 FAMOUS INDIANANS

Indiana has contributed one US president and five vice-presidents to the nation. Benjamin Harrison (b.Ohio, 1833–1901), the 23d president, was a Republican who served one term (1889–93) and then returned to Indianapolis, where his home is now a national historic landmark. Three vice-presidents were Indiana residents: Thomas Hendricks (b.Ohio, 1819–85), who served only eight months under President Cleveland and died in office; Schuyler Colfax (b.New York, 1823–85), who served under President Grant; and Charles Fairbanks (b.Ohio, 1852–1918), who served under Theodore Roosevelt. Two vice-presidents were native sons: Thomas Marshall of North Manchester (1854–1925), who served two four-year terms with President Wilson; and J(ames) Danforth Quayle of Indianapolis (b. 1947), who served with President George Bush during 1989–93.

Only one Hoosier, Sherman Minton (1890–1965), has served on the US Supreme Court. Ambrose Burnside (1824–81) and Lew Wallace (1827–1905) were Union generals during the Civil War.

Harold C. Urey (1893–1981) won the Nobel Prize in chemistry in 1934, and Wendell Stanley (1904–71) won it in 1946. The Nobel Prize in economics was awarded to Paul Samuelson (b. 1915) in 1970. Booth Tarkington (1869–1946) won the Pulitzer Prize for fiction in 1918 and 1921. A. B. Guthrie (1901–91) won it for fiction in 1950. Aviation pioneer Wilbur Wright (1867–1912) was born in Millville.

Juvenile writer Annie Fellows Johnston (1863–1931) produced the "Little Colonel" series. Other notable Indiana novelists include Theodore Dreiser (1871–

Photo credit: EPD Photos

James Whitcomb Riley (1849–1916) was one of Indiana's best known poets.

1945), Jessamyn West (1907–84), and Kurt Vonnegut (b.1922).

Composers of Indiana origin have worked mainly in popular music: Cole Porter (1893–1964) and Howard Hoagland "Hoagy" Carmichael (1899–1981). Entertainers from Indiana include David Letterman (b.1947) and singer Michael Jackson (b.1958).

Hoosier sports heroes include Knute Rockne (b.Norway, 1888–1931), famed as a football player and coach at Notre

Dame. Larry Bird (b.1956) was college basketball's player of the year at Indiana State University in 1978/79 and went on to play for the Boston Celtics of the NBA in the 1980s; in 1998 he became head coach of the NBA's Indiana Pacers.

40 BIBLIOGRAPHY

Aylesworth, Thomas G. *Eastern Great Lakes: Indiana, Michigan, Ohio.* New York: Chelsea House, 1996.

Brill, Marlene Targ. *Indiana.* New York: Benchmark Books, 1997.

Fish, Bruce. *Indy Car Racing.* Philadelphia, Penn.: Chelsea House, 2000.

Heinrichs, Ann. *Indiana.* New York: Children's Press, 2000.

Nelson, Julie. *Indianapolis Colts.* Mankato, Minn.: Creative Education, 2000.

Rambeck, Richard. *Indiana Pacers.* Mankato, Minn.: Creative Education, 1998.

Rudolph, L. C. *Hoosier Faiths: A History of Indiana Churches and Religious Groups.* Bloomington: Indiana University Press, 1995.

Vander Hook, Sue. *Hail Hoosiers: the Indiana Hoosiers Story.* Mankato, Minn.: Creative Education, 1999.

Web sites

Access Indiana Information Network. The Official Website of the State of Indiana. [Online] Available http://www.ai.org/ Accessed May 14, 2001.

Indiana Tourism. Indiana Travel Information. [Online] Available http://www.indianatourism.com Accessed May 14, 2001.

IOWA

State of Iowa

ORIGIN OF STATE NAME: From a Siouan term meaning "beautiful land." Named for Iowa Indians of the Siouan family.

NICKNAME: The Hawkeye State.

CAPITAL: Des Moines.

ENTERED UNION: 28 December 1846 (29th).

SONG: "The Song of Iowa."

MOTTO: Our Liberties We Prize and Our Rights We Will Maintain.

FLAG: There are three vertical stripes of blue, white, and red; in the center a spreading eagle holds in its beak a blue ribbon with the state motto.

OFFICIAL SEAL: A sheaf and field of standing wheat and farm utensils represent agriculture; a lead furnace and a pile of pig lead are to the right. In the center stands a citizen-soldier holding a US flag with a liberty cap atop the staff in one hand and a rifle in the other. Behind him is the Mississippi River with the steamer *Iowa* and mountains; above him an eagle holds the state motto. Surrounding this scene are the words "The Great Seal of the State of Iowa" against a gold background.

BIRD: Eastern goldfinch.

FLOWER: Wild rose.

TREE: Oak.

STONE: Geode.

TIME: 6 AM CST = noon GMT.

1 LOCATION AND SIZE

Located in the western north-central US, Iowa is the smallest of the midwestern states situated west of the Mississippi River, and ranks 25th in size among the 50 states. The total area of Iowa is 56,275 square miles (145,752 square kilometers). The state extends 324 miles (521 kilometers) east-west. Its maximum extension north-south is 210 miles (338 kilometers). Its total boundary length is 1,151 miles (1,853 kilometers).

2 TOPOGRAPHY

The physical terrain of Iowa consists of a gently rolling plain. Iowa has the richest and deepest topsoil in the US. The state is drained by the Mississippi River and Missouri rivers and has 13 natural lakes.

3 CLIMATE

Iowa lies in the humid continental zone and generally has hot summers, cold winters, and wet springs. Temperatures vary widely during the year, with an annual average of 49°F (9°C). Des Moines, in the central part of the state, has a normal daily maximum temperature of 86°F (30°C) in July and a normal daily minimum of 10°F (–4°C) in January. The record low temperature for the state of Iowa is –47°F (–44°C). The record high is 118°F (48°C). Rainfall averages 32 inches (81 centimeters) annually, and snowfall, 30 inches (76 centimeters).

4 PLANTS AND ANIMALS

Although most of Iowa is under cultivation, such unusual wild specimens as bunchberry and bearberry can be found in the northeast. Other notable plants are pink lady's slipper and twinleaf.

Common Iowa mammals include red and gray foxes, raccoon, opossum, and woodchuck. Common birds include the cardinal, rose-breasted grosbeak, and eastern goldfinch (the state bird). Game fish include rainbow trout, smallmouth bass, and walleye. Among endangered species listed by the state are the red-backed vole, black bear, bobcat, and piping plover.

5 ENVIRONMENTAL PROTECTION

In the 1980s and 1990s, Iowans were particularly concerned with improving air quality, preventing chemical pollution, and preserving water supplies. The state regulates the operation of its 140 solid waste disposal sites. In 1998, the state had 17 hazardous waste sites.

6 POPULATION

Iowa ranked 30th of the 50 states in population in 2000, falling behind states such as Connecticut, Oregon, Oklahoma, and

Iowa Population Profile

Total population in 2000:	2,926,324
Population change, 1990–2000:	5.4%
Hispanic or Latino†:	2.8%
Population by race	
One race:	98.9%
White:	93.9%
Black or African American:	2.1%
American Indian/Alaska Native:	0.3%
Asian:	1.3%
Native Hawaiian/Pacific Islander:	—
Some other race:	1.3%
Two or more races:	1.1%

Population by Age Group

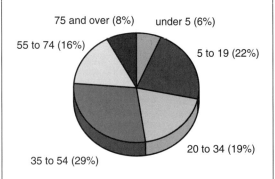

75 and over (8%)
under 5 (6%)
55 to 74 (16%)
5 to 19 (22%)
20 to 34 (19%)
35 to 54 (29%)

Top Cities by Population

City	Population	% change 1990–2000
Des Moines	198,682	2.8
Cedar Rapids	120,758	11.0
Davenport	98,359	3.2
Sioux City	85,013	5.6
Waterloo	68,747	3.4
Iowa City	62,220	4.2
Council Bluffs	58,268	7.3
Dubuque	57,686	0.2
Ames	50,731	7.5
West Des Moines	46,403	46.4

Notes: †A person of Hispanic or Latino origin may be of any race. NA indicates that data are not available.
Sources: U.S. Census Bureau. Public Information Office. *Demographic Profiles.* [Online] Available http://www.census.gov/Press-Release/www/2001/demoprofile.html. Accessed June 1, 2001. U.S. Census Bureau. *Census 2000: Redistricting Data.* Press release issued by the Redistricting Data Office. Washington, D.C., March, 2001.

IOWA

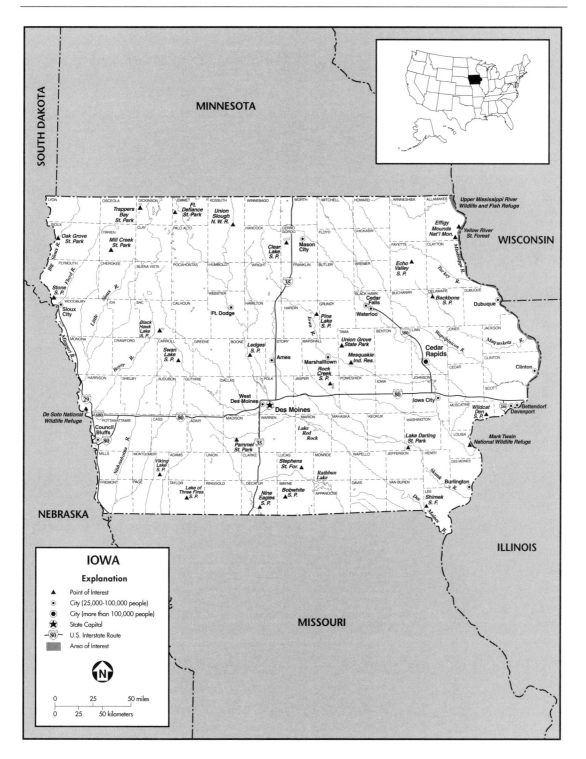

MINNESOTA

SOUTH DAKOTA

WISCONSIN

NEBRASKA

ILLINOIS

MISSOURI

LYON OSCEOLA DICKINSON EMMET KOSSUTH WINNEBAGO WORTH MITCHELL HOWARD WINNESHIEK ALLAMAKEE

Upper Mississippi River
Wildlife and Fish Refuge

Trappers
Bay
St. Park

Ft.
Defiance
St. Park

Union
Slough
N. W. R.

Effigy
Mounds
Nat'l Mon.

Yellow River
St. Forest

SIOUX O'BRIEN CLAY PALO ALTO HANCOCK CERRO
GORDO FLOYD CHICKASW FAYETTE CLAYTON

Oak Grove
St. Park

Mill Creek
St. Park

Clean
Lake
S.P.

Mason
City

Echo
Valley
S. P.

PLYMOUTH CHEROKEE BUENA VISTA POCAHONTAS HUMBOLDT WRIGHT FRANKLIN BUTLER BREMER

Stone
S. P.

WEBSTER Ft. Dodge HAMILTON HARDIN GRUNDY Cedar
Falls BLACK HAWK BUCHANAN DELAWARE DUBUQUE

Sioux
City

WOODBURY IDA SAC CALHOUN

Black
Hawk
Lake
S. P.

Waterloo

Backbone
S. P.

Dubuque

MONONA CRAWFORD CARROLL GREENE BOONE STORY MARSHALL TAMA BENTON LINN JONES JACKSON

Swan
Lake
S. P.

Ledges
S. P.

Ames

Pine
Lake
S. P.

Union Grove
State Park

Cedar
Rapids

Maquoketa

Clinton

HARRISON SHELBY AUDUBON GUTHRIE DALLAS POLK JASPER POWESHIEK IOWA JOHNSON CEDAR CLINTON

Marshalltown

Rock
Creek
S. P.

Mesquakie
Ind. Res.

SCOTT

West
Des Moines

Des Moines

Iowa City

MUSCATINE

Wildcat
Den
S. P.

Bettendorf
Davenport

De Soto National
Wildlife Refuge

POTTAWATTAMIE CASS ADAIR MADISON WARREN MARION MAHASKA KEOKUK WASHINGTON LOUISA

Council
Bluffs

Pammel
St. Park

Lake
Red
Rock

Lake Darling
St. Park

Mark Twain
National Wildlife Refuge

MILLS MONTGOMERY ADAMS UNION CLARKE LUCAS MONROE WAPELLO JEFFERSON HENRY DES MOINES

Viking
Lake
S. P.

Stephens
St. For.

Rathbun
Lake

Burlington

FREMONT PAGE TAYLOR RINGGOLD DECATUR WAYNE APPANOOSE DAVIS VAN BUREN LEE

Lake of
Three Fires
S. P.

Nine
Eagles
S. P.

Bobwhite
S. P.

Shimek
S. F.

IOWA

Explanation

▲ Point of Interest
◉ City (25,000-100,000 people)
◉ City (more than 100,000 people)
★ State Capital
─◯80◯─ U.S. Interstate Route
▨ Area of Interest

N

| 0 | 25 | 50 miles |
| 0 | 25 | 50 kilometers |

Iowa Population by Race

Census 2000 was the first national census in which the instructions to respondents said, "Mark one or more races." This table shows the number of people who are of one, two, or three or more races. For those claiming two races, the number of people belonging to the various categories is listed. The U.S. government conducts a census of the population every ten years.

	Number	Percent
Total population	2,926,324	100.0
One race	2,894,546	98.9
Two races	29,959	1.0
White *and* Black or African American	7,856	0.3
White *and* American Indian/Alaska Native	7,075	0.2
White *and* Asian	4,369	0.1
White *and* Native Hawaiian/Pacific Islander	468	—
White *and* some other race	7,049	0.2
Black or African American *and* American Indian/Alaska Native	577	—
Black or African American *and* Asian	266	—
Black or African American *and* Native Hawaiian/Pacific Islander	46	—
Black or African American *and* some other race	634	—
American Indian/Alaska Native *and* Asian	198	—
American Indian/Alaska Native *and* Native Hawaiian/Pacific Islander	24	—
American Indian/Alaska Native *and* some other race	299	—
Asian *and* Native Hawaiian/Pacific Islander	275	—
Asian *and* some other race	750	—
Native Hawaiian/Pacific Islander *and* some other race	73	—
Three or more races	1,819	0.1

Source: U.S. Census Bureau. *Census 2000: Redistricting Data.* Press release issued by the Redistricting Data Office. Washington, D.C., March, 2001. A dash (—) indicates that the percent is less than 0.1.

South Carolina. The total population that year was 2,926,324. Population density was 52.4 persons per square mile (20.2 persons per square kilometer). In 1990, 60.6% of all Iowans lived in urban areas. Iowa has one of the highest concentrations of people over 75 at 8%. In 2000, the largest cities were: Des Moines, 193,422; Cedar Rapids, 120,758; Davenport, 98,359; and Sioux City, 85,013.

7 ETHNIC GROUPS

In 1997, Iowa's population was estimated to be 96.5% white, the fifth highest ratio among the states. There were an estimated 55,600 black Americans (2%), 35,800 Asians (1.3%), and 8,500 American Indians (0.3%). About 53,000 people with Hispanic origins were living in Iowa in 1997. According to the 1990 census, Iowans of European descent included 1,394,542 Germans; 536,720 English, Scottish, or Welsh; 527,428 Irish; and 152,084 Norwegians. The foreign-born population numbered 43,316 in 1990, and their main countries of origin included Germany, Mexico, Laos, Canada, Korea, and Vietnam.

8 LANGUAGES

Iowa English reflects the three major migration streams: Northern in that half of the

Des Moines has the largest skywalk system per capita in the world.

state above Des Moines and North Midland in the southern half, with a slight South Midland trace in the extreme southeastern corner. In 1990, 96.1% of all Iowans aged five or older spoke only English at home. Other languages reported by Iowans, and the number speaking each at home, included Spanish, 31,620; German, 21,429; and French, 7,941.

9 RELIGIONS

In 1990 there were more than 1,154,034 Protestants, including 272,098 members of the United Methodist Church, 124,021 adherents of the Lutheran Church-Missouri Synod, and 50,771 adherents of the Disciples of Christ (Christian Church). Roman Catholic membership totaled 520,322 and the Jewish population was 6,701.

10 TRANSPORTATION

As of 1998, Iowa had 4,195 rail miles (6,759 kilometers) of railroad track. Amtrak operates the long-distance California Zephyr (Chicago–Oakland, California), with 43,016 Iowa riders in 1995/96. Iowa ranked 11th among the states in road mileage in 1997. The state had 103,383 miles (294,935 kilometers) of rural roads and 9,421 miles (15,158 kilometers) of urban roads, including 783 miles (1,260 kilometers) of interstate highways. There were 1.65 million registered automobiles and 1.28 million trucks and buses in the state in 1997.

Iowa Governors: 1846–2001

1846–1850	Ansel Briggs	Democrat	1913–1917	George W. Clarke	Republican
1850–1854	Stepehn P. Hempstead	Democrat	1917–1921	William Lloyd Harding	Republican
1854–1858	James Wilson Grimes	Whig	1921–1925	Nathan Edward Kendall	Republican
1858–1860	Ralph Phillips Lowe	Republican	1925–1931	John Hammill	Republican
1860–1864	Samuel Jordan Kirkwood	Republican	1931–1933	Daniel Webster Turner	Republican
1864–1868	William Milo Stone	Republican	1933–1937	Clyde LaVerne Herring	Democrat
1868–1872	Samuel Merrill	Republican	1937–1939	Nelson George Kraschel	Democrat
1872–1876	Cyrus Clay Carpenter	Republican	1939–1943	George Allison Wilson	Republican
1876–1877	Samuel Jordan Kirkwood	Republican	1943–1945	Bourke Blakemore Hickenlooper	Republican
1877–1878	Joshua G. Newbold	Republican	1945–1949	Robert Donald Blue	Republican
1878–1882	John Henry Gear	Republican	1949–1954	William S. Beardsley	Republican
1882–1886	Buren Robinson Sherman	Republican	1954–1955	Leo Elthon	Republican
1886–1890	William Larrabee	Republican	1955–1957	Leo Arthur Hoegh	Republican
1890–1894	Horace Boies	Democrat	1957–1961	Herschel Celiel Loveless	Democrat
1894–1896	Frank Darr Jackson	Republican	1961–1963	Norman Arthur Erbe	Republican
1896–1898	Francis Marion Drake	Republican	1863–1969	Harold Everett Hughes	Democrat
1898–1902	Leslie Mortier Shaw	Republican	1969	Robert David Fulton	Democrat
1902–1908	Albert Baird Cummins	Republican	1969–1983	Robert D. Day	Republican
1908–1909	Warren Garst	Republican	1983–1999	Terry Edward Branstad	Republican
1909–1913	Beryl Franklin Carroll	Republican	1999–	Thomas J. Vilsack	Democrat

Iowa is bordered by two great navigable rivers, the Mississippi and the Missouri. Freight is still transported by water as far east as Pennsylvania and west to Oklahoma. The busiest airfield is Des Moines Municipal Airport, which handled 14,412 departures and 905,405 boarded passengers in 1996.

11 HISTORY

The first permanent settlers of the land were the Woodland Indians, who built villages in the forested areas along the Mississippi River and introduced agriculture. Not until June 1673 did the first known white men, explorer Louis Jolliet and the Catholic priest Jacques Marquette, come to the territory. Iowa was part of the vast Louisiana Territory that extended from the Gulf of Mexico to the Canadian border and was ruled by the French until the title was transferred to Spain in 1762.

Napoleon took the territory back in 1800 and then promptly sold all of Louisiana Territory to the amazed American envoys who had come to Paris seeking only the purchase of New Orleans and the mouth of the Mississippi. After Iowa had thus come under US control in 1803, the Lewis and Clark expedition worked its way up the Missouri River to explore the newly purchased land.

Placed under the territorial jurisdiction of Michigan in 1834, and then two years later under the newly created Territory of Wisconsin, Iowa became a separate territory in 1838. The first territorial governor, Robert Lucas, began planning for statehood by drawing aggressive boundary lines that extended county boundaries and local government westward and northward. Under the Missouri Compromise, Iowa came into the Union with Florida as its slaveholding counterpart. A serious dispute, concerning how large the state would be, delayed Iowa's admission into the Union until 28 December 1846.

State Development

The settlement of Iowa was rapidly accomplished. With one-fourth of the nation's fertile topsoil located within its borders, Iowa was a powerful magnet that drew farmers by the thousands from many areas. The settlers were overwhelmingly Protestant in religion and remarkably uniform in ethnic and cultural backgrounds. Fiercely proud of its claim to be the first free state created out of the Louisiana Purchase, Iowa was an important center of abolitionist sentiment throughout the 1850s. The Underground Railroad for fugitive slaves from the South ran across the southern portion of Iowa to the Mississippi River. When the Civil War came, Iowa overwhelmingly supported the Union cause.

The railroad had been lavishly welcomed by Iowans in the 1850s. By the 1870s, Iowa farmers were battling the railroad interests for effective regulatory legislation. The National Grange (an association of farmers) was powerful enough in Iowa to push through the so-called Granger laws regulating the railroads. Following World War I, conservatives regained control of the ruling Republican Party and remained in control until the 1960s. Then new liberal leadership was forced on the party after the disastrous 1964 presidential campaign of Barry Goldwater and effective opposition from a revitalized Democratic Party led by Harold Hughes.

Iowa Presidential Vote by Political Parties, 1948–2000

Year	Iowa Winner	Democrat	Republican	Progressive	Prohibition	Socialist Labor
1948	*Truman (D)	522,380	494,018	12,125	3,382	4,274
1952	*Eisenhower (R)	451,513	808,906	5,085	2,882	—
						Constitution
1956	*Eisenhower (R)	501,858	729,187	—	—	3,202
1960	Nixon (R)	550,565	722,381	—	—	—
1964	*Johnson (D)	733,030	449,148	—	1,902	—
				Soc. Workers	American Ind.	
1968	*Nixon (R)	476,699	619,106	3,377	66,422	—
					American	Peace and Freedom
1972	*Nixon (R)	496,206	706,207	—	22,056	1,332
						Libertarian
1976	Ford (R)	619,931	632,863	—	3,040	1,452
				Citizens		
1980	*Reagan (R)	508,672	676,026	2,191	—	12,324
1984	*Reagan (R)	605,620	703,088	—	—	—
1988	Dukakis (D)	670,557	545,355	755	540	2,494
				Ind. (Perot)		
1992	*Clinton (D)	586,353	504,891	253,468	3,079	1,177
1996	*Clinton (D)	620,258	492,644	105,159	—	2,315
					Reform	
2000	Gore (D)	638,517	634,373	29,374	5,731	190

* Won US presidential election.

The five-domed state capitol in Des Moines has a 23-karat gold center dome.

After Hughes gave up the governorship in 1969 to become a US senator, he was succeeded in office by Robert Ray, a liberal Republican who dominated the state throughout the 1970s. Iowa's economy suffered in the 1980s from a combination of high debt and interest rates, numerous droughts, and low crop prices. Businesses departed or shrank their work forces. By the 1990s, however, the companies that had survived were in a much stronger position, and Iowa began enjoying a period of cautious prosperity. The state's unemployment rate in 1992 was 4.7 percent, lower than the national average.

In 1993, unusually heavy spring and summer rains produced record floods along the Mississippi River by mid-July. The entire state of Iowa was declared a disaster area. The floods forced 11,200 people to evacuate their homes and caused $2.2 billion in damages.

12 STATE GOVERNMENT

The state legislature, or general assembly, consists of a 50-member senate and a 100-member house of representatives. Each house may introduce or amend legislation, with a simple majority vote required for passage. The governor's veto of a bill may be overridden by a two-thirds majority in both houses. The state's elected executives are the governor, lieutenant governor, secretary of state, auditor, treasurer, attorney general, and secretary of agriculture.

13 POLITICAL PARTIES

For 70 years following the Civil War, a majority of Iowa voters supported the Republicans over the Democrats in nearly all state and national elections. During the Great Depression of the 1930s, Iowa briefly turned to the Democrats, supporting Franklin D. Roosevelt in two presidential elections. However, from 1940 through 1984, the majority of Iowans voted Republican in 10 of 12 presidential elections. Democrats have carried the state in the last four presidential contests. Republicans won 35 of the 44 gubernatorial elections from 1900 through 1998 and controlled both houses of the state legislature for 112 of the 130 years from 1855 to 1984.

In the 2000 elections, Iowa gave Democrat Al Gore 49% of the vote, while Republican George W. Bush received 48%. As of 2001, Republicans had a 4–1 edge in the US House delegation, while a Democrat and a Republican both served in the US Senate—Republican Charles Grassley, who won election to a fourth term in 1998, and Democrat Tom Harkin, who won re-election in 1996. Tom Vilsack, a Democrat, won election to a fourth term as governor in 1998. After the November 2000 elections, there were 20 Democrats and 30 Republicans in the state senate, and 56 Republicans and 44 Democrats in the state house.

Iowa's presidential caucuses are held in January of presidential campaign years.

Photo credit: EPD Photos/CSU Archives

Iowa was the birthplace of Herbert Clark Hoover (1874–1964), the first US president born west of the Mississippi. Hoover was buried in West Branch, the town of his birth.

This is earlier than any other state, thus giving Iowans a degree of influence in national politics.

14 LOCAL GOVERNMENT

The state's 99 counties are governed by boards of supervisors consisting of three to five members. County officials enforce state laws, collect taxes, supervise welfare activities, and manage roads and bridges.

Local government was exercised by 951 municipal units in 1997. The mayor-council system functioned in the great majority of these municipalities. The power to tax is authorized by the general assembly.

15 JUDICIAL SYSTEM

The Iowa supreme court consists of nine justices appointed by the governor, who select one of their number as chief justice. The court exercises appeals jurisdiction in civil and criminal cases, supervises the trial courts, and establishes the rules of civil and appeals procedure. The supreme court transfers certain cases to the five-member court of appeals. Iowa's total crime rate in June 1999 was 3,500.6 per 100,000 population. As of 1999 there were 7,231 prisoners in federal and state institutions.

16 MIGRATION

Iowa was opened, organized, and settled by a generation of migrants from other states. After 1850 they were joined by immigrants from northern Europe. During and immediately after the Civil War, some former slaves fled the South for Iowa, and more blacks settled in Iowa cities after 1900. Many of the migrants who came to Iowa did not stay long. Some Iowans left to join the gold rush, and others settled lands in the West. Migration out of the state has continued to this day, as retired Iowans seeking warmer climates have moved to California and other southwestern states. From 1970 through 1990, Iowa's net loss through migration amounted to over 266,000. During 1990–98, the net loss from interstate migration was 13,000, but the net gain from interna-tional migration was about 19,000. In 1998, 1,655 foreign immigrants arrived in the state.

An important migratory trend within the state has been from the farm to the city. Although Iowa has remained a major agricultural state, the urban population increased to over 60.6% of the total population by 1990.

17 ECONOMY

Iowa's economy is based on agriculture. Although the value of the state's manufactures exceeds the value of its farm production, manufacturing is basically farm-centered. The major industries are food processing and the manufacture of agriculture-related products, such as farm machinery.

Technological progress in agriculture and the growth of manufacturing industries have enabled Iowans to enjoy general prosperity since World War II. In the early 1980s, high interest rates and falling land prices created serious economic difficulties for farmers and contributed to the continuing decline of the farm population. By the early 1990s, the state had recovered.

Of the state's total economic output, about $20 billion comes from manufacturing industries, $12 billion from private services-producing industries, and $9 billion from government.

18 INCOME

With a personal income per capita (per person) of $24,745 in 1998, Iowa ranked 32nd among the 50 states. Total disposable personal income was $70.8 billion in

1998. Some 9.4% of the population was living below the federal poverty level in 1998.

19 INDUSTRY

Because Iowa was primarily a farm state, the first industries were food processing and the manufacture of farm implements. These industries have retained a key role in the economy. In recent years, Iowa has added a variety of others—including pens, washing machines, and even mobile homes.

The estimated total value of shipments by manufacturers was $64 billion in 1997.

20 LABOR

Since 1950, Iowa has consistently ranked above the national average in employment of its work force. Iowa's unemployment rate of 2.8% for 1998 was well below the overall US rate of 4.5%. The civilian labor force in mid-1998 totaled 1.57 million. As of 1998, 12.5% of all workers were union members.

21 AGRICULTURE

Iowa recorded a gross farm income of $9.7 billion in 1999. Nearly half of all cash receipts from marketing came from the sale of livestock and meat products. In that year, Iowa ranked first nationwide in output of corn for grain and soybeans, and 5th for oats. In 1998, Iowa had 97,000 farms, with an average size of 340 acres (138 hectares) per farm.

Nearly all of Iowa's land is tillable, and about 90% of it is given to farmland. Corn is grown practically everywhere, and wheat is raised in the southern half of the state and in counties bordering the Mississippi and Missouri rivers. In 1998, agricultural production included corn for grain, 1.8 billion bushels; soybeans, 501.6 million bushels; oats, 10.9 million bushels; and hay, 5.33 million tons.

22 DOMESTICATED ANIMALS

Iowa produced about 25% of the nation's pork in 1995. In that year, hog production accounted for 22% of agricultural receipts; cattle production, 15%. Iowa had an estimated 3.65 million cattle and calves in 1999, valued at $2.2 billion. The state also ranked first in the number of hogs and pigs that year, at 15.3 million, valued at $719.1 million. Iowa's 244,000 dairy cows produced 3.9 billion pounds of milk in 1997. In that year, turkey production totaled 187.6 million pounds.

23 FISHING

Fishing has little commercial importance in Iowa. However, game fishing in the rivers and lakes is a popular sport. There were 408,805 sport fishermen licensed in the state in 1998.

24 FORESTRY

Iowa has 2 million acres (0.8 million hectares) of forestland, representing 5.7% of the state's land area. The state's lumber industry produced 76 million board feet of lumber in 1998.

25 MINING

The value of nonfuel mineral production in Iowa was estimated at $524 million in 1998. Crushed stone (mostly limestone-

Des Moines skyline.

dolomite) continued as the state's leading mineral commodity, accounting for about 45% of the estimated total nonfuel mineral value.

26 ENERGY AND POWER

Although Iowa's fossil fuel resources are extremely limited, the state's energy supply has been adequate for consumer needs. In 1997, Iowa consumed 397.9 million Btu per person. According to 1997 estimates, oil supplied about 33% of the state's energy requirements, natural gas, 23%; coal, 34%; nuclear energy, hydropower, and ethanol, 10%. The state's production of electricity totaled 37.1 billion kilowatt hours in 1998. Of this total, coal-fired plants supplied 31.9 billion kilowatt hours.

27 COMMERCE

Iowa had 1997 wholesale sales of $38 billion and retail sales of $26 billion. The most valuable categories of goods traded were agricultural raw materials, durable goods, groceries and related products, and farm supplies. Iowa's exports of goods originating within the state had an estimated value of $4.9 billion in 1998.

28 PUBLIC FINANCE

The public budget is prepared by the state comptroller with the governor's approval and is adopted or revised by the general assembly.

Iowa's fiscal year 1997 budget included revenues of $9.51 billion and expenditures of $9.35 billion. The state had an outstanding debt of $706 per capita (per person) in 1997, or $2.01 billion total.

29 TAXATION

In 1996, Iowa's personal income tax ranged from 0.4% to 9.98%. The state also taxes corporate income, retail sales, gasoline, cigarettes, alcoholic beverages, insurance premiums, inheritances, chain stores, and business franchises. Iowa's total state tax burden in 1997/98 was $4.8 billion, or $1,677 per person.

30 HEALTH

The death rate in 1998 was 990.8 per 100,000 population, higher than the national rate. Leading causes of death—heart and cerebrovascular diseases were both higher than the national rate. In 1998, Iowa's 116 community hospitals admitted some 374,245 patients, and hospital expenses averaged $747 per inpatient day with an average cost per stay of $5,163. As of 1997, there were 171 licensed doctors per 100,000 people. That same year, there were 940 full-time licensed nurses.

31 HOUSING

Iowa ranks high in the number of housing units that are family-owned and occupied. In 1999, there were an estimated 1.2 million housing units. In 1998, the state authorized the construction of 13,100 new privately owned housing units, valued at $1.3 billion. The median monthly cost for owners with a mortgage in 1990 was $553, one of the lowest amounts in the nation. The monthly median cost of housing for renters in 1990 was $336. The median value of a home in 1990 was $45,900, lower than any state except Mississippi and South Dakota.

32 EDUCATION

Iowa's public school system has been an innovator in school curriculum development, teaching methods, educational administration, and school financing. In fall 1997, Iowa had a total of 501,054 pupils enrolled in the public school system. Expenditures for public elementary and secondary schools amounted to $5,919 per student in 1999/00.

In fall 1997, 180,967 students were enrolled in institutions of higher learning. Iowa has three state universities, with 65,617 students; 35 private colleges; and 23 vocational schools and area community colleges. Small liberal arts colleges and universities include Cornell College, Mt. Vernon; Drake University, Des Moines; Briar Cliff College, Sioux City; Grinnell College, Grinnell; and Iowa Wesleyan College, Mt. Pleasant.

33 ARTS

There is an opera company in Des Moines, and there are art galleries, little theater groups, symphony orchestras, and ballet companies in the major cities and college towns. The Des Moines Arts Center is a leading exhibition gallery for native painters and sculptors. There are regional theater groups in Des Moines, Davenport, and Sioux City. The Writers' Workshop at the University of Iowa (Iowa City) has an international reputation. One problem for the arts in Iowa is the continued migration of native artists to cultural centers in New York, California, and elsewhere.

34 LIBRARIES AND MUSEUMS

Beginning with the founding in 1873 of the state's first tax-supported library at Independence, Iowa's public library system has grown to about 520 libraries with total book holdings of 12 million volumes in 1998. Iowa had 134 museums and zoological parks in 2000. The Herbert Hoover National Historical Site, in West Branch, houses the birthplace and grave of the 31st US president and a library and museum with papers and memorabilia.

35 COMMUNICATIONS

In 1999, about 95.8% of all occupied units had telephones. In 2000, there were 244 radio stations, including 86 AM stations and 158 FM stations. In that same year, Iowa had a total of 34 television stations. A statewide fiberoptic telecommunications system links all 99 counties.

36 PRESS

Overall, Iowa had 38 dailies (23 evening, 15 morning) and 12 Sunday papers in 1998. The *Des Moines Register* remained the leader, with a morning circulation of 163,292 and a Sunday circulation of 236,662 as of 1998. Also published in Iowa were 127 periodicals, among them *Better Homes and Gardens* (circulation, 7.4 million), and *Successful Farming* (500,000).

37 TOURISM, TRAVEL, AND RECREATION

The Mississippi and Missouri rivers offer popular water sports facilities for both out-of-state visitors and resident vacationers. Notable tourist attractions include the Effigy Mounds National Monument (near Marquette), which has hundreds of prehistoric Indian mounds and village sites. Tourist sites in the central part of the state include the state capitol and the Herbert Hoover National Historic Site (West Branch), with its Presidential Library and Museum. Iowa has about 85,000 acres (34,400 hectares) of lakes and reservoirs and 19,000 miles (30,600 kilometers) of fishing streams. There are 52 state parks and 7 state forests. In 1998, Iowa attracted 18 million visitors, who spent over $3.6 billion.

38 SPORTS

Iowa has no major league professional sports teams. High school and college basketball and football teams draw thousands of spectators, particularly to the state high school basketball tournament at Des Moines in March. In intercollegiate competition, the University of Iowa Hawkeyes belong to the Big Ten Conference. They have a legendary wrestling program that has won the NCAA Championship 18 times since 1969. Iowa has over 350 golf courses, eight major ski areas, and is the nation's leading state in pheasant hunting.

39 FAMOUS IOWANS

Among Iowa's most influential governors were the first territorial governor, Robert Lucas (b.Virginia, 1781–1853); William

William F. "Buffalo Bill" Cody (1846–1917), standing second from left, is shown here with members of his family. He earned his infamous nickname after killing over 5,000 buffalo to feed railroad workers laying track for the Kansas Pacific Railway. After serving as an army scout and pony express rider, he toured with his own "Wild West" show. Buffalo Bill was born in Scott County, Iowa.

Larrabee (b.Connecticut, 1832–1912); and Harold Hughes (1863–1969). Iowa has produced a large number of radical dissenters and social reformers. Abolitionists, strong in Iowa before the Civil War, included Josiah B. Grinnell (b.Vermont, 1821–91), and Asa Turner (b.Massachusetts, 1799–1885). William "Billy" Sunday (1862–1935) was an evangelist with a large following among rural Americans. John L. Lewis (1880–1969), head of the United Mine Workers, founded the Congress of Industrial Organizations (CIO).

Iowa can claim two winners of the Nobel Peace Prize: religious leader John R. Mott (b.New York, 1865–1955), and agronomist and plant geneticist Norman E. Borlaug (b.1914). Distinguished scientist George Washington Carver (b.Missouri 1864–1943) was an Iowa resident..

Iowa writers of note include Hamlin Garland (b.Wisconsin, 1860–1940) and Wallace Stegner (1909–93). Two Iowa playwrights, Susan Glaspell (1882–1948) and her husband, George Cram Cook (1873–1924), were instrumental in founding influential theater groups. Columnists Abigail Van Buren (Pauline Esther Friedman, b.1918) and her twin sister Ann Landers (Esther Pauline Friedman Lederer,

Iowa's contributions to the field of popular entertainment include William F. "Buffalo Bill" Cody (1846–1917); circus promoter Charles Ringling (1863–1926) and his four brothers; and one of America's best-loved movie actors, John Wayne (Marion Michael Morrison, 1907–79). Johnny Carson (b.1925), host of the *Tonight Show* for 30 years, was born in Corning. Iowa sports figures of note are baseball Hall of Famers Adrian C. "Cap" Anson (1851–1922) and Robert "Bob" Feller (b.1918), and football All-American Nile Kinnick (1918–44).

Photo credit: EPD Photos/CSU Archives

George H. Gallup (1904–84), a public-opinion analyst, originated the Gallup Polls.

b.1918) are from Sioux City. Iowans who have contributed to America's musical heritage include popular composers Meredith Willson (1902–84) and Peter "PDQ Bach" Schickele (b.1935), jazz musician Leon "Bix" Beiderbecke (1903–31), bandleader Glenn Miller (1904–44), and opera singer Simon Estes (b.1938). Iowa's artists of note include Grant Wood (1892–1942), whose *American Gothic* is one of America's best-known paintings.

40 BIBLIOGRAPHY

Aylesworth, Thomas G. *Western Great Lakes: Illinois, Iowa, Minnesota, Wisconsin.* New York: Chelsea House, 1996.

Genoways, Ted and Hugh H. Genoways, eds. *A Perfect Picture of Hell: Eyewitness Accounts by Civil War Prisoners from the 12th Iowa.* Iowa City: University of Iowa Press, 2001.

Kule, Elaine A. *Iowa Facts and Symbols.* Mankato, Minn.: Hilltop Books, 2001.

Kummer, Patricia K. *Iowa.* Mankato, Minn.: Capstone, 1999.

Morrice, Polly Alison. *Iowa.* New York: Benchmark Books, 1998.

Web sites

Iowa Tourism - Iowa Facts. Iowa, You Make Me Smile. [Online] Available http://iowa.tourism.knewell.com/iowa_facts Accessed May 14, 2001.

State of Iowa. Official Web Site of the State of Iowa. [Online] Available http://www.state.ia.us// Accessed May 14, 2001.

KANSAS

State of Kansas

ORIGIN OF STATE NAME: Named for the Kansa (or Kaw) Indians, the "people of the south wind."

NICKNAME: The Sunflower State. (Also: the Wheat State; the Jayhawker State; and Midway, USA.)

CAPITAL: Topeka.

ENTERED UNION: 29 January 1861 (34th).

SONG: "Home on the Range."

MARCH: "The Kansas March."

MOTTO: *Ad astra per aspera* (To the stars through difficulties).

FLAG: The flag consists of a dark blue field with the state seal in the center; a sunflower on a bar of twisted gold and blue is above the seal; the word "Kansas" is below it.

OFFICIAL SEAL: A sun rising over mountains in the background symbolizes the east; commerce is represented by a river and a steamboat. In the foreground, agriculture, the basis of the state's prosperity, is represented by a settler's cabin and a man plowing a field. Beyond this is a wagon train heading west and a herd of buffalo fleeing from two Indians. Around the top is the state motto above a cluster of 34 stars; the circle is surrounded by the words "Great Seal of the State of Kansas, January 29, 1861."

ANIMAL: American buffalo.

BIRD: Western meadowlark.

FLOWER: Wild native sunflower.

TREE: Cottonwood.

INSECT: Honeybee.

TIME: 6 AM CST = noon GMT; 5 AM MST = noon GMT.

1 LOCATION AND SIZE

Located in the western north-central US, Kansas is the second-largest midwestern state (following Minnesota) and ranks 14th among the 50 states. The total area of Kansas is 82,277 square miles (213,097 square kilometers). The state has a maximum extension east-west of about 411 miles (661 kilometers) and an extreme north-south distance of about 208 miles (335 kilometers). Kansas has a total boundary length of 1,219 miles (1,962 kilometers).

2 TOPOGRAPHY

Three main land regions define the state: the eastern third, consisting of plains, hills, and lowlands; the central third, comprised of the Smoky Hills to the north and the Great Bend Prairie and Red Hills to the south; and the high plains to the west. More than 50,000 streams run through the state, and there are hundreds of artificial lakes. Major rivers include the Missouri, the Arkansas, and the Kansas.

3 CLIMATE

Kansas's continental climate is highly changeable. The average mean temperature is 55°F (13°C). The record high in the state is 121°F (149°C), and the record low is –40°F (–40°C). The normal annual precipitation ranges from slightly more than 40 inches (101.6 centimeters) in the southeast to as little as 16 inches (40.6 centimeters) in the west. Tornadoes are a regular fact of Kansas life.

4 PLANTS AND ANIMALS

Native grasses cover one-third of Kansas, which is much overgrazed. Bluestem—both big and little—grows in most parts of the state. One native conifer, eastern red cedar, is found generally throughout the state. Hackberry, black walnut, and sycamore grow in the east, while box elder and cottonwood predominate in western Kansas. The wild native sunflower, the state flower, is found throughout the state. Other characteristic wildflowers include coneflower and black-eyed Susan.

Kansas's native mammals include the common cottontail, black-tailed jackrabbit, and black-tailed prairie dog. The western meadowlark is the state bird. The black-footed ferret, gray bat, and bald eagle are threatened or endangered as of 1997.

5 ENVIRONMENTAL PROTECTION

No environmental problem is more crucial to Kansas than water quality. The state's

Kansas Population Profile

Total population in 2000:	2,688,418
Population change, 1990–2000:	8.5%
Hispanic or Latino†:	7.0%
Population by race	
One race:	97.9%
White:	86.1%
Black or African American:	5.7%
American Indian/Alaska Native:	0.9%
Asian:	1.7%
Native Hawaiian/Pacific Islander:	—
Some other race:	3.4%
Two or more races:	2.1%

Population by Age Group

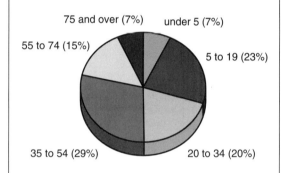

75 and over (7%) under 5 (7%)
55 to 74 (15%)
5 to 19 (23%)
35 to 54 (29%)
20 to 34 (20%)

Top Cities by Population

City	Population	% change 1990–2000
Wichita	344,284	13.2
Overland Park	149,080	33.4
Kansas City	146,866	–1.9
Topeka	122,377	2.1
Olathe	92,962	46.7
Lawrence	80,098	22.1
Shawnee	47,996	26.3
Salina	45,679	8.0
Manhattan	44,831	18.9
Hutchinson	40,787	3.8

Notes: †A person of Hispanic or Latino origin may be of any race. NA indicates that data are not available.
Sources: U.S. Census Bureau. Public Information Office. *Demographic Profiles.* [Online] Available http://www.census.gov/Press-Release/www/2001/demoprofile.html. Accessed June 1, 2001. U.S. Census Bureau. *Census 2000: Redistricting Data.* Press release issued by the Redistricting Data Office. Washington, D.C., March,

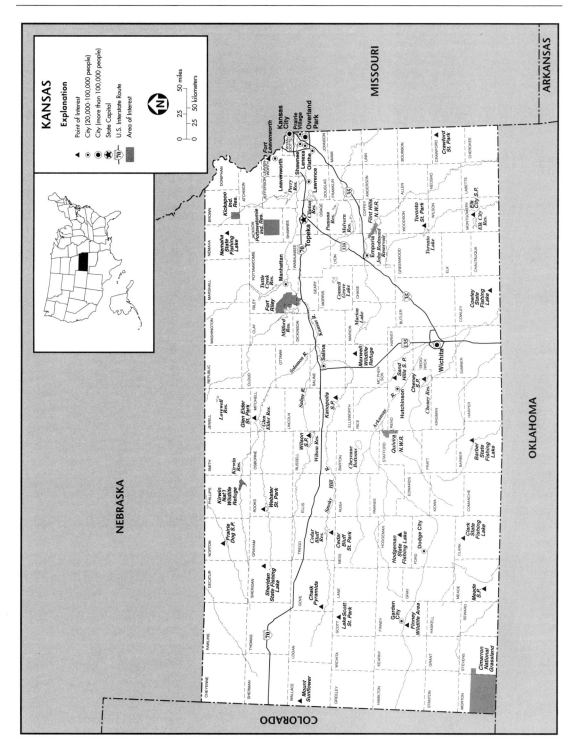

Photo credit: Kansas Division of Travel and Tourism.

The American Buffalo, Kansas's state animal.

environmental efforts focus on regulatory and remedial programs for surface and groundwater sources.

Strip mining for coal is decreasing in southeast Kansas. A 1969 law requires immediate leveling and seeding of the disturbed land. As of 1998, there were 11 hazardous waste sites in Kansas.

6 POPULATION

With a population in 2000 of nearly 2.7 million, Kansas ranked 32nd among the states. The population density in the same year was 32.9 persons per square mile (12.7 persons per square kilometer), only about 40% of the national average (79.6 persons per square mile; 30.7 per square

kilometer). About 69.1% of the population lived in urban areas and 30.9% in rural areas. Estimates for 2000 showed 344,284 residents in Wichita, 149,080 in Overland Park, and 146,866 in Kansas City.

7 ETHNIC GROUPS

There were an estimated 23,200 Native Americans in Kansas as of 1997. Black Americans in Kansas were estimated at 152,800—5.9% of the population—in 1997, when the state also had 44,000 residents (1.7%) of Asian-Pacific origin, primarily Vietnamese, Laotians, and Cambodians. The 1997 federal estimate put the number of Hispanics (who may be

Kansas Population by Race

Census 2000 was the first national census in which the instructions to respondents said, "Mark one or more races." This table shows the number of people who are of one, two, or three or more races. For those claiming two races, the number of people belonging to the various categories is listed. The U.S. government conducts a census of the population every ten years.

	Number	Percent
Total population	2,688,418	100.0
One race	2,631,922	97.9
Two races	53,344	2.0
White *and* Black or African American	9,970	0.4
White *and* American Indian/Alaska Native	17,539	0.7
White *and* Asian	5,781	0.2
White *and* Native Hawaiian/Pacific Islander	613	—
White *and* some other race	12,631	0.5
Black or African American *and* American Indian/Alaska Native	1,951	0.1
Black or African American *and* Asian	661	—
Black or African American *and* Native Hawaiian/Pacific Islander	132	—
Black or African American *and* some other race	1,514	0.1
American Indian/Alaska Native *and* Asian	242	—
American Indian/Alaska Native *and* Native Hawaiian/Pacific Islander	41	—
American Indian/Alaska Native *and* some other race	581	—
Asian *and* Native Hawaiian/Pacific Islander	433	—
Asian *and* some other race	1,104	—
Native Hawaiian/Pacific Islander *and* some other race	151	—
Three or more races	3,152	0.1

Source: U.S. Census Bureau. *Census 2000: Redistricting Data.* Press release issued by the Redistricting Data Office. Washington, D.C., March, 2001. A dash (—) indicates that the percent is less than 0.1.

of any race) at 132,600, or 5.1% of the population.

8 LANGUAGES

Regional features of Kansas speech are almost entirely those of the Northern and North Midland dialects. Kansans typically play as children on a *teetertotter,* make *white bread* sandwiches, carry water in a *pail,* and may designate the time 2:45 as a quarter *to,* or *of,* or *till* three. The migration by Southerners in the mid-19th century is evidenced in southeastern Kansas by such South Midland terms as *pullybone* (wishbone) and *light bread* (white bread). In 1990, 2,158,011 Kansans—94.3%—

spoke only English at home. Kansans who spoke another language at home included Spanish, 62,059; German, 22,887; and French, 7,851.

9 RELIGIONS

The leading Protestant denominations in 1990 were United Methodist, 238,029; Southern Baptist Convention, 96,524; and Christian Church (Disciples of Christ), 58,314. Roman Catholics constitute the largest single religious group in the state, with 369,241 adherents in 1990. Kansas's estimated Jewish population in 1994 was 14,000.

Photo credit: Kansas Division of Travel and Tourism.

Young member of the Kickapoo Tribe at the All Mid-American Indian Center.

10 TRANSPORTATION

In the heartland of the nation, Kansas is at the crossroads of US road and railway systems. In 1998, the state had 5,799 miles (9,331 kilometers) of railroad track. An Amtrak passenger train crosses Kansas en route from Chicago to Los Angeles. The total number of riders through the state in 1996 was 32,944. In 1997, the state had 133,540 miles (214,866 kilometers) of public roads. There were 1.14 million autos, 1.01 million trucks, 48,835 motorcycles, and 3,813 buses registered in Kansas in 1997. The busiest airport, at Wichita, had 17,217 departing flights carrying 678,337 passengers. The chief river ports are Atchison, Leavenworth, and Kansas City.

11 HISTORY

Plains tribes—the Wichita, Pawnee, Kansa, and Osage—were living or hunting in Kansas when the earliest Europeans arrived. Around 1800, they were joined on the Central Plains by the nomadic Cheyenne, Arapaho, Comanche, and Kiowa. The first European, explorer Francisco Coronado, entered Kansas in 1541. Between 1682 and 1739, French explorers established trading contacts with the Native Americans. France ceded its claims to the area to Spain in 1762 but received it back from Spain in 1800.

Most of Kansas was sold to the US by France as part of the Louisiana Purchase of 1803. (The extreme southwestern corner was gained after the Mexican War.) Early settlement of Kansas was sparse, limited to a few thousand Native Americans—including Shawnee, Delaware, Ojibwa, and Wyandot. These tribes were forcibly removed from their lands and relocated in what is now eastern Kansas.

The Santa Fe Trail was opened to wagon traffic in 1822, and for 50 years that route, two-thirds of which lay in Kansas, was of commercial importance to the West. During the 1840s and 1850s, thousands of migrants crossed northeastern Kansas on the California-Oregon Trail. Kansas Territory was created by the Kansas-Nebraska Act (30 May 1854). Almost immediately, disputes arose as to whether

Bullwhacker Days in Olathe. Bullwhackers were men who drove teams of oxen during Oregon Trail days.

Kansas would enter the Union as a free or slave state. Both free-staters and pro-slavery settlers were brought in, and a succession of governors tried to mediate between the two groups.

Statehood

Kansas entered the Union on 29 January 1861 as a free state, and Topeka was named the capital. Although Kansas lay west of the major Civil War action, more than two-thirds of its adult males served in the Union Army and gave it the highest military death rate among the northern states. Following the Civil War, settlement expanded in Kansas, particularly in the central part of the state. White settlers encroached on the hunting grounds of the Plains tribes, and their settlements were attacked in retaliation. Most of the Native Americans were eventually removed to the Indian Territory in what is now Oklahoma.

By 1872, both the Union Pacific and the Santa Fe railroads had crossed Kansas, and other lines were under construction. Rail expansion brought more settlers, who established new communities. It also led to the great Texas cattle drives that meant prosperity to a number of Kansas towns—including Abilene, Ellsworth, Wichita, Caldwell, and Dodge City—from 1867 to 1885. This was when Bat Masterson, Wyatt Earp, and Wild Bill Hickok reigned

Kansas Governors: 1861–2001

1861–1863	Charles Lawrence Robinson	Republican
1863–1865	Thomas Carney	Republican
1865–1868	Samuel Johnson Crawford	Republican
1868–1869	Nehemiah Green	Republican
1869–1873	James Madison Harvey	Republican
1873–1877	Thomas Andrew Osborn	Republican
1877–1879	George Tobey Anthony	Republican
1879–1883	John Pierce St. John	Republican
1883–1885	George Washington Glick	Democrat
1885–1889	John Alexander Martin	Republican
1889–1893	Lyman Underwood Humphrey	Republican
1893–1895	Lorenzo Dow Lewelling	Populist
1895–1897	Edmund Needham Morrill	Republican
1897–1899	John Whitnah Leedy	Populist
1899–1903	William Eugene Stanley	Republican
1903–1905	Willis Joshua Bailey	Republican
1905–1909	Edward Wallis Hoch	Republican
1909–1913	Walter Roscoe Stubbs	Republican
1913–1915	George Hartshorn Hodges	Democrat
1915–1919	Arthur Capper	Republican
1919–1923	Henry Justin Allen	Republican
1923–1925	Johathan McMillan Davis	Democrat
1925–1929	Benjamin Sanford Paulen	Republican
1929–1931	Clyde Martin Reed	Republican
1931–1933	Harry Hines Woodring	Democrat
1933–1937	Alfred Mossman Landon	Republican
1937–1939	Walter Augustus Huxman	Democrat
1939–1943	Payne Harry Ratner	Republican
1943–1947	Andrew Frank Schoeppel	Republican
1947–1950	Frank Carlson	Republican
1950–1951	Frank Leslie Hagaman	Republican
1951–1955	Edward Ferdinand Arn	Republican
1955–1957	Frederick Lee Hall	Republican
1957	John Berridge McCuish	Republican
1957–1961	George Docking	Democrat
1961–1965	John Anderson, Jr.	Republican
1965–1967	William Henry Avery	Republican
1967–1975	Robert Blackwell Docking	Democrat
1975–1979	Robert Frederick Bennett	Republican
1979–1987	John Carlin	Democrat
1987–1991	John Michael Hayden	Republican
1991–1995	Joan Finney	Democrat
1995–	Bill Graves	Republican

in Dodge City and Abilene—the now romantic era of the Old West.

A strain of hard winter wheat that proved particularly well-suited to the state's soil was brought to Kansas in the 1870s by Russian Mennonites fleeing czarist rule, and Plains agriculture was transformed. Significant changes in agriculture, industry, transportation, and communications came after 1900. Mechanization became commonplace in farming, and vast areas were opened to wheat production, particularly during World War I. The Progressive movement of the early 1900s focused attention on control of monopolies, public health, labor legislation, and more representative politics.

1930s–1990s

Kansas suffered through the Great Depression of the 1930s. The state's western region, part of the Dust Bowl, was hardest hit. Improved weather conditions and the demands of World War II revived Kansas agriculture in the 1940s. The World War II era also saw the development of industry, especially in transportation. Other heavy industry grew, and mineral production—oil, natural gas, salt, coal, and gypsum—expanded greatly.

Since World War II, Kansas has become increasingly urban. Agriculture has become highly commercialized, and there are dozens of large industries that process and market farm products and supply materials to crop producers. Livestock production, especially in closely controlled feedlots, is a major enterprise. Recent governors have worked to expand international exports of Kansas products, and by 1981/82, Kansas ranked seventh among the states in agricultural exports, with sales of more than $1.6 billion.

The late 1980s and early 1990s brought dramatic extremes of weather. A severe drought in 1988 drove up commodity prices and depleted grain stocks. From April through September of 1993, Kansas experienced the worst floods of the century. Some 13,500 people evacuated their homes, and the floods caused $574 million dollars worth of damage.

12 STATE GOVERNMENT

The Kansas legislature consists of a 40-member senate and a 125-member house of representatives. Officials elected statewide include the governor, lieutenant governor, secretary of state, attorney general, and treasurer. A bill becomes law when it has been approved by 21 senators and 63 representatives and signed by the governor. A veto can be overridden by one more than two-thirds of the members of both houses.

13 POLITICAL PARTIES

Although the Republicans remain the dominant force in state politics, the Democrats controlled several state offices in the mid–1990s. Democrats held the governorship for 18 of the 28 years between 1957 and 1985. The most recent Democratic governor was Joan Finney, elected in 1990. Republican Bill Graves was reelected governor in 1998. Republicans have regularly controlled the legislature, however. In 1998, the state had 683,108 registered Republicans (45% of registered voters) and 432,074 registered Democrats (29%).

In the 2000 election, Republican George W. Bush won 58% of the vote while Democrat Al Gore received 37%. In the 1996 elections, Republican Bob Dole, first elected to the US Senate in 1968 and elected Senate majority leader in 1984, was reelected in 1992. He reclaimed the

Kansas Presidential Vote by Political Parties, 1948–2000

YEAR	KANSAS WINNER	DEMOCRAT	REPUBLICAN	PROGRESSIVE	SOCIALIST	PROHIBITION
1948	Dewey (R)	351,902	423,039	4,603	2,807	6,468
1952	*Eisenhower (R)	273,296	616,302	6,038	530	6,038
1956	*Eisenhower (R)	296,317	566,878	—	—	3,048
1960	Nixon (R)	363,213	561,474	—	—	4,138
1964	*Johnson (D)	464,028	386,579		1,901	5,393
				AMERICAN IND.		
1968	*Nixon (R)	302,996	478,674	88,921	—	2,192
1972	*Nixon (R)	270,287	619,812	21,808	—	4,188
					LIBERTARIAN	
1976	Ford (R)	430,421	502,752	4,724	3,242	1,403
1980	*Reagan (R)	326,150	566,812	7,555	14,470	—
1984	*Reagan (R)	333,149	677,296	—	3,329	—
1988	*Bush (R)	422,636	554,049	3,806	12,553	—
				IND. (Perot)		
1992	Bush (R)	390,434	449,951	312,358	4,314	—
1996	Dole (R)	387,659	583,245	92,639	4,557	—
					REFORM	LIBERTARIAN
2000	*Bush (R)	399,276	622,332	36,086	7,370	4,525

* Won US presidential election.

Wheat harvest. Kansas is one of the highest wheat-producing states in the US.

post of Senate majority leader when the Republicans gained control of the Senate in the elections of 1994. In a surprise move in May 1996, Dole suddenly retired from the Senate to concentrate on his presidential campaign. In November, the race to fill his remaining term was won by Republican Sam Brownback. Brownback was quickly reelected in 1998. Kansas's other Republican senator, is Pat Roberts, elected in 1996. Following the 2000 election, Republicans held three of four US congressional seats. In the state legislature in 2001, there were 27 Republicans and 13 Democrats in the senate, and 79 Republicans and 46 Democrats in the state house.

14 LOCAL GOVERNMENT

As of 1997, Kansas had 105 counties, 628 incorporated cities, 1,362 townships, and 324 school districts. Each county government is headed by three elected county commissioners. Most cities are run by mayor-council or mayor-commission systems.

15 JUDICIAL SYSTEM

The supreme court, the highest court in the state, is composed of a chief justice and six other justices. An intermediate-level court of appeals consists of a chief judge and six other judges. There are 31 district courts. Kansas's crime rate was 4,858.8 per 100,000 inhabitants in 1998.

The state had a prison population of 8,494 in 1999.

16 MIGRATION

Steady migration from farms to cities has been a feature of Kansas life throughout this century, with urban population surpassing farm population after World War II. From 1980 to 1990, Kansas had a net loss of 63,411 from migration. As of 1990, 61.3% of all Kansans had been born within the state. During 1990–98, the net loss from interstate migration was 13,000, while the net gain from international migration was 24,000.

17 ECONOMY

Today, agricultural products and meat-packing industries are rivaled by the large aircraft industry centered in Wichita. Four Kansas companies, all located in Wichita, manufacture 70% of the world's general aviation aircraft. Kansas leads all states and trails only seven countries in wheat production. The Kansas City metropolitan area is a center of automobile production and printing. Metal fabrication, printing, and mineral products are the main industries in the nine southeastern counties.

18 INCOME

In 1998, Kansas's income per capita (per person) was $25,537 (27th in the US). In that year, total personal income was $67.4 billion. Median household income was $35,867 in 1998. About 10.1% of all Kansans lived below the federal poverty level as of 1998.

19 INDUSTRY

Food products, transportation equipment, printing and publishing, petroleum and coal products, and chemicals accounted for about 70% of the estimated value of shipments, which totaled $49 billion in 1997. Kansas is a world leader in aviation, claiming a large share of both US and world production and sales of commercial aircraft.

20 LABOR

Kansas has traditionally had a fairly low unemployment rate. In 1998, the civilian labor force was 1.41 million, with an unemployment rate of 3.8%. The Wichita area accounts for about 20% of the labor force. As of 1998, 9.7% of all workers were union members.

21 AGRICULTURE

Known as the Wheat State and the bread-basket of the nation, Kansas typically produces more wheat than any other state. It ranked fifth in total farm income in 1999, with cash receipts of over $7.6 billion. Between 1940 and 1998, the number of farms declined from 159,000 to 65,000, while the average size of farms more than doubled. The following table shows figures for several leading crops in 1998:

CROP	PRODUCTION (BUSHELS)	VALUE
Wheat	494.9 million	$1.26 billion
Sorghum (grain)	264 million	$448.8 million
Corn (grain)	418.9 million	$816.9 million
Soybeans	75 million	$401.2 million

Other leading crops are alfalfa, hay, oats, barley, popcorn, rye, dry edible beans, corn and sorghums for silage, wild hay, red clover, and sugar beets.

22 DOMESTICATED ANIMALS

In 1997, Kansas ranchers had an estimated 6.55 million head of cattle (third among the states), valued at $3.34 billion. There were 1.59 million hogs and pigs in 1998, valued at $58.8 million. Cattle production in 1999 was valued at about $3.34 billion.

The total production of milk in 1995 was 1.27 billion pounds from 81,000 dairy cows. Poultry farms produced 2.4 million pounds of chicken that year.

23 FISHING

There is little commercial fishing in Kansas. Sport fishermen can find bass, crappie, catfish, perch, and walleye in the state's reservoirs and artificial lakes. In 1998, there were 329,115 fishing licenses issued by the state.

24 FORESTRY

Kansas was at one time so barren of trees that early settlers were offered 160 acres (65 hectares) free if they would plant trees on their land. Today much of Kansas is still treeless. Kansas has 1.5 million acres (625,700 hectares) of forestland, 2.9% of the total state area.

25 MINING

The value of nonfuel mineral production in Kansas was estimated at $535 million in 1998. Portland cement, salt, crushed stone, and grade-A helium are the most valuable commodities; together these accounted for nearly 86% of the 1998 value.

26 ENERGY AND POWER

In 1999, Kansas's electrical output was 41.5 billion kilowatt hours, of which 68% was coal-fired. In 1999, Kansas produced a total of 29 million barrels of crude petroleum, ninth among the states. There were proven reserves of 275 million barrels at the end of 1995. Natural gas production was 603.6 billion cubic feet (17 billion cubic meters) in 1998. Two surface mines produced 341,000 tons of bituminous coal in 1998.

27 COMMERCE

The state's wholesale sales totaled $44 billion in 1997; retail sales totaled $23 billion. Kansas's agricultural and manufactured goods have an important role in US foreign trade. Exports of goods originating in Kansas totaled $4 billion in 1998.

28 PUBLIC FINANCE

The total indebtedness of state government exceeded $1.21 billion as of 1997, or about $466 per capita (per person). Kansas's ratio of state public debt per person was the lowest of any state that year.

The state revenues for fiscal year 1997 were $7.95 billion; expenditures were $7.5 billion.

29 TAXATION

Kansas ranked 21st in state taxes per capita (per person) in 1997, at $1,630. The state taxes the income of individuals (3.5% to 6.45%) and corporations (4%). The state sales tax rate was 4.9% in 2000. Kansas also collects liquor and bingo

Photo credit: © Cotton Coulson/Woodfin Camp.

A worker assembles a small jet aircraft at the Beechcraft Manufacturing Plant in Wichita.

taxes, cigarette and tobacco products taxes, inheritance taxes, and other types of tax. Property taxes are the largest source of income for local governments. Local government collected $2.2 billion in taxes in 1996. In 1995, Kansans paid almost $10 billion in federal taxes.

30 HEALTH

Heart disease, the leading cause of death in the state, occurred at a rate of 274.1 per 100,000 people in 1998. In 1998, Kansas had 129 community hospitals with 10,923 beds. Kansas had 8,221 full-time nurses in 1998, and 202 physicians per 100,000 population in 1997.

Topeka, a major US center for psychiatric treatment, is home to the world-famous Menninger Clinic. The Mid-America Cancer Center and Radiation Therapy Center at the University of Kansas are the state's major cancer research and treatment facilities.

31 HOUSING

By 1998, there were an estimated 1.13 million housing units in Kansas. The median monthly cost in 1990 of housing for owners with a mortgage was $628. The median monthly rent was $372. The median sales price of existing one-family homes in the Kansas City, Missourir/Kansas area in 1998 was $114,000.

Photo credit: © Cotton Coulson/Woodfin Camp.

An oil rig in Butler County.

32 EDUCATION

Enrollment in the state's 1,479 public schools in fall 1997 was 468,687: 141,142 students were in high school and 327,545 were in kindergarten through eighth grade. There were about 16,423 elementary-school teachers and 14,306 secondary-school teachers. Expenditures for public elementary and secondary schools amounted to $6,112 per student in 1999/00. Attendance at private and parochial schools in fall 1997 was 40,573.

In 1998, 28.5% of the Kansas population had completed four or more years of college, compared with the national average of 23%. In 1997, there were 6 state universities, 19 two-year community colleges, 5 private two-year colleges, 17 church-affiliated universities and four-year colleges, and 12 vocational-technical schools. In fall 1997, 177,544 students were enrolled in institutions of higher education.

33 ARTS

The Kansas Arts Commission is a 12-member panel appointed by the governor, which annually awards grants to more than 300 arts organizations. Wichita has a resident symphony orchestra.

34 LIBRARIES AND MUSEUMS

The Dwight D. Eisenhower Library in Abilene houses the collection of papers and memorabilia from the 34th president. There is also a museum. The Menninger Foundation Museum and Archives in Topeka maintains various collections pertaining to psychiatry. Kansas had 35 public library systems in 1998, with 10.2 million volumes and a circulation of over 20 million. Additionally there were 10 bookmobiles, 28 college libraries, and 24 junior college libraries. Seven regional library systems serve state residents who have no local library service.

There were about 188 museums, historical societies, and art galleries scattered across the state in 2000. Among the art museums are the Mulvane Art Center in Topeka, the Helen Foresman Spencer Museum of Art at the University of Kansas (Lawrence), and the Wichita Art Museum.

35 COMMUNICATIONS

About 93.8% of all households had telephone service in 1999. The state had 61 AM and 147 FM radio stations, 21 commercial television stations, and 4 public television stations in 2000. That year, there were 42,009 registered Internet domain names in the state.

36 PRESS

In 1998, Kansas had 46 daily newspapers and 15 Sunday papers. Leading newspapers and their daily circulations in 1998 were the *Wichita Eagle* (87,915) and the *Topeka Capital-Journal* (59,858).

37 TOURISM, TRAVEL, AND RECREATION

Kansas has 23 state parks, 24 federal reservoirs, and more than 100 privately owned campsites. Over 2.1 million visitors annually use the state park system. There are two national historic sites, Fort Larned and Fort Scott, both 19th century frontier army bases.

Topeka features a number of tourist attractions, including the Kansas Museum of History and the Menninger Foundation. Dodge City offers a reproduction of Old Front Street as it was when the town was the "cowboy capital of the world." In Hanover stands the only remaining original and unaltered Pony Express station. A recreated "Little House on the Prairie," near the childhood home of author Laura Ingalls Wilder, is 13 miles (21 kilometers) southwest of Independence. The Eisenhower

Photo credit: Kansas Division of Travel and Tourism.

Bernard Warkentin House in Newton. Warkentin brought the hardy "Turkey Red" winter wheat to Kansas and 5,000 German-speaking Mennonites to help farm it.

Center in Abilene contains the 34th president's family home, library, and museum.

38 SPORTS

There are no major professional sports teams in Kansas. The Wichita Wings play in the National Professional Soccer League, an indoor league. During spring, summer, and early fall, horses are raced at Eureka Downs. The University of Kansas and Kansas State both play collegiate football in the Big 12 Conference.

Photo credit: National Archives.

Dwight D. Eisenhower (1890–1969), shown here with his wife, Mamie, was born in Texas but grew up in Abilene, Kansas. He was elected the 34th president in 1952 and was reelected in 1956.

39 FAMOUS KANSANS

Kansas claims only one US president and one US vice-president. Dwight D. Eisenhower (b.Texas, 1890–1969) was elected the 34th president in 1952 and was reelected in 1956. Charles Curtis (1860–1936) was vice-president during the Hoover administration. Two Kansans have been associate justices of the US Supreme Court: David J. Brewer (1837–1910) and Charles E. Whittaker (1901–73).

Prominent US senators include Robert "Bob" Dole (b.1923), who was the Republican candidate for vice-president in 1976, twice served as Senate majority leader, and was his party's presidential candidate in 1996; and Nancy Landon Kassebaum Baker (b.1932), who was first elected to the US Senate in 1978 but retired in 1997. Gary Hart (b.1936) was a senator and a presidential candidate in 1984 and 1988.

Other prominent Kansan political figures included Alfred M. Landon (1887–1984), a former governor who ran for US president on the Republican ticket in 1936; and Carrie Nation (b. Kentucky, 1846–1911), the prohibition activist.

Leaders in medicine and science include the Menninger doctors—C. F. (1862–1953), William (1899–1966), and Karl (1893–1990)—who established the Menninger Foundation, a leading center for mental health; and Clyde Tombaugh (1906–97), who discovered the planet Pluto. Kansas also had several pioneers in aviation including Clyde Cessna (b.Iowa, 1880–1954), Walter Beech (1891–1950), and Amelia Earhart (1898–1937). William Coleman (1870–1957) was an innovator in lighting, and Walter Chrysler (1875–1940) was a prominent automotive developer.

Most famous of Kansas writers was William Allen White (1868–1944), whose son William L. White (1900–73) also had a distinguished literary career. Damon Runyon (1884–1946) was a popular journalist and storyteller, Gordon Parks (b.1912) is a well-known photographer, and Mort Walker (Mortimer Walker Addison, b.1923) is a famous cartoonist. William Inge (1913–73) was a prize-winning playwright who contributed to the Broadway stage.

Notable painters include John Noble (1874–1934) and John Steuart Curry (1897–1946). Jazz great Charlie "Bird" Parker (Charles Christopher Parker, Jr., 1920–55) was born in Kansas City.

Stage and screen notables include Joseph "Buster" Keaton (1895–1966), Louise Brooks (1906–85), Edward Asner (b.1929), and Kirstie Alley (b.1955).

Glenn Cunningham (1909–88) and Jim Ryun (b.1947) both set running records for the mile. Also prominent in sports history were James Naismith (b.Ontario, Canada, 1861–1939), the inventor of basketball; and baseball pitcher Walter Johnson (1887–1946).

40 BIBLIOGRAPHY

Averill, Thomas Fox, editor. *What Kansas Means to Me: Twentieth-Century Writers on the Sunflower State.* Lawrence: University Press of Kansas, 1991.

Averill, Thomas Fox. *Soldier of Democracy: A Biography of Dwight Eisenhower.* New York: Doubleday, 1945, 1952.

Bjorklund, Ruth. *Kansas.* New York: Benchmark Books, 2000.

Deady, Kathleen W. *Kansas Facts and Symbols.* Mankato, Minn.: Hilltop Books, 2001.

Howes, Charles C. *This Place Called Kansas.* Norman: University of Oklahoma Press, 1984.

Moody, Ralph. *Horse of a Different Color: Reminiscenses [sic] of a Kansas Drover.* Lincoln: University of Nebraska Press, 1994.

Nelson, Julie. *Kansas City Chiefs.* Mankato, Minn.: Creative Education, 2000.

Sturman, Susan. *Kansas City.* Minneapolis, Minn.: Dillon Press, 1990.

Zeinert, Karen. *Tragic Prelude: Bleeding Kansas.* North Haven, Conn.: Linnet, 2001.

Web sites

Information Network of Kansas. Welcome to the State of Kansas: Enjoy Your Visit. [Online Available http://www.50states.com/kansas.htm Accessed May 15, 2001.

Kansas Department of Commerce & Housing. General Information about Kansas. [Online] Available http://www.kansascommerce.com/ Accessed May 15, 2001.

KENTUCKY

Commonwealth of Kentucky

ORIGIN OF STATE NAME: Possibly derived from the Wyandot Indian word *Kah-ten-tah-teh* (land of tomorrow).

NICKNAME: The Bluegrass State.

CAPITAL: Frankfort.

ENTERED UNION: 1 June 1792 (15th).

SONG: "My Old Kentucky Home."

MOTTO: United We Stand, Divided We Fall.

FLAG: A simplified version of the state seal on a blue field.

OFFICIAL SEAL: In the center are two men exchanging greetings; above and below them is the state motto. On the periphery are two sprigs of goldenrod and the words "Commonwealth of Kentucky."

COLORS: Blue and gold.

BIRD: Cardinal.

WILD ANIMAL: Gray squirrel.

FISH: Bass.

FLOWER: Goldenrod.

INSECT: Viceroy butterfly.

TREE: Tulip poplar.

TIME: 7 AM EST = noon GMT; 6 AM CST = noon GMT.

1 LOCATION AND SIZE

Located in the eastern south-central US, the Commonwealth of Kentucky is the smallest of the eight south-central states and ranks 37th in size among the 50 states. The total area of Kentucky is 40,409 square miles (104,659 square kilometers). The state extends about 350 miles (563 kilometers) east-west; its maximum north-south extension is about 175 miles (282 kilometers). Its total boundary length is 1,290 miles (2,076 kilometers). Because of a double bend in the Mississippi River, about 10 square miles (26 square kilometers) of southwest Kentucky is separated from the rest of the state by a narrow strip of Missouri.

2 TOPOGRAPHY

The eastern quarter of the state is dominated by the Cumberland Plateau, which is on the western border of the Appalachian Mountains. The western coalfields are the most level part of the state. In the far west are the coastal plains of the Mississippi River. The highest point in Kentucky is Black Mountain in Harlan County, at 4,145 feet (1,263 meters).

The only large lakes in Kentucky are artificial. The biggest is Lake Cumberland at 79 square miles (205 square kilometers). Including the Ohio and Mississippi rivers on its borders and the tributaries of the Ohio, Kentucky claims at least 3,000 miles (4,800 kilometers) of navigable rivers. This is more than any other state except Alaska. The Cumberland Falls, 92 feet (28 meters) high and 100 feet (30 meters) wide, are located in Whitley County.

3 CLIMATE

Kentucky has a moderate, relatively humid climate, with abundant rainfall. The southern and lowland regions are slightly warmer than the uplands. In Louisville, the normal monthly mean temperature ranges from 33°F (1°C) in January to 76°F (24°C) in July. The record high for the state was 114°F (46°C) in 1930. The record low, –37°F (–40°C), was set in 1994. The normal annual precipitation is 43 inches (109 centimeters). Snowfall totals about 18 inches (46 centimeters) a year.

4 PLANTS AND ANIMALS

Kentucky's forests are mostly of the oak/hickory variety, with some beech/maple areas. Four species of magnolia are found, and the tulip poplar, eastern hemlock, and eastern white pine are also common. Kentucky's famed bluegrass is actually blue only in May, when dwarf iris and wild columbine are in bloom.

Game mammals include the raccoon, muskrat, and opossum. The eastern chipmunk and flying squirrel are common small mammals. At least 300 bird species have been recorded, including blackbirds, cardinals (the state bird), and robins. Eagles are winter visitors. The Indiana bat, cougar, and brown bear are among Kentucky's endangered species.

Kentucky Population Profile

Total population in 2000:	4,041,769
Population change, 1990–2000:	9.7%
Hispanic or Latino†:	1.5%
Population by race	
One race:	98.9%
White:	90.1%
Black or African American:	7.3%
American Indian/Alaska Native:	0.2%
Asian:	0.7%
Native Hawaiian/Pacific Islander:	—
Some other race:	0.6%
Two or more races:	1.1%

Population by Age Group

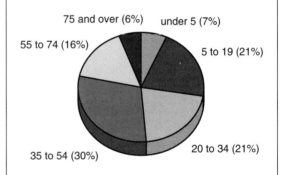

75 and over (6%)
under 5 (7%)
55 to 74 (16%)
5 to 19 (21%)
20 to 34 (21%)
35 to 54 (30%)

Top Cities by Population

City	Population	% change 1990–2000
Lexington-Fayette	260,512	15.6
Louisville	256,231	–4.8
Owensboro	54,067	1.0
Bowling Green	49,296	21.3
Covington	43,370	0.2
Hopkinsville	30,089	0.9
Frankfort	27,741	6.8
Henderson	27,373	5.5
Richmond	27,152	28.3
Jeffersontown	26,633	14.7

Notes: †A person of Hispanic or Latino origin may be of any race. NA indicates that data are not available.
Sources: U.S. Census Bureau. Public Information Office. *Demographic Profiles.* [Online] Available http://www.census.gov/Press-Release/www/2001/demoprofile.html. Accessed June 1, 2001. U.S. Census Bureau. *Census 2000: Redistricting Data.* Press release issued by the Redistricting Data Office. Washington, D.C., March, 2001.

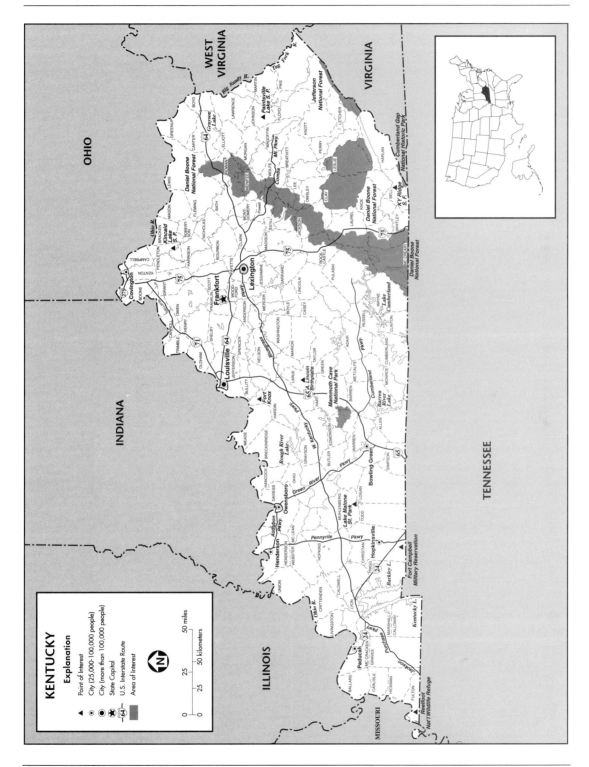

Kentucky Population by Race

Census 2000 was the first national census in which the instructions to respondents said, "Mark one or more races." This table shows the number of people who are of one, two, or three or more races. For those claiming two races, the number of people belonging to the various categories is listed. The U.S. government conducts a census of the population every ten years.

	Number	Percent
Total population	4,041,769	100.0
One race	3,999,326	98.9
Two races	39,863	1.0
White *and* Black or African American	11,084	0.3
White *and* American Indian/Alaska Native	12,842	0.3
White *and* Asian	4,728	0.1
White *and* Native Hawaiian/Pacific Islander	633	—
White *and* some other race	6,166	0.2
Black or African American *and* American Indian/Alaska Native	1,174	—
Black or African American *and* Asian	571	—
Black or African American *and* Native Hawaiian/Pacific Islander	141	—
Black or African American *and* some other race	1,126	—
American Indian/Alaska Native *and* Asian	174	—
American Indian/Alaska Native *and* Native Hawaiian/Pacific Islander	30	—
American Indian/Alaska Native *and* some other race	233	—
Asian *and* Native Hawaiian/Pacific Islander	251	—
Asian *and* some other race	592	—
Native Hawaiian/Pacific Islander *and* some other race	118	—
Three or more races	2,580	0.1

Source: U.S. Census Bureau. *Census 2000: Redistricting Data.* Press release issued by the Redistricting Data Office. Washington, D.C., March, 2001. A dash (—) indicates that the percent is less than 0.1.

5 ENVIRONMENTAL PROTECTION

The most serious environmental concern in Kentucky is damage to land and water from strip-mining. The first comprehensive attempts at control did not begin until the passage in 1977 of the Federal Surface Mining Control and Reclamation Act. Flooding is a chronic problem in southeastern Kentucky, where strip-mining has worsened soil erosion. Leakage of radioactive materials had been discovered at Maxey Flats, a closed nuclear waste disposal facility in Fleming County.

In 1996, Kentucky's production of solid waste averaged 17 million pounds (7.7 million kilograms) per day, or 4.4 pounds (2 kilograms) a day per person. There are 24 municipal landfills, and 115 of the state's 120 counties have recycling centers. In 1998, Kentucky had 16 hazardous waste sites.

6 POPULATION

Kentucky fell behind Alabama and Colorado to rank 25th in population among the states in 2000, with a census population of over 4 million. At the time of the 1990 census, Kentucky's population was 51% urban, far below the national norm of 75.2%. The projected population for 2005 is 4.1 million. The population den-

Photo credit: James Archambeault.

The green fields and white fences of Lexington's notable Thoroughbred farms.

sity in 2000 was 101.7 persons per square mile (39.3 persons per square kilometer).

Lexington-Fayette, the state's largest city, had a 2000 population of about 260,512. Other cities and their 2000 populations include Louisville, 256,231; Owensboro, 54,067; Bowling Green, 49,296; and Covington, 43,370. Approximately 28% of the population was 19 years of age and younger.

7 ETHNIC GROUPS

Since there was relatively little opportunity for industrial employment, Kentucky attracted small numbers of foreign immigrants in the 19th and 20th centuries. Among persons reporting a single ancestry

in the 1990 census, a total of 552,802 claimed English descent, 798,001 German, 695,853 Irish, 222,428 African-American, and 92,588 French. Kentucky had an estimated black population of 263,000 (7.2%) in 1997.

There were an estimated 5,970 (0.2%) Native Americans in 1997. However, 208,938 Kentuckians reported at least some Native American ancestry in 1990. In 1997, Asian-Pacific peoples were estimated at 25,500 (0.7%). The 1990 census recorded 4,264 Koreans, 2,367 Asian Indians, 3,275 Japanese, 1,340 Vietnamese, and 3,137 Chinese. An estimated 30,100 state residents were of Hispanic origin in 1997 (primarily Mexican and Puerto Rican).

8 LANGUAGES

Speech patterns in the state generally reflect the first settlers' Virginia and Kentucky backgrounds. South Midland features are best preserved in the mountains, but some common to Midland and Southern are widespread. In 1990, 97.5% of all residents five years old and older spoke only English at home. Other languages spoken at home included Spanish, German, Korean, and Chinese.

9 RELIGIONS

As of 1990 there were 1,847,667 known Protestants in Kentucky, of whom 962,945 belonged to the Southern Baptist Convention; 227,143 to the United Methodist Church; 66,798 to the Christian Church (Disciples of Christ); and 90,520 to the Christian Churches and Churches of Christ. The Roman Catholic Church had 365,270 members at the beginning of 1990. There were an estimated 11,000 Jews in Kentucky in 1994.

10 TRANSPORTATION

As of 1998, Kentucky had 2,811 rail miles (4,523 kilometers) of railroad track, 80% of which was Class I track. In 1995/96, the total number of Amtrak riders came to 7,330. In 1997, Kentucky had 73,031 miles (117,507 kilometers) of public roads. There were 762 miles (1,226 kilometers) of interstate highway. That same year, 1.63 million automobiles, 1.13 million trucks, and 11,812 buses were registered in the state.

Louisville, on the Ohio River, is the chief port. In 1998, traffic through the port totaled 8.6 million tons. Paducah is the outlet port for traffic on the Tennessee River. Greater Cincinnati Airport, located in northern Kentucky west of Covington, serves 22 million passengers annually. Standiford Field in Louisville boarded 3.8 million passengers in 1999.

11 HISTORY

No Native American nations resided in central and eastern Kentucky when these areas were first explored by British-American surveyors Thomas Walker and Christopher Gist in 1750 and 1751. The dominant Shawnee and Cherokee tribes utilized the region as a hunting ground, returning to homes in the neighboring territories of Ohio and Tennessee. The first permanent colonial settlement in Kentucky was established at Harrodstown (now Harrodsburg) in 1774.

North Carolina speculator Richard Henderson, assisted by famed woodsman Daniel Boone, purchased a huge tract of land in central Kentucky from the Cherokee and established Fort Boonesborough. Henderson sought approval for creation of a 14th colony, but the plan was blocked by Virginians, who in 1776 incorporated the region as the County of Kentucky.

Kentucky became the principal gateway for migration into the Mississippi Valley. By the late 1780s, its settlements were growing, and it was obvious that Kentucky could not long remain under the control of Virginia. In June 1792, Kentucky entered the Union as the 15th state.

Kentucky Governors: 1792–2001

1792–1796	Isaac Shelby	Dem-Rep		1895–1899	William O'Connell Bradley	Republican
1796–1804	James Garrard	Dem-Rep		1899–1900	William Sylvester Taylor	Republican
1804–1808	Christopher Greenup	Republican		1900	William Goebel	Democrat
1808–1812	Charles Scott	Dem-Rep		1900–1907	John Crepps Wickliffe Beckham	Democrat
1812–1816	Isaac Shelby	Dem-Rep		1907–1911	Augustus Everett Willson	Republican
1816	George Madison	Dem-Rep		1911–1915	James Bennett McCreary	Democrat
1816–1820	Gabriel Slaughter	Dem-Rep		1915–1919	Augustus Owsley Stanley	Democrat
1820–1824	John Adair	Dem-Rep		1919	James Dixon Black	Democrat
1824–1828	Joseph Desha	Dem-Rep		1919–1923	Edwin Porch Morrow	Republican
1828–1832	Thomas Metcalfe	Nat-Rep		1923–1927	William Jason Fields	Democrat
1832–1834	John Breathitt	Democrat		1927–1931	Flem Davis Sampson	Republican
1834–1836	James Turner Morehead	Democrat		1831–1835	Ruby Laffoon	Democrat
1836–1839	James Clark	Whig		1835–1839	Albert Benjamin Chandler	Democrat
1839–1840	Charles Anderson Wickliffe	Whig		1839–1843	Keen Johnson	Democrat
1840–1844	Robert Perkins Letcher	Whig		1943–1947	Simeon Slavens Willis	Republican
1844–1848	William Owsley	Whig		1947–1950	Earle Chester Clements	Democrat
1848–1850	John Jordan Crittenden	Whig		1950–1955	Lawrence Winchester Wetherby	Democrat
1850–1851	John Larue Helm	Democrat		1955–1959	Albert Benjamin Chandler	Democrat
1851–1855	Lazarus Whitehead Powell	Democrat		1959–1963	Bertram Thomas Combs	Democrat
1855–1859	Charles Slaughter Morehead	American		1963–1967	Edward Thompson Breathitt	Democrat
1859–1862	Beriah Magoffin	Democrat		1967–1971	Louie Broady Nunn	Republican
1862–1863	James Fisher Robinson	Democrat		1971–1974	Wendell Hampton Ford	Democrat
1863–1867	Thomas E. Bramlette	Union-Dem		1974–1979	Julian Morton Carroll	Democrat
1867	John Larue Helm	Democrat		1979–1983	John Young Brown, Jr.	Democrat
1867–1871	John White Stevenson	Democrat		1983–1987	Martha Layne Collins	Democrat
1871–1875	Preston Hopkins Leslie	Democrat		1987–1991	Wallace G. Wilkinson	Democrat
1875–1879	James Bennett McCreary	Democrat		1991–1995	Brereton Chandler Jones	Democrat
1879–1883	Luke Pryor Blackburn	Democrat		1995–	Paul E. Patton	Democrat
1883–1887	James Procter Knott	Democrat				
1887–1891	Simon Bolivar Buckner	Democrat			Democratic Republican – Dem-Rep	
1891–1895	John Young Brown	Democrat			National Republican – Nat-Rep	
					Union Democrat – Union-Dem	

State Development

Kentucky became a center for breeding and racing fine thoroughbred horses, an industry that still thrives today. More important was the growing and processing of tobacco, which accounted for half the agricultural income of Kentucky farmers by 1860. Finally, whiskey began to be produced in vast quantities by the 1820s, culminating in the development of a fine, aged amber-red brew known throughout the world as bourbon, after Bourbon County.

During the Civil War, Kentuckians were forced to choose sides between the Union, led in the North by Kentucky native Abraham Lincoln, and the Confederacy, led in the South by Kentucky native Jefferson Davis. Although the state legislature finally opted for the Union side, approximately 40,000 men went south to Confederate service, while 100,000—including nearly 24,000 black soldiers—served in the Union army.

In the decades following the war, railroad construction increased threefold and exploitation of timber and coal reserves began in eastern Kentucky. By 1900, Kentucky ranked first among southern states in per capita (per person) income. However, wealth remained very unevenly distributed—a third of all Kentucky farmers were landless tenants. The gubernatorial election scandal of 1899, in which Republican William S. Taylor was charged with fraud and reform-minded Democrat William Goebel was assassinated, polarized the state. Outside investment plummeted, and Kentucky fell into a prolonged economic depression. By 1940, the state ranked last among the 48 states in per capita income and was burdened by an image of poverty and feuding clans. The Great Depression hit the state hard, though an end to Prohibition revived the inactive whiskey industry.

Post-World War II

Kentucky has changed greatly since World War II. Between 1945 and 1980, the number of farms decreased by 53%, while the number of manufacturing plants increased from 2,994 to 3,504 between 1967 and 1982. Although Kentucky remains one of the poorest states in the nation, positive change is evident even in relatively isolated rural communities—a result of better roads, education, television, and government programs.

In the early 1990s, public corruption became a major issue in Kentucky politics. In a sting operation code-named Boptrot, legislators were filmed by hidden cameras accepting payments from lobbyists. Fifteen state legislators, lobbyists, and public figures were convicted or charged with bribery, extortion, fraud, and racketeering. An investigation carried out at the same time charged the husband of former Governor Martha Layne Collins, Dr. William Collins, with collecting $1.7 million in bribes while his wife was in office.

Kentucky Presidential Vote by Political Parties, 1948–2000

YEAR	KENTUCKY WINNER	DEMOCRAT	REPUBLICAN	STATES' RIGHTS DEMOCRAT	PROHIBITION	PROGRESSIVE	SOCIALIST
1948	*Truman (D)	466,756	341,210	10,411	1,245	1,567	1,284
1952	Stevenson (D)	495,729	495,029	—	1,161	—	—
1956	*Eisenhower (R)	476,453	572,192	—	2,145	—	—
1960	Nixon (R)	521,855	602,607	—	—	—	—
				STATES' RIGHTS			
1964	*Johnson (D)	669,659	372,977	3,469	—	—	—
				AMERICAN IND.			SOC. WRKRS
1968	*Nixon (R)	397,541	462,411	193,098	—	—	2,843
					AMERICAN	PEOPLE'S	
1972	*Nixon (R)	371,159	676,446	—	17,627	1,118	—
1976	*Carter (D)	615,717	531,852	2,328	8,308	—	—
						LIBERTARIAN	CITIZENS
1980	*Reagan (R)	617,417	635,274	—	—	5,531	1,304
1984	*Reagan (R)	539,539	821,702	—	—	1,776	599
1988	*Bush (R)	580,368	734,281	4,994	1,256	2,118	—
				IND. (Perot)			
1992	*Clinton (D)	665,104	617,178	203,944	430	4,513	989
1996	*Clinton (D)	636,614	623,283	120,396	—	4,009	—
				LIBERTARIAN	REFORM		
2000	*Bush (R)	638,898	872,492	2,896	4,173	23,192	—

*Won US presidential election.

Photo credit: Louisville and Jefferson County Convention & Visitors Bureau.

Hillerich & Bradsby, makers of the "Louisville Slugger" baseball bat.

12 STATE GOVERNMENT

The state legislature, called the general assembly, consists of the house of representatives, which has 100 members elected for two-year terms, and the senate, with 38 members elected for staggered four-year terms. Except for revenue-raising measures, which must be introduced in the house of representatives, either chamber may introduce or amend a bill. Most bills may be passed by majority votes equal to at least two-fifths of the membership of each house. A majority of the members of each house is required to override the governor's veto. The elected executive officers of Kentucky include the governor, lieutenant governor, secretary of state, attorney general, and treasurer. All serve four-year terms and may succeed themselves one time only.

13 POLITICAL PARTIES

Regional divisions in party affiliation during the Civil War era, based upon sympathy with the South (Democrats) or with the Union (Republicans), have persisted in the state's voting patterns. In general, the poorer mountain areas tend to vote Republican, while the more affluent lowlanders in the Bluegrass and Pennyroyal areas tend to vote Democratic.

In 1999, Kentucky had 1,576,949 registered Democrats or 60% of the total number of registered voters. There were

842,041 registered Republicans, or 32%; and 184,623 independents, or 7%. In 1983, Martha Layne Collins, a Democrat, defeated Republican candidate Jim Bunning to become Kentucky's first woman governor. Democrat Paul E. Patton was elected governor in 1995. Republican George W. Bush defeated Democrat Al Gore 57% to 41% in the 2000 US presidential campaign.

After the November 1998 elections, Democrats held 20 seats in the state senate, and Republicans held 18. The Democrats continued to dominate the house of representatives, with 65 seats to the Republicans' 34 (there was one vacancy). At the national level, Kentucky was represented by Republican Senators Mitch McConnell (reelected in 1996) and Jim Bunning (elected in 1998). In the US House of Representatives, there is one Democrat and five Republicans.

14 LOCAL GOVERNMENT

The chief governing body of Kentucky's counties is the fiscal court. Elected officials include magistrates, commissioners, and sheriffs. Cities are assigned by the general assembly to one of six classes on the basis of population. Kentucky has two first-class cities, Louisville and Lexington. There are 14 second-class cities and 22 third-class cities. The mayor or other chief executive officer in the top three classes must be elected. In the bottom classes, the executive may be either elected by the people or appointed by a city council or commission. Other units of local government in Kentucky include urban counties and special-purpose districts.

15 JUDICIAL SYSTEM

Judicial power in Kentucky is vested in a unified court of justice. The highest court is the supreme court, consisting of a chief justice and six associate justices. It has appeals jurisdiction and also bears responsibility for the budget and administration of the entire system. The court of appeals consists of 14 judges, 2 elected from each supreme court district.

Circuit courts, with original and appellate jurisdiction, are held in each county. There are 56 judicial circuits. Under the revised judicial system, district courts, which have limited and original jurisdiction, replaced various local and county courts. The total crime rate in 1998 was 2,889.4 crimes per 100,000. In June 1999 there were 15,055 prisoners in state and federal prisons in Kentucky.

16 MIGRATION

Until the early 1970s there was a considerable out-migration of whites, especially from eastern Kentucky to industrial areas of Ohio, Indiana, and other nearby states. From 1980 to 1990, net loss to migration came to about 22,000. During 1990–98, Kentucky had net gains of 90,000 from domestic migration and 14,000 from international migration. As of 1990, 77.4% of the state's residents had been born in Kentucky.

17 ECONOMY

Although agriculture is still important in Kentucky, manufacturing has grown rapidly since World War II and was, by the mid-1980s, the most important area of the economy as a source of both employment and personal income. Kentucky leads the nation in the production of coal and whiskey, and ranks second in tobacco output. In contrast to the generally prosperous Bluegrass area and the growing industrial cities, eastern Kentucky, highly dependent on coal mining, is one of the poorest regions in the US.

18 INCOME

Kentucky has long been one of the poorest of the 50 states, and in 1998, per capita (per person) income was $22,183, for a rank of 43rd. Total personal income was $87.3 billion. In 1998, 15.5% of all Kentuckians were living below the federal poverty line.

19 INDUSTRY

Manufacturing industries are concentrated in Louisville and Jefferson County and other cities along the Ohio River. The value of manufactured shipments was $88 billion in 1997. Kentucky is the leading producer of American whiskey. It also produces about 10% of the nation's trucks in assembly plants at Louisville; automobiles are produced at Bowling Green and Georgetown. Transportation equipment accounted for 30% of manufactured shipments in 1995.

20 LABOR

According to federal statistics, Kentucky's civilian labor force in December 1998 was about 1.92 million. There was an unemployment rate of 4.6%.

Mining employment amounted to 22,500 in mid-1998; manufacturing, 321,000; construction, 84,000; transportation and public utilities, 102,000; trade, 416,000; finance, insurance, and real estate, 70,000; services, 443,000; and government, 294,000. Union membership amounted to 13.1% of the labor force in 1998.

21 AGRICULTURE

With cash receipts totaling $3.5 billion, Kentucky ranked 21st among the 50 states in farm marketings in 1999. In 1998 there were approximately 90,000 farms in Kentucky. Kentucky farms in 1995 produced about 460.9 million pounds of tobacco. Other leading field crops in 1998 (in bushels) included corn for grain, 135.7 million; soybeans, 36 million; wheat, 24.7 million; sorghum, 1.6 million; and barley, 573,000.

22 DOMESTICATED ANIMALS

The Bluegrass region, which offers excellent pasturage and drinking water, has become renowned as a center for horse breeding and racing. Kentucky has a horse population of over 225,000, including thoroughbreds, quarter horses, American saddle horses, Arabians, and standardbreds. The sale of horses accounts for about 20% of Kentucky's agricultural receipts in 1998.

In 1999, Kentucky had an estimated 2.4 million cattle and calves worth $1.2 billion. There were also 520,000 hogs and pigs worth $18.2 million. The state produced about 1.77 billion pounds of milk from 45,000 dairy cows in 1997.

23 FISHING

Fishing is of little commercial importance in Kentucky. Federal hatcheries distributed

777,324 coldwater species fish (weighing 218,041 pounds/98,903 kilograms) and 2 million fish eggs within the state in 1996.

In 1998, Kentucky had 543,706 fishing license holders.

24 FORESTRY

There are about 12.6 million acres (5.13 million hectares) of forested land in Kentucky—50% of the state's land area. In 1998, Kentucky produced 777 million board feet of lumber, nearly all of it in hardwoods. The Division of Forestry of the Department of Natural Resources operates two forest tree nurseries producing 7–9 million seedling trees a year. There are two national forests—the Daniel Boone and the Jefferson on Kentucky's eastern border—enclosing two national wilderness areas.

25 MINING

The value of nonfuel mineral production in Kentucky in 1998 was a record $489 million. Crushed stone accounted for 58% ($282 million) of the total value.

26 ENERGY AND POWER

In 1999, Kentucky had 29 electric generating plants. In 1998, 86.2 billion kilowatt hours of power were produced. Southern Kentucky shares in the power produced by the Tennessee Valley Authority, which supports a coal-fired steam electric plant in Kentucky at Paducah. In 1998, eastern Kentucky produced an estimated 116.6 million tons of coal; western Kentucky, 33.6 million tons. Kentucky has more underground mines than any other state. In 1998, Kentucky held 1.7 billion tons of recoverable coal reserves, or 6.1% of the national total.

In 1999, Kentucky produced 2.77 million barrels of crude petroleum and was estimated to have about 23 million barrels of proven oil reserves. In 1998, Kentucky marketed 81.9 billion cubic feet (2.3 billion cubic meters) of natural gas. As of 1999, the state was estimated to have proven reserves totaling 1.2 trillion cubic feet (34.5 billion cubic meters) of natural gas. Kentucky has no nuclear plants.

27 COMMERCE

Wholesale sales in 1997 totaled $40 billion; retail sales totaled $34 billion. The KFC Corporation, which owns and franchises Kentucky Fried Chicken restaurants, has its headquarters in Louisville, as does Papa John's, a popular pizza chain. Kentucky's exports to foreign countries in 1998 totaled $8 billion.

28 PUBLIC FINANCE

The Kentucky biennial state budget is prepared by the Governor's Office for Policy and Management late in each odd-numbered year and submitted by the Governor to the General Assembly for approval. The fiscal year runs from July 1 to June 30. Revenues in 1997 totaled $15 billion, while expenditures amounted to $12.95 billion. As of 1997, the total state debt was more than $7.12 billion, or about $1,822 per capita (per person).

29 TAXATION

Kentucky collected more than $6.8 billion in state taxes in 1997, or $1,745 per person (the 15th highest rate among the states). The state imposes personal income taxes (2% to 6%) and corporate income taxes (4% to 8.25%) and severance taxes on oil and coal, and also levies a 6% sales and use tax (excluding food and drugs), a gasoline tax, and other taxes. In 1995, Kentucky's total share of the federal income tax burden was $5.6 billion. In 1999, tax reductions eliminated the inheritance tax.

30 HEALTH

In 1996, Kentucky ranked higher than the national averages in death rates from heart diseases, cancer, cerebrovascular diseases, accidents, and suicide. Black lung (pneumoconiosis) has been recognized as a serious work-related illness among coal miners. In 1998, Kentucky's 106 community hospitals had 15,240 beds. As of 1998, there were 205 physicians per 100,000 people. Licensed nurses in Kentucky numbered close to 15,000 the same year. Some 14% of state residents did not have health insurance in 1998.

31 HOUSING

According to a 1999 estimate, Kentucky had 1.66 million year-round housing units. In 1998, 20,600 new housing units worth $1.7 billion were authorized for construction. The median cost for an owner with a mortgage was $536 per month in 1990. Median rent was $319 per month.

32 EDUCATION

In 1998, 77.9% of all adults had completed four years of high school; only 20.1% had completed four or more years of college, placing Kentucky well below the national average of 24.4%. The Kentucky Education Reform Act of 1990 addressed the problems of the state's education system.

In fall 1997, 669,332 students attended public schools in Kentucky. Expenditures for public elementary and secondary schools amounted to $5,876 per student in 1999/00, below the national average of $6,356. As of fall 1997, Kentucky had 37 four-year colleges and universities (8 public, 29 private) and 24 two-year institutions (including 14 public community colleges). Total enrollment at these institutions was 178,924 students. The University of Kentucky is the state's largest public institution, with an enrollment of 30,900 in the fall of 2000.

33 ARTS

The Actors Theater of Louisville holds a yearly festival of new American plays. The city also has a resident ballet company. The Louisville Orchestra has recorded numerous works by contemporary composers. Bluegrass, a form of country music featuring fiddle and banjo and played at a rapid tempo, is named after the style pioneered by Kentuckian Bill Monroe and his Blue Grass Boys.

The Kentucky Arts Council receives state funding for the promotion of the arts. The state has over 200 arts associations and over 50 local art associations.

34 LIBRARIES AND MUSEUMS

In 1999 there were 13 public library systems in Kentucky, with a total of over 7.6

million volumes. The regional library system of 14 districts included university libraries and the state library at Frankfort, as well as city and county libraries. The state has 107 museums. The Kentucky Historical Society in Frankfort maintains the State History Museum. Art museums include the University of Kentucky Art Museum and the Headley-Whitney Museum, both in Lexington.

Among Kentucky's horse-related museums is the Kentucky Derby Museum in Louisville. The John James Audubon Museum is located in Audubon State Park at Henderson. Leading historical sites include Abraham Lincoln's birthplace at Hodgenville and the Mary Todd Lincoln and Henry Clay homes in Lexington.

35 COMMUNICATIONS

Only 92.8% of all occupied housing units in the state had a telephone in 1999. In 2000 there were 327 radio stations, 134 AM and 193 FM. That year there were 39 television broadcasting stations. As of 1996 there were seven large cable television systems serving Kentucky. By 2000, Kentucky had registered a total of 39,264 Internet domain names.

36 PRESS

In 1998, Kentucky had 23 daily newspapers (9 morning, 14 evening), and 14 Sunday papers. The leading Kentucky newspapers with their 1998 daily circulations are the Louisville *Courier-Journal* (228,144); the Lexington *Herald-Leader* (113,036); and the Frankfort *State Journal* (8,829).

37 TOURISM, TRAVEL, AND RECREATION

One of the state's top tourist attractions is Mammoth Cave National Park, which contains an estimated 150 miles (241 kilometers) of underground passages. Other units of the national park system in Kentucky include Abraham Lincoln's birthplace in Hodgenville, and Cumberland Gap National Historical Park, which extends into Tennessee and Virginia. As of 1999, the state operated 15 resort parks and 15 recreational parks.

38 SPORTS

There are no major league professional sports teams in Kentucky. There is a minor league baseball team in Louisville, however. The annual Kentucky Derby at Churchill Downs, first run on 17 May 1875, has become the single most famous event in US thoroughbred racing. Keeneland Race Course in Lexington is the site of the Blue Grass Stakes and other major thoroughbred races. In 1996, thoroughbred horse racing in Kentucky drew an attendance of over 2.3 million.

Rivaling horse-racing as a spectator sport is collegiate basketball. The University of Kentucky Wildcats won the NCAA Division I basketball championship in 1947, 1948, 1951, 1958, and 1978; the University of Louisville Cardinals captured the NCAA crown in 1980 and 1986; and Kentucky Wesleyan, at Owensboro, was the NCAA Division II titleholder in 1966, 1968, 1969, 1973, 1987, 1990, and 1999.

Photo credit: Louisville and Jefferson County Convention & Visitors Bureau.

Churchill Downs in Louisville, home of the Kentucky Derby.

39 FAMOUS KENTUCKIANS

Kentucky has been the birthplace of one US president, four US vice-presidents, the only president of the Confederacy, and several important jurists, statesmen, writers, artists, and sports figures. Abraham Lincoln, (1809–65) the 16th president of the US, was born in Hodgenville. His wife, Mary Todd Lincoln (1818–82), was a native of Lexington. Kentucky-born US vice-presidents have all been Democrats. The best known were Adlai Stevenson (1835–1914), who served with Grover Cleveland, and

Alben W. Barkley (1877–1956) who, before his election with President Harry S Truman in 1948, was a US senator and longtime Senate majority leader.

Frederick M. Vinson (1890–1953) was the only Kentuckian to serve as chief justice of the US. Noteworthy associate justices were John Marshall Harlan (1833–1911), famous for his dissent from the segregationist *Plessy v. Ferguson* decision (1896); and Louis B. Brandeis (1856–1941), the first Jew to serve on the Supreme Court and a champion of social reform.

A figure prominently associated with frontier Kentucky is the explorer and surveyor Daniel Boone (b.Pensylvania, 1734–1820). Other frontiersmen include Kit Carson (1809–68) and Roy Bean (1825?–1903).

Other personalities of significance include James G. Birney (1792–1857) and Cassius Marcellus Clay (1810–1903), both major antislavery spokesmen. Clay's daughter Laura (1849–1941) and Madeline Breckinridge (1872–1920) were important contributors to the women's suffrage movement. During the 1920s, Kentuckian John T. Scopes (1900–70) gained fame as the defendant in the "monkey trial" in Dayton, Tennessee. Scopes was charged with teaching Darwin's theory of evolution.

Thomas Hunt Morgan (1866–1945), honored for his work in heredity and genetics, and chemist William N. Lipscomb (b.Ohio, 1919) are Kentucky's lone Nobel Prize winners. Notable businessmen include "Colonel" Harland Sanders

Photo credit: EPD Photos.

Cassius Marcellus Clay, one of the richest men in Kentucky in his time, spoke out against slavery in the 1800s. A latter-day Cassius Clay, also from Kentucky, is a world-famous boxer who changed his name to Muhammad Ali.

(b.Indiana, 1890–1980), founder of Kentucky Fried Chicken restaurants. Robert Penn Warren (1905–89), a novelist, poet laureate, and critic, won the Pulitzer Prize three times and was the first author to win the award in both the fiction and poetry categories.

Among Kentuckians well recognized in the performing arts are film innovator D.

W. Griffith (David Lewelyn Wark Griffith, 1875–1948); Academy Award-winning actress Patricia Neal (b.1926); and country music singers Loretta Lynn (b.1932) and her sister Crystal Gayle (Brenda Gail Webb, b.1951). Kentucky's sports figures include basketball coach Adolph Rupp (b.Kansas, 1901–77); shortstop Harold ("Pee Wee") Reese (1919–99); football great Paul Hornung (b.1935); and world heavyweight boxing champions Jimmy Ellis (b.1940) and Muhammad Ali (Cassius Clay, b.1942).

40 BIBLIOGRAPHY

Aylesworth, Thomas G. *The Southeast: Georgia, Kentucky, Tennessee*. New York: Chelsea House, 1996.

Barrett, Tracy. *Kentucky*. New York: Benchmark Books, 1999.

Deady, Kathleen W. *Kentucky Facts and Symbols*. Mankato, Minn.: Hilltop Books, 2001.

Goldstein, Joel. *Kentucky Government and Politics*. Bloomington, Ind.: Tichenor, 1984.

Hollingsworth, Kent. *The Kentucky Thoroughbred*. Lexington: University Press of Kentucky, 1976.

Kummer, Patricia K. *Kentucky*. Mankato, Minn.: Capstone, 1999.

Rennick, Robert M. *Kentucky Place Names*. Lexington: University Press of Kentucky, 1984.

Williams, Suzanne M. *Kentucky*. New York: Children's Press, 2001.

Web sites

Kentucky Symbols. [Online] Available http://www.state.ky.us/agencies/gov/symbols.htm Accessed May 15, 2001.

Official Kentucky Vacation Guide. Kentucky Facts. [Online] Available http://www.kytourism.com/ Accessed May 15, 2001.

State of Kentucky. Commonwealth of Kentucky Homepage. [Online] Available http://www.kydirect.net/ Accessed May 15, 2001.

LOUISIANA

State of Louisiana

ORIGIN OF STATE NAME: Named in 1682 for France's King Louis XIV.

NICKNAME: The Pelican State.

CAPITAL: Baton Rouge.

ENTERED UNION: 30 April 1812 (18th).

SONGS: "Give Me Louisiana," "You are My Sunshine," and "State March Song."

MOTTO: Union, Justice and Confidence.

COLORS: Gold, white, and blue.

FLAG: On a blue field, fringed on three sides, a white pelican feeds her three young, symbolizing the state providing for its citizens; the state motto is inscribed on a white ribbon.

OFFICIAL SEAL: In the center, pelican and young are as depicted on the flag; the state motto encircles the scene, and the words "State of Louisiana" surround the whole.

BIRD: Eastern brown pelican.

FLOWER: Magnolia.

TREE: Bald cypress.

GEM: Agate.

FOSSIL: Petrified palmwood.

INSECT: Honeybee.

TIME: 6 AM CST = noon GMT.

1 LOCATION AND SIZE

Situated in the western south-central US, Louisiana ranks 31st in size among the 50 states. The total area of Louisiana is 48,523 square miles (125,675 square kilometers). The state extends 237 miles (381 kilometers) east-west; its maximum north-south extension is 280 miles (451 kilometers). Louisiana is shaped roughly like a boot, with the heel in the southwest corner and the toe at the extreme southeast. The state's total boundary length is 1,486 miles (2,391 kilometers).

2 TOPOGRAPHY

Louisiana lies wholly within the Gulf Coastal Plain. In the northern part of the state, east and west of a central alluvial plain, are the upland districts. The coastal-delta section, in the southernmost portion of the state, consists of the Mississippi Delta and the coastal lowlands. The highest elevation in the state is Driskill Mountain at 535 feet (163 meters), in Bienville Parish.

Louisiana has the most wetlands of all the states, including floodplains, coastal swamps, and marshes. The largest lake is

Lake Pontchartrain, with an area of more than 620 square miles (1,600 square kilometers). The most important rivers are the Mississippi, Red, Pearl, Atchafalaya, and Sabine. Louisiana has nearly 2,500 coastal islands covering some 2,000 square miles (5,000 square kilometers).

3 CLIMATE

Louisiana has a relatively constant semi-tropical climate. The temperature in New Orleans ranges from 52°F (11°C) in January to 82°F (28°C) in July. The all-time high temperature is 114°F (46°C), recorded in 1936. The all-time low, −16°F (−27°C), was set in 1899. New Orleans has an average annual rainfall of 60 inches (152 centimeters). Snow falls occasionally in the north, but rarely in the south. During the summer and fall, tropical storms and hurricanes frequently batter the state, especially along the coast.

4 PLANTS AND ANIMALS

Forests in Louisiana consist of four major types: shortleaf pine uplands; pine flats and hills; hardwood forests; and cypress and tupelo swamps. Important commercial trees also include beech, eastern red cedar, and black walnut. Among the state's wildflowers are the ground orchid and several hyacinths. Spanish moss grows profusely in the southern regions but is rare in the north.

Louisiana's varied habitats—tidal marshes, swamps, woodlands, and prairies—offer a diversity of animals. Deer, squirrel, and bear are hunted as game, while muskrat, mink, and skunk are commercially valuable furbearers. Prized game

Louisiana Population Profile

Total population in 2000:	4,468,976
Population change, 1990–2000:	5.9%
Hispanic or Latino†:	2.4%
Population by race	
One race:	98.9%
White:	63.9%
Black or African American:	32.5%
American Indian/Alaska Native:	0.6%
Asian:	1.2%
Native Hawaiian/Pacific Islander:	—
Some other race:	0.7%
Two or more races:	1.1%

Population by Age Group

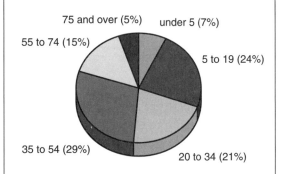

75 and over (5%) under 5 (7%)
55 to 74 (15%)
5 to 19 (24%)
35 to 54 (29%)
20 to 34 (21%)

Top Cities by Population

City	Population	% change 1990–2000
New Orleans	484,674	−2.5
Baton Rouge	227,818	3.8
Shreveport	200,145	0.8
Lafayette	110,257	16.7
Lake Charles	71,757	1.7
Kenner	70,517	−2.1
Bossier City	56,461	7.1
Monroe	53,107	−3.3
Alexandria	46,342	−5.8
New Iberia	32,623	2.5

Notes: †A person of Hispanic or Latino origin may be of any race. NA indicates that data are not available.
Sources: U.S. Census Bureau. Public Information Office. *Demographic Profiles.* [Online] Available http://www.census.gov/Press-Release/www/2001/demoprofile.html. Accessed June 1, 2001. U.S. Census Bureau. *Census 2000: Redistricting Data.* Press release issued by the Redistricting Data Office. Washington, D.C., March, 2001.

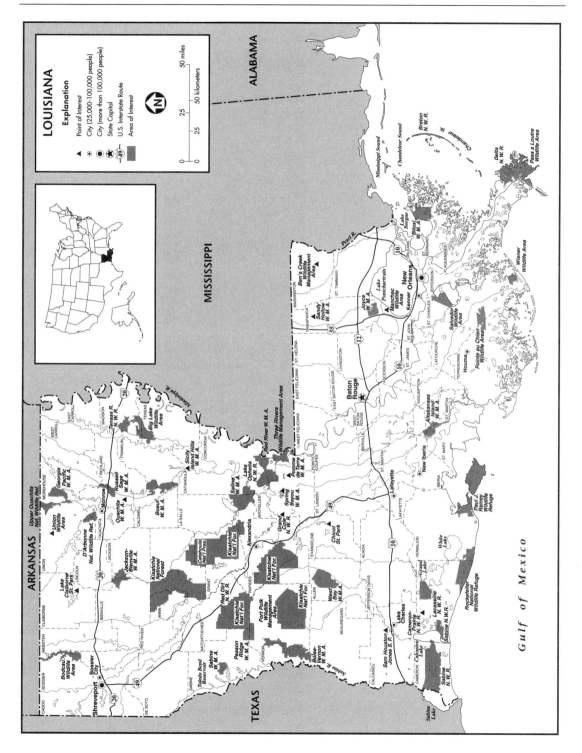

Photo credit: Louisiana Office of Tourism.

Swamp of the Atchafalaya River. Louisiana has the most wetlands of all the states.

birds include quail, turkey, and various waterfowl, of which the mottled duck and wood duck are native. Coastal beaches are inhabited by sea turtles, and whales may be seen offshore. Freshwater fish include bass, crappie, and bream. In 1997, endangered animals included the American alligator, the Sei and sperm whales, and the eastern brown pelican (the state bird).

5 ENVIRONMENTAL PROTECTION

Louisiana's earliest and most pressing environmental problem was the chronic danger of flooding by the Mississippi River. In the 1920s, the US Congress funded construction of a system of floodways and spillways to divert water from the Mississippi when necessary. However, these flood control measures created another environmental problem, as salt water from the Gulf of Mexico has seeped into the wetlands. Louisiana's wetlands are more than wildlife refuges. They are central to the state's agriculture and fishing industries.

In 1984, Louisiana consolidated much of its environmental protection effort into a new state agency—The Department of Environmental Quality (DEQ). With approximately 100 major chemical and petrochemical manufacturing and refining facilities located in Louisiana, many DEQ programs deal with the regulation of hazardous waste generation, management and disposal, and chemical releases to the air

Louisiana Population by Race

Census 2000 was the first national census in which the instructions to respondents said, "Mark one or more races." This table shows the number of people who are of one, two, or three or more races. For those claiming two races, the number of people belonging to the various categories is listed. The U.S. government conducts a census of the population every ten years.

	Number	Percent
Total population	4,468,976	100.0
One race	4,420,711	98.9
Two races	44,657	1.0
White *and* Black or African American	7,099	0.2
White *and* American Indian/Alaska Native	11,666	0.3
White *and* Asian	5,345	0.1
White *and* Native Hawaiian/Pacific Islander	466	—
White *and* some other race	11,212	0.3
Black or African American *and* American Indian/Alaska Native	2,675	0.1
Black or African American *and* Asian	1,133	—
Black or African American *and* Native Hawaiian/Pacific Islander	270	—
Black or African American *and* some other race	2,504	0.1
American Indian/Alaska Native *and* Asian	335	—
American Indian/Alaska Native *and* Native Hawaiian/Pacific Islander	28	—
American Indian/Alaska Native *and* some other race	450	—
Asian *and* Native Hawaiian/Pacific Islander	349	—
Asian *and* some other race	974	—
Native Hawaiian/Pacific Islander *and* some other race	151	—
Three or more races	3,608	0.1

Source: U.S. Census Bureau. *Census 2000: Redistricting Data.* Press release issued by the Redistricting Data Office. Washington, D.C., March, 2001. A dash (—) indicates that the percent is less than 0.1.

and water. In 1998, there were 15 hazardous waste sites in Louisiana.

The two largest wildlife refuges in the state are the Rockefeller Wildlife Refuge in Cameron and Vermilion parishes, covering 84,000 acres (34,000 hectares). The other is the Marsh Island Refuge, 82,000 acres (33,000 hectares) of marshland in Iberia Parish.

6 POPULATION

In 2000, Louisiana's population was 4,468,976, falling behind Minnesota and ranking 22nd among the 50 states. The US Census Bureau estimates that the state's population will be 4.53 million in 2005.

Louisiana's population density in 2000 was 102.6 persons per square mile (39.6 persons per square kilometer). About 75% of Louisianians lived in metropolitan areas in 1992. In 2000, 31% of the population was 19 years of age and younger, and one-fifth are over the age of 55. New Orleans is the largest city, with a 2000 population of 484,674 (ranking 31st among all US cities), followed by Baton Rouge, 227,818; and Shreveport, 200,145.

7 ETHNIC GROUPS

Louisiana, especially the Delta region, is more ethnically diverse than other areas of the South. Two groups that have been highly identified with the culture of Louisiana are Creoles and Acadians (also called Cajuns). Both descend from early French immigrants to the state. The Cajuns trace their origins to rural Acadia (Nova Scotia), and the Creoles tend to be city people from France and, in some cases, from Nova Scotia, Spain, or the Caribbean island of Hispaniola. Acadians still speak a French patois (dialect) and retain a distinctive culture and cuisine. In 1990, 432,549 residents claimed Acadian/Cajun ancestry.

Blacks made up an estimated 32.1% of the population in 1997, the third highest percentage in the nation. Many are of mixed blood, referred to locally as "colored Creoles," who traditionally formed a black elite in both urban and rural Louisiana. As of 1997, there were an estimated 19,500 Native Americans (0.4%) in Louisiana, along with 53,500 Asians and Pacific Islanders (1.2%), many of whom are Vietnamese.

8 LANGUAGES

Louisiana English is predominantly Southern. In 1990, 3,494,359 Louisiana residents—89.9% of the population—spoke only English at home. Other languages spoken at home (with number of speakers) included French, 261,678; Spanish, 72,173; and Vietnamese, 14,352. In 1990, about 495 Louisiana residents spoke a Native American language at home.

Unique to Louisiana is a large French-speaking area. West of New Orleans the French dialect called Acadian (Cajun) is used as the first language. From it, and from early colonial French, English has taken such words as *pirogue* (dugout canoe), *armoire* (wardrobe), and *lagniappe* (extra gift).

9 RELIGIONS

As of 1990, the Roman Catholic Church was the largest Christian denomination, with 1,369,154 church members. The leading Protestant denominations in 1990 were Southern Baptist, 757,639; United Methodist, 172,676; Episcopal, 33,423; and Presbyterian, 27,105. In 1994, 17,000 Jews resided in Louisiana, about 70% of them in New Orleans. Voodoo, in some cases blended with Christian ritual, is more widespread in Louisiana than anywhere else in the US.

10 TRANSPORTATION

As of 1998, Louisiana had a total railroad mileage of 2,728 route miles (4,389 kilometers), 90% of which was Class I track. As of 1995/96, Amtrak provided passenger links with Los Angeles, Chicago, and New York and carried 165,888 passengers from nine stations through the state. At the end of 1997, Louisiana had a total of 60,699 miles (97,665 kilometers) of public roads, 77% of them rural. That same year, 1.93 million automobiles and 1.46 million trucks were registered in the state.

Four of the nation's ten busiest ports are in Louisiana. New Orleans is a major center of domestic and international freight traffic. In volume of domestic and foreign cargo handled, it was the busiest port on the Gulf of Mexico and the fourth leading port in the US in 1996. The Louisiana Offshore Oil Port (LOOP) opened in 1981 as the first deepwater oil port in the

A ship in the port of New Orleans.

US. In 1996, LOOP handled over 300 million barrels of crude oil from 279 supertankers, or 13% of the nation's crude oil imports. In 1996, the busiest air facility was New Orleans International Airport, which boarded 4.2 million passengers and 17,894 tons of freight.

11 HISTORY

When European exploration and settlement of North America began, Louisiana was inhabited by a number of different Native American groups, including various tribes of the Caddo people, small Tunican-speaking groups, the Atakapa group, and the Chitimacha. The Spaniard Hernando de Soto was probably the first to penetrate the state's present boundaries, in 1541. Robert Cavelier, Sieur de la Salle reached the mouth of the Mississippi on 9 April 1682, named the land there Louisiana in honor of King Louis XIV, and claimed it for France. In 1714, Louis Juchereau de St. Denis established Natchitoches, the first permanent European settlement in Louisiana; Iberville's brother, the Sieur de Bienville, established New Orleans four years later.

Although Louisiana did not thrive economically under French rule, French culture was firmly implanted there and absorbed by non-French settlers, especially Germans from Switzerland and the Rhineland. In 1762, France ceded Louisiana to

Louisiana Governors: 1812–2001

1812–1816	William Charles Cole Claiborne	Dem-Rep		1892–1900	Murphy James Foster	Anti–Lottery-Dem
1816–1820	Jacques Philippe Villere	Dem-Rep		1900–1904	William Wright Heard	Democrat
1820–1824	Thomas Bolling Robertson	Dem-Rep		1904–1908	Newton Crain Blanchard	Democrat
1824	Henry Schuyler Thibodeaux	Dem-Rep		1908–1912	Jared Young Sanders	Democrat
1824–1828	Henry Johnson	Dem-Rep		1912–1916	Luther Egbert Hall	Democrat
1828–1829	Pierre Auguste Charles Derbigny	Nat-Rep		1916–1920	Ruffin Golson Pleasant	Democrat
1829–1830	Armand Beauvais	Nat-Rep		1920–1924	John Milliken Parker	Democrat
1830–1831	Jacques Dupre	Nat-Rep		1924–1926	Henry Luce Fuqua	Democrat
1831–1835	Andre Bienvenu Roman	Whig		1926–1928	Oramel Hinckley Simpson	Democrat
1835–1839	Edward Douglass White, Sr.	Whig		1928–1932	Huey Pierce Long	Democrat
1839–1843	Andre Bienvenu Roman	Whig		1932	Alvin Olin King	Democrat
1843–1846	Alexandre Mouton	Democrat		1932–1936	Oscar Kelly Allen	Democrat
1846–1850	Isaac Johnson	Democrat		1936	James Albert Noe	Democrat
1850–1853	Joseph Marshall Walker	Democrat		1936–1939	Richard Webster Leche	Democrat
1853–1856	Paul Octave Herbert	Democrat		1939–1940	Earl Kemp Long	Democrat
1856–1860	Robert Charles Wickliffe	Democrat		1940–1944	Sam Houston Jones	Democrat
1860–1862	Thomas Overton Moore	Democrat		1944–1948	James Houston Davis	Democrat
1862–1864	Gen. George Foster Shepley	Military		1948–1952	Earl Kemp Long	Democrat
1864–1865	Henry Watkins Allen	Democrat		1952–1956	Robert Floyd Kennon	Democrat
1864–1865	Michael Hahn	State Rights Free Trader		1956–1960	Earl Kemp Long	Democrat
1865–1867	James Madison Wells	Democrat		1960–1964	James Houston Davis	Democrat
1867–1868	Benjamin Franklin Flanders	Military-Rep		1964–1972	John Julian McKeithen	Democrat
1868	Joshua Baker	Military-Dem		1972–1980	Edwin Washington Edwards	Democrat
1868–1872	Henry Clay Warmouth	Republican		1980–1984	David Conner Treen	Republican
1872–1873	Pinkney Benton Pinchback	Republican		1984–1988	Edwin Washington Edwards	Democrat
	John McEnery (elected but ruled out)			1988–1992	Charles Elson Roemer III	Republican
1873–1877	William Pitt Kellogg (de facto)	Republican		1992–1996	Edwin Washington Edwards	Democrat
1877–1880	Francis Redding Tillou Nicholls	Democrat		1996–	Michael J. Foster	Republican
1880–1881	Louis Alfred Wiltz	Democrat				
1881–1888	Samuel Douglas McEnery	Democrat			Democratic Republican – Dem-Rep	
1888–1892	Francis Redding Tillou Nicholls	Democrat			National Republican – Nat-Rep	

Spain. Governed by Spaniards, the colony was much more prosperous. New settlers—including Acadian refugees from Nova Scotia—added to the population. The territory grew to about 50,000 inhabitants by 1800, when Napoleon forced the Spanish government to return Louisiana to France. Three years later, Napoleon sold Louisiana to the US to keep it from falling into the hands of Great Britain.

President Thomas Jefferson concluded what was probably the best real estate deal in history, purchasing 800,000 square miles (2,100,000 square kilometers) for $15,000,000 and thus more than doubling the size of the US at a cost of about 3 cents per acre. The next year, that part of the purchase south of 33°N was separated from the remainder and designated the Territory of Orleans. When its population reached the level required for statehood in 1810, the people of the territory drew up a constitution, and Louisiana entered the Union on 30 April 1812.

State Development

American control of Louisiana was threatened soon afterward when British troops tried to take New Orleans in 1814 but were soundly defeated by a mixed contingent of forces under the command of Andrew Jackson. From

1815 to 1861, Louisiana was one of the most prosperous states in the South, producing sugar and cotton, and raising hogs and cattle. Wealthy planters, whose slaves made up almost half the population, dominated Louisiana politically and economically. When the secession crisis came in 1861, they led Louisiana into the Confederacy and, after four bloody years, to total defeat.

After the Civil War, Radical Republican governments elected by black voters ruled the state, but declining support from the North and fierce resistance from Louisiana whites brought the Reconstruction period to an end. Blacks and their few white allies lost control of state government and, in 1898, blacks were deprived almost entirely of their voting rights by a new state constitution drawn up primarily for that purpose. This constitution also significantly reduced the number of poorer whites who voted in Louisiana elections. Just as before the Civil War, large landowners—combined with New Orleans bankers, businessmen, and politicians—dominated state government, effectively blocking political and social reform.

Not until 1928, with the election of Huey P. Long as governor, did the winds of major change strike Louisiana. The years from 1928 through 1960 could well be called the Long Era. Three Longs dominated state politics for most of the period: Huey, who became governor but was assassinated in 1935; his brother Earl, who served as governor three times; and his son Russell, who became a powerful US senator. From a backward agricultural state, Louisiana evolved into one of the

Louisiana Presidential Vote by Political Parties, 1948–2000

YEAR	LOUISIANA WINNER	DEMOCRAT	REPUBLICAN	STATES' RIGHTS DEMOCRAT	PROGRESSIVE	AMERICAN INDEPENDENT
1948	Thurmond (SRD)	136,344	72,657	204,290	3,035	—
1952	Stevenson (D)	345,027	306,925	—	—	—
				UNPLEDGED		
1956	*Eisenhower (R)	243,977	329,047	44,520	—	—
				NAT'L. STATES' RIGHTS		
1960	*Kennedy (D)	407,339	230,980	169,572	—	—
1964	Goldwater (R)	387,068	509,225	—	—	—
1968	Wallace (AI)	309,615	257,535	—	—	530,300
				AMERICAN	SOC. WORKERS	
1972	*Nixon (R)	298,142	686,852	44,127	12,169	—
				LIBERTARIAN	COMMUNIST	
1976	*Carter (D)	661,365	587,446	3,325	7,417	10,058
					CITIZENS	
1980	*Reagan (R)	708,453	792,853	8,240	1,584	10,333
1984	*Reagan (R)	651,586	1,037,299	1,876	9,502	—
					POPULIST	NEW ALLIANCE
1988	*Bush (R)	717,460	883,702	4,115	18,612	2,355
					IND. (Perot)	AMERICA FIRST
1992	*Clinton (D)	815,971	733,386	3,155	211,478	18,545
1996	*Clinton (D)	927,837	712,586	7,499	123,293	—
				REFORM		Constitutional
2000	*Bush (R)	792,344	927,871	14,356	20,473	5,483

* Won US presidential election.

The capitol building in Baton Rouge.

world's major petrochemical-manufacturing centers. What had been one of the most frugal states became one of the most liberal in welfare spending, care for the aged, highway building, and education. The state could afford these expanding programs because of ever-increasing revenues from oil and gas.

In the mid-1980s, the major problems confronting the state were racial and labor tensions, inadequate disposal sites for industrial wastes, and (despite important new discoveries) the depletion of oil and gas resources. In 1989, racial tensions took a new turn when white supremacist

David Duke, running as a Republican, narrowly won a seat in the Louisiana state legislature. He then ran for the US Senate—with a showing of 44 percent among voters—and, in 1991, for governor. (He was defeated by former governor Edwin Edwards.) In opposing affirmative action, Duke appealed to whites' frustrations with the high unemployment brought on by the collapse of oil prices in the mid- and late 1980s, when the number of jobs in the state declined by 8%.

12 STATE GOVERNMENT

The state legislature consists of a 39-member senate and a 105-member house of representatives. All legislators are elected for four-year terms. Major elected executive officials include the governor and lieutenant governor (independently elected), secretary of state, attorney general, and treasurer, all elected for four-year terms.

To become law, a bill must receive majority votes in both the senate and the house and be signed by the governor; or be left unsigned but not vetoed by the governor; or be passed again by two-thirds votes of both houses over the governor's veto. Appropriation bills must originate in the house but may be amended by the senate. The governor has an item veto on appropriation bills. Constitutional amendments require approval by two-thirds of the elected members of each house and ratification by a majority of the people voting on it at the next general election.

13 POLITICAL PARTIES

The major political organizations are the Democratic Party and the Republican

Party, each affiliated with the national party. However, differences in culture and economic interests have made Louisiana's politics extremely complex. After an extended period of Democratic dominance under the Long family, the 1960s and 1970s saw a resurgence of the Republican Party and the election in 1979 of David C. Treen, the state's first Republican governor since Reconstruction. However, Treen was succeeded by Democrats Edwin Edwards in 1983 and Charles Roemer in 1987, and Edwards again in 1991.

As of 1999 there were 1,653,450 registered Democrats, 570,953 registered Republicans, and 432,666 unaffiliated. Both US senators—John Breaux and Mary Landrieu—were Democrats in 1999. Louisiana's delegation of US representatives consisted of three Democrats and four Republicans. In 2001, 25 of the state senators were Democrats, and 14 were Republicans; 71 of the state representatives were Democrats while 31 were Republicans. In the 2000 presidential election, Louisianians gave Republican George W. Bush 53% of the vote, while Democrat Al Gore received 45%.

Photo credit: EPD Photos/CSU Archives

Without question, the most important state officeholder in Louisiana history was Huey P. Long (1893–1935) who is shown here making a speech. He was elected to the governorship in 1928 and inaugurated a period of social and economic reform. In the process, he made himself very nearly an absolute dictator within Louisiana. Huey's brother Earl K. Long (1895–1960) served three times as governor. Huey's son, US Senator Russell B. Long (b.1918), was chairman of the Finance Committee from 1965 to 1980.

14 LOCAL GOVERNMENT

The church districts, called parishes, into which Louisiana was divided in the late 17th century remain the primary political divisions in the state, serving functions similar to those of counties in other states. In 1997 there were 60 parishes, many of them governed by police jury. Other parish officials are the sheriff, clerk of court, assessor, and coroner. As of 1997, Louisiana also had 301 municipal governments.

Prominent local officials include the mayor, chief of police, and a council or board of aldermen.

15 JUDICIAL SYSTEM

The highest court in Louisiana is the supreme court, with appeals jurisdiction.

There are five appeals circuits in the state, each divided into three districts. Each of the state's district courts serves at least one parish and has at least one district judge, elected for a six-year term. District courts have original jurisdiction in criminal and civil cases. City courts are the principal courts of limited jurisdiction. According to the FBI Crime Index in 1998, Louisiana had a crime index total of 6,098.3 per 100,000. As of June 1999, 33,463 prisoners were in Louisiana's state and federal prisons—a ratio of 763 per 100,000 residents.

16 MIGRATION

Beginning in World War II, large numbers of both black and white farm workers left Louisiana and migrated north and west. During the 1960s, the state had a net out-migration of 15% of its black population, but the trend had slowed somewhat by 1975. Recent migration within the state has been from north to south, and from rural to urban areas, especially to Shreveport, Baton Rouge, and the suburbs of New Orleans. Overall, Louisiana suffered a net loss from migration of about 368,000 from 1940 to 1990. During 1990–98, Louisiana had a net loss of 117,000 from interstate migration and a net gain of 25,000 from international migration. By 1990, 79% of all state residents were native-born, a proportion exceeded only by Pennsylvania.

17 ECONOMY

With the rise of the petrochemical industry, Louisiana's economy has regained much of the vitality it enjoyed before the Civil War. Today, Louisiana ranks second only to Texas in the value of its mineral products.

Louisiana is primarily an industrial state, but its industries are to a large degree based on its natural resources, principally oil, water, and timber. Industrial expansion suffered a severe blow in the early 1980s, when the price of oil dropped from $37 a barrel in 1981 to $15 a barrel in 1986. Energy-related industries, such as barge-building, machinery-manufacturing, and rig/platform production suffered. In an attempt to offset losses in employment, Louisiana planned to build several casinos.

18 INCOME

Louisiana's per capita (per person) income in 1998 was $22,206, for a rank of 42nd in the US. Total personal income was $96.9 billion in 1998. Median household income in 1998 was $32,317. In 1998, about 18.6% of all Louisianians were living below the federal poverty level.

19 INDUSTRY

A huge and still-growing petrochemical industry has become a dominant force in the state's economy. Other expanding industries are wood products and, especially since World War II, shipbuilding. In 1997, the total value of shipments of manufactured goods was $81 billion. Chemicals accounted for 33% of the total, and petroleum products contributed 31%. The state's main industrial regions are along the Mississippi River from north of Baton Rouge to New Orleans, and also include the Monroe, Shreveport, Morgan City, and Lake Charles areas.

20 LABOR

In mid-1998, Louisiana had a total civilian labor force of 2.07 million, or about 63% of the population. There was an unemployment rate of 5.7%. In 1998, about 10% of all workers were union members.

21 AGRICULTURE

With a farm income of over $1.85 billion in 1999—66% from crops—Louisiana ranked 32nd among the 50 states. Nearly every crop grown in North America can be raised somewhere in Louisiana. In the south are strawberries, oranges, and sweet potatoes; in the southeast, sugarcane; and in the southwest, rice and soybeans. Soybeans are also raised in the cotton-growing area of the northeast. Oats, alfalfa, corn, potatoes, and peaches are among the other crops grown in the north.

As of 1998 there were an estimated 30,000 farms covering 8.2 million acres (3.3 million hectares). Louisiana ranks second in the US in sugarcane production after Florida. Cash receipts for the sugar crop in 1997 were about $290.4 million for 10.7 million tons. Louisiana ranked third in the value of its rice production in 1998 with about $250.2 million.

22 DOMESTICATED ANIMALS

Livestock production in 1999 accounted for about 34% of agricultural income. In 1999 there were 900,000 cattle and 30,000 hogs. Fur trapping has some local importance. In 1981, a month-long statewide alligator season was held for the first time in 18 years.

23 FISHING

In 1998, Louisiana was second only to Alaska in the size of its commercial fish landings, with over 1.1 billion pounds, and ranked second by value of catch at $291.9 million. The most important species caught in Louisiana are shrimp, menhaden, and oysters. In 1998, shrimp landings amounted to 34.6% of the national total.

Louisiana produces most of the US crayfish harvest. In 1998, crayfish farms covered some 100,000 acres (40,500 hectares). Spring water levels of the Atchafalaya Basin cause the wild crayfish harvest to vary from year to year. As of 1999, there were also 98 catfish farms covering 13,728 acres (6,221 hectares) with about 32.4 million stocker-sized catfish.

24 FORESTRY

There are 13.8 million acres (5.6 million hectares) of forestland in Louisiana, representing almost half the state's land area in 1997. The principal forest types are loblolly and shortleaf pine in the northwest, longleaf and slash pine in the south, and hardwood in a wide area along the Mississippi River. In 1996, forest land-owner income from sales of timber was estimated at $568.4 million. Louisiana has one national forest, Kisatchie, with a gross area of over 1.02 million acres (413,875 hectares).

25 MINING

Louisiana's nonfuel mineral value totaled an estimated $379 million in 1998. The four leading mineral commodities, in

Photo credit: © Nathan Benn/Woodfin Camp.

The Shell Oil refinery in Burnside, Louisiana.

terms of value, were salt, sulfur, and construction sand/gravel.

26 ENERGY AND POWER

In 1998, power plants in Louisiana generated a total of 66.11 billion kilowatt hours of power, and 1997 energy consumption was 4.1 quadrillion Btu, or 940 million Btu per person. Louisiana ranked second nationally in per person energy consumption. About 45% of the state's energy needs were supplied by natural gas, 39% by oil, and 16% by other sources. As of 1999, Louisiana had two nuclear power plants.

Oil and gas production has expanded greatly since World War II, but production reached its peak in the early 1970s and proven reserves are declining. Louisiana produced 120 million barrels of crude oil during 1999, 5.6% of the national total. At the end of 1998, remaining proven reserves of oil in Louisiana amounted to 551 million barrels, 2.6% of the national total. Natural gas marketed production in 1998 was 5.29 trillion cubic feet.

27 COMMERCE

Louisiana had 1997 wholesale sales of $49 billion, and retail sales of $37 billion. In 1998, Louisiana ranked ninth among the 50 states in value of its goods exported abroad, with $17 billion.

28 PUBLIC FINANCE

The budget is prepared by the state executive budget director and submitted annually by the governor to the legislature for amendment and approval. Revenues for fiscal year 1997 were $15.93 billion; expenditures were $14.29 billion. As of 1997, Louisiana had a total debt of $7.03 billion, or about $1,615 per capita (per person).

29 TAXATION

For most of the state's history, Louisianians paid little in taxes. Despite increases in taxation and expenditures since the late 1920s, when Huey Long introduced the graduated income tax, Louisiana's state tax burden per capita (per person), $1,297 in 1997, is still below the national average of $1,660. Income taxes accounted for $1.5 billion of the state's $5.65 billion in state revenues in 1997.

The state's 4% sales and use tax yielded nearly $1.8 billion to the state in 1997. Louisiana also taxes gasoline sales (20¢ per gallon), gifts and inheritances, soft drinks, alcoholic beverages, and tobacco products, among other items. Taxes on beer and chain stores contribute to local revenues, as does the property tax, although Louisiana relies less on this than do most other states.

30 HEALTH

In 1997, there were 15 births per 1,000 women (aged 15–44), slightly higher than the national rate. Some 43.4% of births that year were to unmarried women, third-highest after the District of Columbia and Mississippi. Death rates from heart disease, cancer, suicide, cerebrovascular diseases, and accidents were above the national rate. In 1998, the 126 community hospitals in Louisiana had a total of 17,820 beds. There were 239 physicians per 100,000 in 1997. Louisiana's licensed nurses numbered close to 20,000 in 1998.

31 HOUSING

According to a 1999 estimate there were nearly 1.8 million housing units. In 1990, New Orleans had 264,146 housing units, 7.2% of which had been built during the previous decade. In 1998, 16,500 new housing units worth $1.5 billion were authorized for construction in the state. The median value of a home in Louisiana was $58,500 in 1990. Owner-occupied monthly costs (including mortgage) had a median of $595 in 1990, when the median monthly rent was $352.

32 EDUCATION

As of 1998, only 78.6% of adult Louisianians had completed high school and 19.5% had completed four or more years of college. In fall 1997, total enrollment in Louisiana's public elementary and secondary schools was 776,813. Expenditures for public elementary and secondary schools amounted to $5,441 per student in 1999/2000.

As of 1997, in addition to 53 vocational-technical schools, there were 34 institutions of higher education in Louisiana, of which 22 were public and 12 private. The center of the state university system is Louisiana State University (LSU) in Baton Rouge, with a 1999/00 student enrollment of about 30,000. Tulane University in New Orleans is one of the most distinguished private universities in the South.

33 ARTS

New Orleans has long been one of the most important centers of artistic activity in the South. In the mid-1980s, Louisiana's principal theaters included the New Orleans Theater of the Performing Arts, Le Petit Theatre du Vieux Carre, and the Tulane Theater. The Free Southern Theatre is a black touring company based in New Orleans. Baton Rouge, Shreveport, Monroe, Lake Charles, and Hammond are among the cities with little theaters, and Baton Rouge, Lafayette, and Lake Charles have ballet companies. There are symphony orchestras in most of the larger cities, of which the Baton Rouge Symphony Orchestra is the best known.

It is probably in music that Louisiana has made its most distinctive contributions to culture. Jazz was born in New Orleans around 1900. Early jazz in the New Orleans style is called Dixieland. Traditional Dixieland may still be heard in New Orleans at Preservation Hall, Dixieland Hall, and the New Orleans Jazz Club. Equally distinctive is Cajun music, dominated by the sound of the fiddle and accordion. The French Acadian Music Festival, held in Abbeville, takes place in April.

Louisiana has an income tax checkoff for arts programs that allows taxpayers to designate part or all of their income tax refunds to be placed in a fund for the arts.

34 LIBRARIES AND MUSEUMS

Louisiana's 64 parishes were served by 65 public libraries in 1998. That year, the public library system held 11 million volumes and had a total circulation of 18.7 million. The New Orleans Public Library features a special collection on jazz and folk music. As of 2000, Louisiana had 89 museums, historic sites, and public gardens, as well as 27 art collections. Leading art museums are the New Orleans Museum of Art, the Lampe Gallery in New Orleans, and the R. W. Norton Art Gallery at Shreveport.

35 COMMUNICATIONS

As of 1999, 91.5% of Louisiana's occupied housing units had telephones. In 2000, the state had 242 radio broadcasting stations (85 AM and 157 FM) and 37 television stations. That year, there were nine large cable television systems. In the same year, a total of 46,786 Internet domain names had been registered in the state.

36 PRESS

In 1998, Louisiana had a total of 13 morning dailies, 13 evening dailies, and 21 Sunday papers. The principal dailies with their 1998 daily circulations are *The New Orleans Times-Picayune* (259,317), *The Baton Rouge Advocate* (93,127), and *The Shreveport Times* (75,683). Two influential literary magazines originated in the state: the *Southern Review,* founded at LSU in the 1930s by Robert Penn Warren and Cleanth Brooks, and the *Tulane Drama Review.*

37 TOURISM, TRAVEL, AND RECREATION

Visitors spend an estimated $5.2 billion in the state per year. New Orleans is one of the major tourist attractions in the US. Known for its fine restaurants, serving such distinctive fare as gumbo, jambalaya, and crayfish, along with an elaborate French-inspired haute cuisine, New Orleans also offers jazz clubs, the graceful buildings of the French Quarter, and a lavish carnival called Mardi Gras ("Fat Tuesday"). Beginning on the Wednesday before Shrove Tuesday (preceding Lent), parades and balls, staged by private organizations called *krewes*, are held almost nightly.

Among the many other annual events that attract visitors to the state are the Natchitoches Christmas Festival, which includes 170,000 Christmas lights and spectacular fireworks displays. Louisiana's 34 state parks and recreation sites total 39,000 acres (15,800 hectares).

38 SPORTS

Louisiana has one major league professional sports team: the Saints of the National Football League. Horse-racing is popular in the state. The principal tracks are the Louisiana Jockey Club at the Fair Grounds in New Orleans and Evangeline Downs at Lafayette. Gambling has long been widespread in Louisiana. The New Orleans Open Golf Tournament is held in April.

In 1935, Tulane University inaugurated the Sugar Bowl, an annual New Year's Day event and one of the most prestigious bowl games in college football. Louisiana

Photo credit: Louisiana Office of Tourism.

Canoeing and fishing in Chicot State Park, one of 34 state parks and recreation areas.

State University last won the Sugar Bowl in 1968.

39 FAMOUS LOUISIANIANS

Zachary Taylor (b. Virginia, 1784–1850) is the only US president to whom Louisiana can lay claim. Taylor owned a large plantation north of Baton Rouge, which was his residence before his election to the presidency in 1848. Edward Douglass White (1845–1921) served as chief justice of the US Supreme Court.

Also prominent in Louisiana history was Robert Cavelier, Sieur de la Salle (b.France, 1643–87), who was the first to claim the region for the French crown. Jean Étienne Boré (1741–1820) laid the foundation of the Louisiana sugar industry by developing a process for granulating sugar from cane; Norbert Rillieux (1806–94), a free black man, developed the much more efficient vacuum pan process of refining sugar.

Biochemist Andrew Victor Schally (b.Poland, 1926) shared the Nobel Prize for medicine in 1977 for his research on hormones. Among other distinguished Louisiana professionals have been historian T. Harry Williams (1909–79), who won the Pulitzer Prize for his biography of Huey Long; architect Henry Hobson Richardson (1838–86); and heart specialist Michael De Bakey (b.1908).

Louisiana's important writers include George Washington Cable (1844–1925), an early advocate of racial justice; Kate O'Flaherty Chopin (b.Missouri, 1851–1904); playwright and memoirist Lillian Hellman (1905–84); and novelists Walker Percy (b.Alabama 1916–90), Truman Capote (1924–84), Shirley Ann Grau (b.1929), and John Kennedy Toole (1937–69). The latter two were both winners of the Pulitzer Prize.

Louisianians in the arts include composer Louis Moreau Gottschalk (1829–69); jazz musicians Jelly Roll Morton (Ferdinand Joseph La Menthe, 1885–1941) and Louis "Satchmo" Armstrong (1900–71), gained nationwide popularity. Other prominent Louisianians in music are gospel singer Mahalia Jackson (1911–72);

pianist-singer-songwriter Antoine "Fats" Domino (b.1928); and pop singer Jerry Lee Lewis (b.1935).

Louisiana baseball heroes include Hall of Famer Melvin Thomas "Mel" Ott (1909–58). Terry Bradshaw (b.1948) quarterbacked the Super Bowl champion Pittsburgh Steelers during the 1970s. Player-coach William F. "Bill" Russell (b.1934) led the Boston Celtics to 10 National Basketball Association championships between 1956 and 1969. Chess master Paul Morphy (1837–84) was born in New Orleans.

40 BIBLIOGRAPHY

Corrick, James A. *The Louisiana Purchase.* San Diego: Lucent Books, 2000.

Gaines, Ann. *The Louisiana Purchase in American History.* Berkeley Heights, N.J.: Enslow, 2000.

Hintz, Martin. *Louisiana.* New York: Children's Press, 1998.

Kein, Sybil, ed. *Creole: The History and Legacy of Louisiana's Free People of Color.* Baton Rouge: Louisiana State University Press, 2000.

LeVert, Suzanne. *Huey Long: the Kingfish of Louisiana.* New York: Facts on File, 1995.

McAuliffe, Emily. *Louisiana Facts and Symbols.* Mankato, Minn.: Hilltop Books, 1999.

Moneyhon, Carl H. *Portraits of Conflict: A Photographic History of Louisiana in the Civil War.* Fayetteville: University of Arkansas Press, 1990.

Web sites

Louisiana Information for Students. [Online] Available http://www.state.la.us/ed_students.htm Accessed May 15, 2001.

Louisiana Secretary of State. Facts. [Online] Available http://www.sec.state.la.us/ Accessed May 15, 2001.

State of Louisiana. INFO Louisiana: Entry Point to State Government Information. [Online] Available http://www.state.la.us/ Accessed May 15, 2001.

MAINE

State of Maine

ORIGIN OF STATE NAME: Derived either from the French for a historical district of France, or from the early use of "main" to distinguish coast from islands.

NICKNAME: The Pine Tree State.

CAPITAL: Augusta.

ENTERED UNION: 15 March 1820 (23d).

SONG: "State of Maine Song."

MOTTO: *Dirigo* (I direct).

COAT OF ARMS: A farmer and sailor support a shield on which are depicted a pine tree, a moose, and water. Under the shield is the name of the state; above it are the state motto and the North Star.

FLAG: The coat of arms is on a blue field, with a yellow fringed border surrounding three sides.

OFFICIAL SEAL: Same as the coat of arms.

ANIMAL: Moose.

BIRD: Chickadee.

FISH: Landlocked salmon.

FLOWER: White pine Cone and Tassel.

TREE: Eastern white pine.

INSECT: Honeybee.

MINERAL: Tourmaline.

TIME: 7 AM EST = noon GMT.

1 LOCATION AND SIZE

Situated in the extreme northeastern corner of the US, Maine is the nation's most easterly state, the largest in New England, and 39th in size among the 50 states. The total area of Maine is 33,265 square miles (86,156 square kilometers). Maine extends 207 miles (333 kilometers) east-west; the maximum north-south extension is 322 miles (518 kilometers). Hundreds of islands dot Maine's coast. The largest is Mt. Desert Island. Others include Deer Isle, Vinalhaven, and Isle au Haut. Maine's total boundary length is 883 miles (1,421 kilometers).

2 TOPOGRAPHY

Maine is divided into four main regions: coastal lowlands extending 10–20 miles (16–32 kilometers) inland; the piedmont, a transitional hilly belt; a mountain region, which marks the northern endpoint of the 2,000-mile (3,200-kilometer) Appalachian Trail; and Maine's uplands, a high, relatively flat plateau extending northward beyond the mountains. Maine has more than 2,200 lakes and ponds. The more than 5,000 rivers and streams include the Penobscot, Androscoggin, Kennebec, and Saco. Mt. Katahdin, at 5,268 feet (1,607 meters), is the highest point in the state.

3 CLIMATE

Maine has three climatic regions: the northern interior zone, comprising roughly the northern half of the state, between Quebec and New Brunswick; the southern interior zone; and the coastal zone. The northern zone is both drier and cooler in all four seasons than either of the other zones, while the coastal zone is more moderate in temperature year-round than the other two. Annual mean temperatures range from about 40°F (5°C) in the northern zone to 46°F (8°C) in the coastal zone. Record temperatures for the state are −48°F (−44°C) registered in 1925, and 105°F (41°C) in 1911. The mean annual precipitation ranges from 40.2 inches (102 centimeters) in the north to 45.7 inches (116 centimeters) on the coast.

4 PLANTS AND ANIMALS

Maine's forests are largely softwoods, comprising chiefly red and white spruces, eastern hemlock, and white and red pine. Important hardwoods include beech, white oak, and black willow. Maine is home to most of the flowers and shrubs common to the north temperate zone, including an important commercial resource, the low-bush blueberry. Maine has 17 rare orchid species (one, the small whorled pogonia, is on the federal endangered list).

Maine Population Profile

Total population in 2000:	1,274,923
Population change, 1990–2000:	3.8%
Hispanic or Latino†:	0.7%
Population by race	
One race:	99.0%
White:	96.9%
Black or African American:	0.5%
American Indian/Alaska Native:	0.6%
Asian:	0.7%
Native Hawaiian/Pacific Islander:	—
Some other race:	0.2%
Two or more races:	1.0%

Population by Age Group

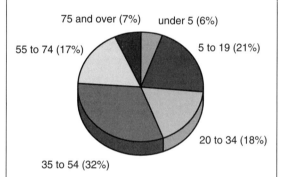

75 and over (7%) under 5 (6%)
55 to 74 (17%)
5 to 19 (21%)
20 to 34 (18%)
35 to 54 (32%)

Top Cities by Population

City	Population	% change 1990–2000
Portland	64,249	−0.2
Lewiston	35,690	−10.2
Bangor	31,473	−5.1
South Portland	23,324	0.7
Auburn	23,203	−4.5
Brunswick	21,172	1.3
Biddeford	20,942	1.1
Sanford	20,806	1.7
Augusta	18,560	−13.0
Scarborough	16,970	35.6

Notes: †A person of Hispanic or Latino origin may be of any race. NA indicates that data are not available.
Sources: U.S. Census Bureau. Public Information Office. *Demographic Profiles.* [Online] Available http://www.census.gov/Press-Release/www/2001/demoprofile.html. Accessed June 1, 2001. U.S. Census Bureau. *Census 2000: Redistricting Data.* Press release issued by the Redistricting Data Office. Washington, D.C., March, 2001.

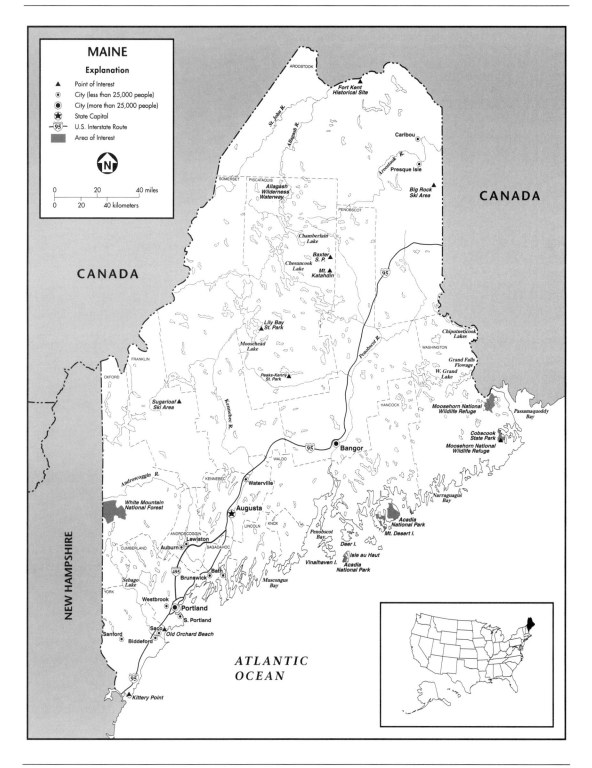

MAINE

Explanation

▲ Point of Interest
⊙ City (less than 25,000 people)
◉ City (more than 25,000 people)
★ State Capital
—95— U.S. Interstate Route
▨ Area of Interest

N

| 0 | 20 | 40 miles |
| 0 | 20 | 40 kilometers |

AROOSTOOK

CANADA

CANADA

NEW HAMPSHIRE

St. John R.

Allagash R.

Fort Kent
Historical Site

Caribou

Aroostook R.

Presque Isle

Big Rock
Ski Area

SOMERSET

PISCATAQUIS

Allagash
Wilderness
Waterway

PENOBSCOT

Chamberlain
Lake

Baxter
S. P. ▲

Chesuncook
Lake

Mt. ▲
Katahdin

95

Chiputneticook
Lakes

Lily Bay
St. Park ▲

Moosehead
Lake

Penobscot R.

WASHINGTON

Grand Falls
Flowage

W. Grand
Lake

FRANKLIN

OXFORD

Peaks-Kenny
St. Park ▲

Sugarloaf ▲
Ski Area

Kennebec R.

HANCOCK

Moosehorn National
Wildlife Refuge

Passamaquoddy
Bay

Cobscook
State Park

Moosehorn National
Wildlife Refuge

Androscoggin R.

KENNEBEC

95

Bangor

WALDO

Waterville

Narraguagus
Bay

White Mountain
National Forest

Augusta

LINCOLN

KNOX

Penobscot
Bay

Deer I.

Acadia
National Park

Mt. Desert I.

ANDROSCOGGIN

Lewiston

CUMBERLAND

Auburn

SAGADAHOC

Bath

495

Brunswick

Muscongus
Bay

Vinalhaven I.

Isle au Haut

Acadia
National Park

Sebago
Lake

YORK

Westbrook

Portland

S. Portland

Saco ▲

Old Orchard Beach

Sanford

Biddeford

ATLANTIC
OCEAN

95

Kittery Point

About 30,000 white-tailed deer are killed by hunters in Maine each year, but the herd does not appear to diminish. Other common forest animals include the bobcat, beaver, and snowshoe hare. Seals and porpoises are found in coastal waters, along with practically every variety of North Atlantic fish and shellfish, including the famous Maine lobster. Coastal waterfowl include the osprey, and herring and great black-backed gulls. Matinicus Rock is the only known North American nesting site of the common puffin, or sea parrot. Endangered species include the cougar, bald eagle, and shortnose sturgeon.

5 ENVIRONMENTAL PROTECTION

The Department of Environmental Protection administers laws regulating the selection of commercial and industrial sites, air and water quality, the prevention and cleanup of oil spills, the control of hazardous wastes, the licensing of oil terminals, the use of coastal wetlands, and mining. Maine had 12 hazardous waste sites in 1998.

6 POPULATION

Maine's 2000 census population was 1,274,923, falling behind Idaho and Nebraska to rank 40th among the 50 states. The population density for 2000 was 41.3 persons per square mile (15.9 persons per square kilometer), well below the national average of 79.6 persons per square mile (30.7 per square kilometer). More than half the population lives on less than one-seventh of the land within 25 miles (40 kilometers) of the Atlantic coast, and almost half the state is nearly uninhabited. Maine has one of the oldest populations, with almost one-quarter of its residents over the age of 55 (the median age is 38.6, more than 3 years older than the national average). The state's largest cities are Portland, with 64,249 people in 2000; Lewiston, with 35,690; and Bangor, with 31,473.

7 ETHNIC GROUPS

Maine's population is primarily Yankee, of English and Scotch-Irish origins. The largest minority group consists of French-Canadians. Among those reporting at least one specific ancestry group in 1990, 372,042 claimed English ancestry; 223,653 French (not counting 123,857 who claimed Canadian or French-Canadian); and 217,226 Irish. Maine's 1997 population was estimated to be 98.4% white (the second highest ratio among the states). As of 1997, Maine had an estimated 5,600 Native Americans, 6,000 blacks, 8,500 Asians and Pacific Islanders. Some 8,500 residents had Hispanic origins.

8 LANGUAGES

Maine English is celebrated as typical Yankee speech. In 1990, 90.8% of Maine residents five years old or older reported speaking only English in the home. Some 81,012 residents spoke French, down from 95,181 in 1980. Native Algonkian place-names abound, including Saco, Kennebec, and Skowhegan.

9 RELIGIONS

Maine had 264,943 Roman Catholics in 1990 and an estimated 8,160 Jews. The

Maine Population by Race

Census 2000 was the first national census in which the instructions to respondents said, "Mark one or more races." This table shows the number of people who are of one, two, or three or more races. For those claiming two races, the number of people belonging to the various categories is listed. The U.S. government conducts a census of the population every ten years.

	Number	Percent
Total population	1,274,923	100.0
One race	1,262,276	99.0
Two races	11,987	0.9
White *and* Black or African American	1,914	0.2
White *and* American Indian/Alaska Native	5,387	0.4
White *and* Asian	2,054	0.2
White *and* Native Hawaiian/Pacific Islander	182	—
White *and* some other race	1,598	0.1
Black or African American *and* American Indian/Alaska Native	115	—
Black or African American *and* Asian	87	—
Black or African American *and* Native Hawaiian/Pacific Islander	19	—
Black or African American *and* some other race	245	—
American Indian/Alaska Native *and* Asian	47	—
American Indian/Alaska Native *and* Native Hawaiian/Pacific Islander	11	—
American Indian/Alaska Native *and* some other race	65	—
Asian *and* Native Hawaiian/Pacific Islander	68	—
Asian *and* some other race	183	—
Native Hawaiian/Pacific Islander *and* some other race	12	—
Three or more races	660	0.1

Source: U.S. Census Bureau. *Census 2000: Redistricting Data*. Press release issued by the Redistricting Data Office. Washington, D.C., March, 2001. A dash (—) indicates that the percent is less than 0.1.

leading Protestant denominations were United Methodist, with 36,164; United Church of Christ, 33,265; American Baptist USA, with 32,549; and Episcopal, 16,375.

10 TRANSPORTATION

Although Maine had no Class I railroads in 1998, eight regional and local railroads operated on 1,199 rail miles (1,929 kilometers) of track. About three-quarters of all communities and about half the population depend entirely on highway trucking for the overland transportation of freight. In 1997, Maine had 22,643 miles (36,433 kilometers) of public roads. There were nearly 1.1 million registered motor vehicles in 1997. Maine has ten established seaports, with Portland and Searsport the main depots for overseas shipping. Portland International Jetport, the state's largest and most active airport, boarded 433,473 passengers in 1996.

11 HISTORY

Sometime around 1600, English expeditions began fishing the Gulf of Maine regularly. By 1630, however, there were permanent English settlements on several islands and at nearly a dozen spots along the coast. In 1652, the government of the Massachusetts Bay Colony began absorb-

Acadia National Park.

ing the small Maine settlements, and in 1691, Maine became a district of Massachusetts. During the first hundred years of settlement, Maine's economy was based on farming, fishing, trading, and exploitation of the forests.

The first naval encounter of the Revolutionary War occurred in Machias Bay, when, on 12 June 1775, angry colonials captured the British armed schooner *Margaretta*. An expedition through the Maine woods in the fall of 1775 intended to drive the British out of Quebec, but this failed. Another disaster was a 1779 expedition in which Massachusetts forces, failing to dislodge British troops at Castine, abandoned many of its own

ships near the Penobscot River. Popular pressure for separation from Massachusetts mounted after the War of 1812. Admission of Maine to the Union as a free state was joined with the admission of Missouri as a slave state in the Missouri Compromise of 1820.

Textile mills and shoe factories came to Maine between 1830 and 1860. After the Civil War, the revolution in papermaking that substituted wood pulp for rags brought a vigorous new industry to the state. By 1900, Maine was one of the leading papermaking states in the US, and the industry continues to dominate the state today. The rise of tourism and the conflict between economic development and environmental protection have been central in the postwar period.

In the 1980s, the state government paid $81.5 million to the Penobscot and Passamaquoddy tribes. This settled a suit claiming that a 1794 treaty under which the Passamaquoddy handed over most of its land—amounting to the northern two-thirds of Maine—was illegal and had never been ratified by Congress.

12 STATE GOVERNMENT

The legislature, consisting of a senate of 31 to 35 members and a 151-member house of representatives, convenes every two years in joint session to elect the secretary of state, attorney general, and state treasurer. The governor is the only official elected statewide. The governor's veto may be overridden by a two-thirds vote of members present and voting in each legislative chamber.

13 POLITICAL PARTIES

The Republican Party dominated Maine politics for 100 years after its formation in the 1850s. The rise of Democrat Edmund S. Muskie, elected governor in 1954 and 1956 and to the first of four terms in the US Senate in 1960, signaled a change. Muskie appealed personally to many traditionally Republican voters, but his party's revival was also the result of demographic changes, especially an increase in the proportion of French-Canadian voters. In 1994 there were 272,089 registered Democrats, or 33% of the total number of registered voters; 246,277 registered Republicans, or 30%; and 306,292 unaffiliated registered voters, or 37%.

In the November 1998 elections, Independent Angus King won reelection to a second term as governor. Republican Olympia Snowe, in 2000, won reelection in the Senate and Republican Susan E. Collins won the seat left vacant by retiring three-term senator William S. Cohen in 1996. Cohen, a Republican, went on to serve Democratic president Bill Clinton as Secretary of Defense. In 2000, Democrat Al Gore won 49% of the presidential vote and Republican George W. Bush received 44%. The two US House of Representatives seats were held by two Democrats and the Senate by two Republicans in 2000. As of 2001, Democrats held 17 seats in the state senate. There were 17 Republicans and one independent. The state house consisted of 89 Democrats, 61 Republicans, and one independent.

Maine Presidential Vote by Major Political Parties, 1948–2000

YEAR	MAINE WINNER	DEMOCRAT	REPUBLICAN
1948	Dewey (R)	111,916	150,234
1952	*Eisenhower (R)	118,806	232,353
1956	*Eisenhower (R)	102,468	249,238
1960	*Eisenhower (R)	102,468	249,238
1960	Nixon (R)	181,159	240,608
1964	*Johnson (D)	262,264	118,701
1968	Humphrey (D)	217,312	169,254
1972	*Nixon (R)	160,584	256,458
1976	Ford (R)	232,279	236,320
1980	*Reagan (R)	220,974	238,522
1984	*Reagan (R)	214,515	336,500
1988	*Bush (R)	243,569	307,131
1992**	*Clinton (D)	263,420	206,504
1996**	*Clinton (D)	312,788	186,378
2000	Gore (D)	319,951	286,616

*Won US presidential election.

**Independent candidate Ross Perot received 206,820 votes in 1992 and 85,970 votes in 1996.

Maine Governors: 1820–2001

1820–1821	William King	Dem-Rep	1881–1883	Harris Merrill Plaisted	Fusion
1821	William Durkee Williamson	Dem-Rep	1883–1887	Frederick Robie	Republican
1821–1822	Benjamin Ames	Dem-Rep	1887	Joseph Robinson Bodwell	Republican
1822	Daniel Rose	Dem-Rep	1887–1889	Sebastian Streeter Marble	Republican
1822–1827	Albion Keith Parris	Dem-Rep	1889–1893	Edwin Chick Burleigh	Republican
1827–1829	Enoch Lincoln	Republican	1893–1897	Henry B. Cleaves	Republican
1829–1830	Nathan Cutler	Democrat	1897–1901	Llewellyn Powers	Republican
1830	Joshua Hall	Democrat	1901–1905	John Fremont Hill	Republican
1830–1831	Johathan Glidden Hunton	Nat-Rep	1905–1909	William Titcomb Cobb	Republican
1831–1834	Samuel Emerson Smith	Jacksonian	1909–1911	Bert Manfred Fernald	Republican
1834–1838	Robert Pinckney Dunlap	Democrat	1911–1913	Frederick William Plaisted	Republican
1838–1839	Edward Kent	Whig	1913–1915	William Thomas Haines	Republican
1839–1841	John Fairfield	Democrat	1915–1917	Oakley Chester Curtis	Democrat
1841	Richard H. Vose	Democrat	1917–1921	Carl Elias Milliken	Republican
1841–1842	Edward Kent	Whig	1921	Frederic Hale Parkhurst	Republican
1842–1843	John Fairfield	Democrat	1921–1925	Percival Proctor Baxter	Republican
1843–1844	Edward Kavanagh	Democrat	1925–1929	Ralph Owen Brewster	Republican
1844	David Dunn	Democrat	1929–1933	William Tudor Gardiner	Republican
1844	John Winchester Dana	Democrat	1933–1937	Louis Jefferson Brann	Democrat
1844–1847	Hugh Johnston Anderson	Democrat	1937–1941	Lewis Orin Barrows	Republican
1847–1850	John Winchester Dana	Democrat	1941–1945	Sumner Sewall	Republican
1850–1853	John Hubbard	Democrat	1945–1949	Horace Augustus Hildreth	Republican
1853–1855	William George Crosby	Whig	1949–1952	Frederick George Payne	Republican
1855–1856	Anson Peaslee Morrill	Maine Law	1952–1955	Burton Melvin Cross	Republican
1856–1857	Samuel Wells	Democrat	1955–1959	Edmund Sixtus Muskie	Democrat
1857	Hannibal Hamlin	Republican	1959	Robert Nelson Haskell	Republican
1857–1858	Joseph Hartwell Williams	Republican	1959	Clinton Amos Clauson	Democrat
1858–1861	Lot Myrick Morrill	Republican	1959–1967	John Hathaway Reed	Republican
1861–1863	Israel Washburn, Jr.	Republican	1967–1975	Kenneth M. Curtis	Democrat
1863–1864	Abner Coburn	Republican	1975–1979	James Bernard Longley	Independent
1864–1867	Samuel Cony	Republican	1979–1987	Joseph Edward Brennan	Democrat
1867–1871	Jushua Lawrence Chamberlain	Republican	1987–1995	John Rettie McKernan, Jr.	Republican1995
1871–1874	Sidney Perham	Republican	1995–	Angus S. King, Jr.	Independent
1874–1876	Nelson Dingley, Jr.	Republican			
1876–1879	Selden Connor	Republican		Democratic Republican – Dem-Rep	
1879–1880	Alonzo Garcelon	Democrat		National Republican – Nat-Rep	
1880–1881	Daniel Franklin Davis	Republican			

14 LOCAL GOVERNMENT

The principal units of local government in 1997 were the 22 cities and 465 towns. In all, there were 832 local government units. As is customary in New England, the basic instrument of town government is the annual town meeting, with an elective board of selectmen supervising town affairs between meetings. Some of the larger towns employ full-time town managers. There is no local government in roughly half the state. Maine's 16 counties function primarily as judicial districts.

15 JUDICIAL SYSTEM

The highest state court is the supreme judicial court, which has statewide appeals jurisdiction in all civil and criminal matters. The 16-member superior court has original jurisdiction in cases involving trial by jury and also hears some appeals. The district courts hear non-felony criminal cases and small claims and juvenile

Photo credit: Susan D. Rock.

Fishing boats at anchor in Bar Harbor.

cases. Maine's crime rate in 1998 was 3,040.7 per 100,000 persons. There were 1,724 state and federal prisoners in June 1999.

16 MIGRATION

Although net losses from migration have continued through most of this century, there was a net gain of about 80,000 from 1970 to 1990. During 1990–98, the net loss from domestic migration was 15,000. As of 1990, some 68.5% of all state residents had been born in Maine.

17 ECONOMY

Maine's greatest economic strengths are its forests and waters, yielding wood products, waterpower, fisheries, and ocean com-

merce. Today, the largest industry by far is paper manufacturing, for which both forests and waterpower are essential. Maine's greatest current economic weakness is its limited access to the national transportation network that links major production and manufacturing centers with large metropolitan markets. On the other hand, this relative isolation, combined with the state's traditional natural assets, has contributed to Maine's attractiveness as a place for tourism and recreation.

18 INCOME

Personal income in 1998 was $23,499 per capita (per person), 38th in the US. Total personal income in the same year was $29.3 billion. Some 10.6% of the population lived below the federal poverty level in 1998.

19 INDUSTRY

Manufacturing in Maine has always been related to the forests. From the 17th century through much of the 19th, the staples of Maine industry were shipbuilding and lumber. Today they are papermaking and wood products, but footwear, textiles and apparel, shipbuilding, and electronic components and accessories are also important items.

Maine has the largest paper-production capacity of any state in the nation. There are large papermills and pulpmills in more than a dozen towns and cities. Wood-related industries—paper, lumber, wood products—accounted for 46% of the value of manufacturers shipments in 1995. The estimated total value of manufacturers' shipments in 1997 was over $15 billion.

20 LABOR

Maine's civilian labor force totaled 656,400 in mid-1998, with an unemployment rate of 4.4%. Labor union membership among Maine's workers in 1998 amounted to 66,100, or 14.3% of the work force. There were 60 labor unions operating in Maine in 1995.

21 AGRICULTURE

Maine's gross farm income in 1999 was $479 million (44th in the US). There were 6,900 farms in 1998, with an estimated 1.28 million acres (518,000 hectares) of land. Potatoes, grown primarily in Aroostook County, are by far the most important crop. Maine ranks eighth in potato-

production in the US, producing 1.7 billion pounds. Other crops included commercial apples, oats, and hay. Maine is also the leading producer of blueberries.

22 DOMESTICATED ANIMALS

Livestock and livestock products accounted for 57% of Maine's income from farm marketings in 1994. In 1995, egg production totaled 1.4 billion and yielded about $110 million in gross income. There were 100,000 cattle on Maine farms in 1999, worth $76 million. Southcentral Maine is the state's main poultry region.

23 FISHING

Fishing has been important to the economy of Maine since its settlement. In 1998, 183.9 million pounds of finfish and shellfish worth $216.4 million were landed at Maine ports. The value of the catch was the third highest after Alaska and Louisiana. The most valuable Maine fishery product is the lobster. Flounder, halibut, scallops, and shrimp are also caught. In 1996, federal hatcheries distributed over 3 million cold-water-species fish and 1.4 million fish eggs within the state, made up of mostly Atlantic salmon.

24 FORESTRY

Maine's 17.7 million acres (7.2 million hectares) of forest contains an estimated 3.6 billion trees and covers 90% of the state's land area, the largest percentage of any state in the US. Principal commercial hardwoods include ash, hard maple, white and yellow birch, beech, and oak. Commercially significant softwoods include white pine, hemlock, cedar, spruce, and fir.

Photo credit: Maine Office of Tourism.

A statue of Paul Bunyon in Bangor—the lumber capital of the world in the 1880s.

Roundwood harvested in 1993 totaled 776.4 million cubic feet (21.7 million cubic meters), 12th among the states and 3.4% of the US total.

25 MINING

The value of nonfuel mineral production in Maine in 1998 was estimated to be $76.2 million. Leading mineral commodities were construction sand and gravel (valued at $33.1 million), crushed stone, (valued at $16.8 million), and cement. Other mineral commodities produced included clay, peat, dimension stone, and gemstones.

26 ENERGY AND POWER

In recent decades, waterpower has been surpassed in importance by oil-fired steam plants and, most recently, by nuclear power. In 1995, the Maine Yankee Atomic Power Company station in Wiscasset generated 7.4% of the state's electric power. As of 1997, several nuclear plants in the region remained offline and may stay that way pending reviews by the Nuclear Regulatory Commission. Oil-fired steam units accounted for 49% and hydroelectric units for 51%. Electric power production in 1998 totaled 3.55 billion kilowatt hours. All fuel oil and coal must be imported.

27 COMMERCE

Maine had 1997 wholesale sales of $8 billion; retail sales totaled $13 billion. The value of Maine's exports amounted to $1.8 billion of goods in 1998.

28 PUBLIC FINANCE

Maine's biennial budget is prepared by the Bureau of the Budget and submitted by the Governor to the Legislature for consideration. The revenues for fiscal year 1997, were $5.22 billion; expenditures were $4.44 billion. The state had a total debt of nearly $3.2 billion as of 1997, or about $2,579 per capita (per person).

29 TAXATION

The leading sources of tax revenue as of 1997 were a sales and use tax of 5% and a personal income tax of 2% to 8.5%.

Maine also imposes corporate income taxes, taxes on utilities, inheritance and estate taxes, liquor and cigarette taxes, and a tax on gasoline, fuel, and motor carriers. In 1997, the state tax burden amounted to over $2 billion, or $1,626 per person (22nd highest rate among the states). Federal expenditures traditionally outstrip the state's federal tax burden by a large amount.

30 HEALTH

The death rate of 975.3 per 100,000 in 1998 was slightly higher than the US norm, reflecting a higher than average population in the upper age levels. Maine's death rate from Alzheimer's disease was the highest in the country in 1996, at 14.3 per 100,000. The death rates from cancer, heart disease, pulmonary disease, and suicide were higher than their respective national rates in 1998. In 1998, Maine had 38 community hospitals, with 3,768 beds. Licensed medical personnel included 214 physicians per 100,000. Licensed nurses numbered almost 4,000. The average per-inpatient charge for hospital care in 1998 was $1,098 per day, or $6,426 for an average cost per stay. About 12.7% of state residents did not have health insurance in 1998.

31 HOUSING

There were an estimated 626,000 housing units in Maine in 1999. About one-seventh of all Maine homes are for seasonal rather than year-round use. The median home value in Maine was $87,400 in 1990. Maine had the lowest median owner (including mortgage) and renter costs in New England in 1990, at $664 and $419 per month, respectively.

32 EDUCATION

Maine has a long and vigorous tradition of education at all levels, both public and private. In 1998, 86.7% of the adult population had completed high school, but only 19.2% had completed college, the lowest rate in New England. In 1996, Maine's public school enrollment was about 212,526. Expenditures for public elementary and secondary schools amounted to $6,116 per student in 1995/96 (15th among the states).

Since 1968, the state's system of state colleges and universities has been incorporated into a single University of Maine, which in 1999 had over 30,000 undergraduate, graduate, and professional students. Of the state's 16 private colleges and professional schools, Bowdoin College in Brunswick, Colby College in Waterville, and Bates College in Lewiston are the best known.

33 ARTS

Maine has long held an attraction for painters and artists, Winslow Homer and Andrew Wyeth among them. The state abounds in summer theaters, the oldest and most famous of which is at Ogunquit. The Portland Symphony is Maine's leading orchestra; another ensemble is in Bangor. The Maine Arts Commission funds the state's arts education programs and makes grants available to rural arts groups.

34 LIBRARIES AND MUSEUMS

In 1998, Maine public libraries had 5.3 million volumes and a combined circulation of 7.7 million. Leading academic libraries are those of Maine State at Augusta, the University of Maine at Orono, Bowdoin College at Brunswick, and the University of Southern Maine at Portland. Maine has 121 museums and historic sites. The privately supported Maine Historical Society in Portland maintains a research library and the Wadsworth Longfellow House, the boyhood home of Henry Wadsworth Longfellow. The largest of several maritime museums is in Bath.

35 COMMUNICATIONS

In 1999, 97.2% of the occupied housing units had telephones. Maine had 115 commercial radio stations (27 AM, 88 FM) in 2000, along with 16 television stations. Educational television stations broadcast from Augusta, Biddeford, Calais, Orono, and Presque Isle. In 2000, a total of 25,583 Internet domain names had been registered in the state.

36 PRESS

Maine had seven daily newspapers in 1998. The most widely read newspapers were the *Bangor Daily News* (mornings, 69,514; weekend, 82,870) and the *Portland Press Herald* (mornings, 75,686). Maine's largest Sunday newspaper is the *Maine Sunday Telegram* (124,892). The capital is served by the *Augusta Kennebec Journal* (15,708 daily; 14,185 Sundays).

37 TOURISM, TRAVEL, AND RECREATION

Calling itself "Vacationland," the state of Maine is a year-round resort destination. Expenditures by tourists were estimated at over $1.4 billion in 1998. Most out-of-state visitors continue to come in the summer, when the southern coast offers sandy beaches, icy surf, and several small harbors for sailing and saltwater fishing. Northeastward, the scenery becomes more rugged and spectacular, and sailing and hiking are the primary activities. Whitewater canoeing lures the adventurous along the Allagash Wilderness Waterway in northern Maine. Maine has always attracted hunters, especially during the fall deer season. Wintertime recreation facilities include nearly 60 ski areas and countless opportunities for cross-country skiing.

In 2000 there were 12 state parks and beaches. Acadia National Park, a popular attraction, drew 2.7 million visitors in 1996. There are four other federal parks, forests, and wildlife areas, and seven national wildlife refuges. The state fair is at Bangor.

38 SPORTS

Maine has no major league professional sports team. The Portland Pirates (a minor league team) of the American Hockey League play on their home ice at the Cumberland County Civic Center in Portland. The Portland Seadogs, a minor league baseball team, is affiliated with the Florida Marlins. Harness-racing is held at Scarborough Downs and other tracks and fairgrounds throughout the state.

Photo credit: EPD Photos.

Sarah Orne Jewett (1849–1909) wrote about life in Maine, especially that of late nineteenth-century women.

39 FAMOUS MAINERS

The highest federal officeholders born in Maine were Hannibal Hamlin (1809–91), the nation's first Republican vice-president, under Abraham Lincoln; and Nelson A. Rockefeller (1908–79), governor of New York State from 1959 to 1973 and US vice-president under Gerald Ford. Margaret Chase Smith (1897–1995) served longer in the US Senate—24 years—than any other woman.

Maine claims a large number of well-known reformers and humanitarians: Dorothea Lynde Dix (1802–87), who led the movement for hospitals for the insane;

Elijah Parish Lovejoy (1802–37), an abolitionist killed while defending his printing press from a proslavery mob in St. Louis, Missouri; and Harriet Beecher Stowe (b.Connecticut, 1811–96), whose novel *Uncle Tom's Cabin* (1852) was written in Maine. Other important writers include poet Henry Wadsworth Longfellow (1807–82) and Kate Douglas Wiggin (1856–1923), author of *Rebecca of Sunnybrook Farm*. Edwin Arlington Robinson (1869–1935) and Edna St. Vincent Millay (1892–1950) were both Pulitzer Prize-winning poets. E. B. (Elwyn Brooks) White (1899–1985), *New Yorker* essayist and author of the children's classic *Charlotte's Web*, maintained a home in Maine, which inspired much of his writing. Winslow Homer (b.Massachusetts, 1836–1910) had a summer home at Prouts Neck, where he painted many of his seascapes.

40 BIBLIOGRAPHY

Beem, Edgar Allen. *Maine: the Spirit of America.* New York: Harry N. Abrams, 2000.

Dornfeld, Margaret. *Maine.* New York: Benchmark Books, 2001.

Gale, Robert L. *A Sarah Orne Jewett Companion.* Westport, Conn.: Greenwood Press, 1999.

Kent, Deborah. *Maine.* New York: Children's Press, 1999.

Kummer, Patricia K. *Maine.* Mankato, Minn.: Capstone Press, 1998.

McAuliffe, Emily. *Maine Facts and Symbols.* New York: Hilltop Books, 2000.

Web sites

Maine Secretary of State. Kid's Page. [Online] Available http://www.state.me.us/sos/kids/ Accessed May 15, 2001.

State of Maine. Maine State Government Web Site. [Online] Available http://www.state.me.us/ Accessed May 15, 2001.

MARYLAND

State of Maryland

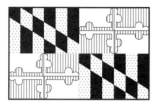

ORIGIN OF STATE NAME: Named for Henrietta Maria, queen consort of King Charles I of England.

NICKNAME: The Old Line State; Free State.

CAPITAL: Annapolis.

ENTERED UNION: 28 April 1788 (7th).

SONG: "Maryland, My Maryland."

MOTTO: *Fatti maschii, parole femine* (Manly deeds, womanly words).

FLAG: Bears the quartered arms of the Calvert and Crossland families (the paternal and maternal families of the founders of Maryland).

OFFICIAL SEAL: REVERSE: A shield bearing the arms of the Calverts and Crosslands is surmounted by an earl's coronet and a helmet and supported by a farmer and fisherman. The state motto (originally that of the Calverts) appears on a scroll below. The circle is surrounded by the Latin legend *Scuto bonæ voluntatis tuæ coronasti nos,* meaning "With the shield of thy favor hast thou compassed us"; and "1632," the date of Maryland's first charter. OBVERSE: Lord Baltimore is seen as a knight in armor on a charger. The surrounding inscription, in Latin, means "Cecilius, Absolute Lord of Maryland and Avalon New Foundland, Baron of Baltimore."

BIRD: Baltimore oriole.

FISH: Rockfish.

FLOWER: Black-eyed Susan.

TREE: White oak.

DOG: Chesapeake Bay retriever.

CRUSTACEAN: Blue crab.

INSECT: Baltimore checkerspot butterfly.

SPORT: Jousting.

TIME: 7 AM EST = noon GMT.

1 LOCATION AND SIZE

Located on the eastern seaboard of the US in the South Atlantic region, Maryland ranks 42d in size among the 50 states. Maryland's total area is 10,460 square miles (27,092 square kilometers). The state extends 199 miles (320 kilometers) east-west and 126 miles (203 kilometers) north-south. The total boundary length of Maryland is 842 miles (1,355 kilometers).

Important islands in Chesapeake Bay, off Maryland's Eastern Shore (part of the Delmarva Peninsula), include Kent, Bloodsworth, South Marsh, and Smith.

2 TOPOGRAPHY

Three distinct regions characterize Maryland's terrain. The first and major area is the coastal plain, nearly cut in half by Chesapeake Bay. The Piedmont Plateau to the west is a broad, rolling upland with several deep gorges. Farther west is the Appalachian Mountain region, containing the state's highest hills. Backbone Mountain in westernmost Maryland is the state's highest point, at 3,360 feet (1,024 meters). A few small islands lie in Chesapeake Bay, Maryland's dominant waterway. The state has 23 rivers and bays. Principal rivers include the Potomac, the Patapsco, the Patuxent, and the Susquehanna.

3 CLIMATE

Despite its small size, Maryland has a diverse climate. Temperatures vary from an annual average of 48°F (9°C) in the extreme western uplands to 59°F (15°C) in the southeast, where the climate is moderated by Chesapeake Bay and the Atlantic Ocean. The mean temperature for Baltimore ranges from 33°F (1°C) in January to 77°F (25°C) in July. The record high temperature for the state is 109°F (43°C), set on 10 July 1936; the record low is −40°F (−40°C), set on 13 January 1912.

Precipitation ranges from 36 inches (91 centimeters) annually in the Cumberland area to about 49 inches (124 centimeters) in the southeast. As much as 100 inches (254 centimeters) of snow falls in western Garrett County, while 8–10 inches (20–25 centimeters) is average for the Eastern Shore.

4 PLANTS AND ANIMALS

Maryland's three life zones—coastal plain, piedmont, and Appalachian—mingle wildlife characteristics of both North and South. Most of the state lies within a hardwood belt in which red and white oaks,

Maryland Population Profile

Total population in 2000:	5,296,486
Population change, 1990–2000:	10.8%
Hispanic or Latino†:	4.3%
Population by race	
One race:	98.0%
White:	64.0%
Black or African American:	27.9%
American Indian/Alaska Native:	0.3%
Asian:	4.0%
Native Hawaiian/Pacific Islander:	—
Some other race:	1.8%
Two or more races:	2.0%

Population by Age Group

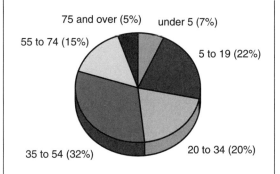

75 and over (5%) under 5 (7%)
55 to 74 (15%)
5 to 19 (22%)
35 to 54 (32%)
20 to 34 (20%)

Top Cities by Population

City	Population	% change 1990–2000
Baltimore	651,154	−11.5
Frederick	52,767	31.4
Gaithersburg	52,613	33.1
Bowie	50,269	33.7
Rockville	47,388	5.7
Hagerstown	36,687	3.5
Annapolis	35,838	8.0
College Park	24,657	12.5
Salisbury	23,743	15.3
Cumberland	21,518	−9.2

Notes: †A person of Hispanic or Latino origin may be of any race. NA indicates that data are not available.
Sources: U.S. Census Bureau. Public Information Office. *Demographic Profiles.* [Online] Available http://www.census.gov/Press-Release/www/2001/demoprofile.html. Accessed June 1, 2001. U.S. Census Bureau. *Census 2000: Redistricting Data.* Press release issued by the Redistricting Data Office. Washington, D.C., March, 2001.

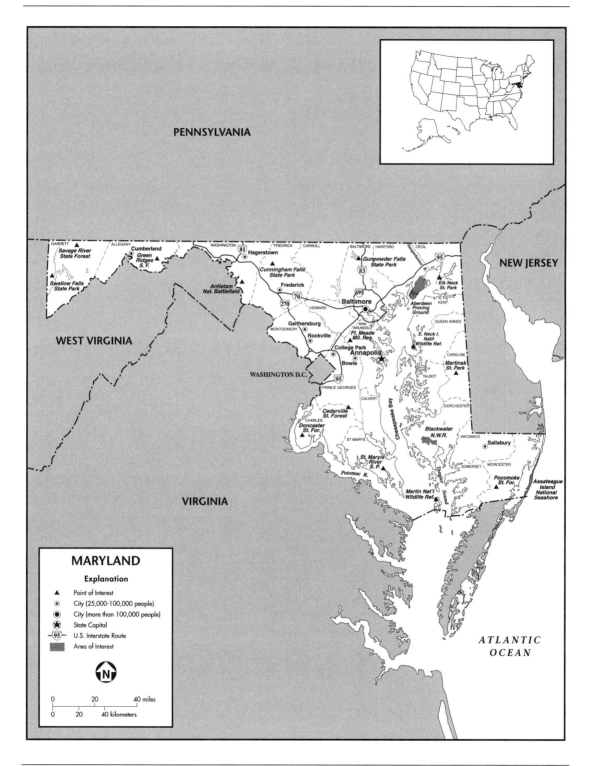

PENNSYLVANIA

NEW JERSEY

WEST VIRGINIA

VIRGINIA

GARRETT
Savage River
State Forest
ALLEGANY
Cumberland
Green
Ridges
S. F.
Swallow Falls
State Park
WASHINGTON
81
Hagerstown
Cunningham Falls
State Park
Antietam
Nat. Battlefield
Frederick
FREDRICK
CARROLL
270
70
HOWARD
Gaithersburg
Rockville
MONTGOMERY
College Park
WASHINGTON D.C.
95
Bowie
PRINCE GEORGES
BALTIMORE
HARFORD
CECIL
Gunpowder Falls
State Park
83
695
Baltimore
ANNE
ARUNDEL
Ft. Meade
Mil. Res.
Annapolis
95
Aberdeen
Proving
Ground
KENT
Elk Neck
St. Park
QUEEN ANNES
E. Neck I.
Nat'l
Wildlife Ref.
CAROLINE
Martinak
St. Park
TALBOT
Chesapeake Bay
CALVERT
Cedarville
St. Forest
CHARLES
Doncaster
St. For.
ST MARYS
St. Mary's
River
S. P.
Potomac R.
Martin Nat'l
Wildlife Ref.
DORCHESTER
Blackwater
N.W.R.
WICOMICO
Salisbury
SOMERSET
WORCESTER
Pocomoke
St. For.
Assateague
Island
National
Seashore

ATLANTIC
OCEAN

MARYLAND

Explanation

▲ Point of Interest
◉ City (25,000-100,000 people)
◉ City (more than 100,000 people)
★ State Capital
—95— U.S. Interstate Route
▨ Area of Interest

N

0   20   40 miles
0   20   40 kilometers

yellow poplar, and beech, among others, are represented. Shortleaf and loblolly pines are the leading softwoods. Honeysuckle, Virginia creeper, and wild raspberry are also common. Wooded hillsides are rich with such wildflowers as trailing arbutus, early blue violet, and wild rose.

The white-tailed (Virginia) deer, eastern cottontail, and raccoon, among others, are native to Maryland, although urbanization has sharply reduced their habitat. Common small mammals are the woodchuck, eastern chipmunk, and gray squirrel. Birds include the cardinal, chestnut-sided warbler, and rose-breasted grosbeak. Among saltwater species, shellfish—especially oysters, clams, and crabs—have the greatest economic importance. The Indiana bat, eastern cougar, and Maryland darter are among the species listed as endangered in the state.

5 ENVIRONMENTAL PROTECTION

The Maryland Department of the Environment (MDE) serves as the state's primary environmental protection agency. Besides protecting and restoring the quality of Maryland's land, air, and water, MDE regulations also control the storage, transportation, and disposal of hazardous wastes and ensure long-term, environmentally sound solid-waste recycling and disposal capabilities. As of 1998, Maryland had 18 hazardous waste sites.

MDE leads the state's efforts to restore the Chesapeake Bay and protect it from the effects of stormwater run-off and both airborne and waterborne pollutants. Additionally, Maryland's Department of

Natural Resources manages water allocation, fish and wildlife, state parks and forests, land reclamation, and open space.

6 POPULATION

The enormous expansion of the federal government and exodus of people from Washington, D.C. to the surrounding suburbs contributed to the rapid growth of Maryland. As of 2000, it was the 19th most populous state, with 5,296,486 people. It is projected that the population will reach 5.47 million by 2005. The population density in 2000 was 541.9 persons per square mile (209.2 persons per square kilometer), considerably higher than the national average of 79.6 persons per square mile (30.7 per square kilometer).

Almost all the growth since World War II has occurred in the four suburban counties around Washington, D.C., and Baltimore. Metropolitan Baltimore, embracing Carroll, Howard, Harford, Anne Arundel, and Baltimore counties, expanded from 2,244,700 to 2,474,100 inhabitants between 1984 and 1996. The city of Baltimore, on the other hand, declined from 763,570 to 675,400 during the same period. Baltimore is the state's only major city, with a 2000 population of 651,154. Other cities and their 2000 populations include Frederick, 52,767; Gaithersburg, 52,613; and Bowie, 50,269. About 29% of the population is 19 years of age and younger.

7 ETHNIC GROUPS

Black Americans, estimated at 1.4 million in 1997, constitute the largest racial minority in Maryland, representing 27.4% of the population (6th highest percentage in the

Maryland Population by Race

Census 2000 was the first national census in which the instructions to respondents said, "Mark one or more races." This table shows the number of people who are of one, two, or three or more races. For those claiming two races, the number of people belonging to the various categories is listed. The U.S. government conducts a census of the population every ten years.

	Number	Percent
Total population	5,296,486	100.0
One race	5,192,899	98.0
Two races	95,262	1.8
White *and* Black or African American	19,270	0.4
White *and* American Indian/Alaska Native	10,388	0.2
White *and* Asian	15,660	0.3
White *and* Native Hawaiian/Pacific Islander	793	—
White *and* some other race	20,812	0.4
Black or African American *and* American Indian/Alaska Native	6,488	0.1
Black or African American *and* Asian	3,330	0.1
Black or African American *and* Native Hawaiian/Pacific Islander	840	—
Black or African American *and* some other race	10,920	0.2
American Indian/Alaska Native *and* Asian	855	—
American Indian/Alaska Native *and* Native Hawaiian/Pacific Islander	70	—
American Indian/Alaska Native *and* some other race	796	—
Asian *and* Native Hawaiian/Pacific Islander	930	—
Asian *and* some other race	3,827	0.1
Native Hawaiian/Pacific Islander *and* some other race	283	—
Three or more races	8,325	0.2

Source: U.S. Census Bureau. *Census 2000: Redistricting Data.* Press release issued by the Redistricting Data Office. Washington, D.C., March, 2001. A dash (—) indicates that the percent is less than 0.1.

nation). Hispanic Americans, mostly from Puerto Rico and Central America, were estimated at 179,000 in 1997. The Asian population estimate of 194,600 in 1997 accounted for 3.8% of the population (8th highest). The leading Asian ethnicities are Korean, Chinese, Filipino, Japanese, and Vietnamese.

Foreign-born residents were estimated at 412,000 (8%) in 1996, many having immigrated to Maryland in the 1970s. The leading countries of origin in 1990 were Korea, India, El Salvador, Germany, and the Philippines. A significant proportion of the German, Polish, and Russian immigrants were Jewish refugees arriving just before and after World War II. Maryland's Native American population is small—only 15,400 (0.3%) in 1997.

8 LANGUAGES

The state's diverse terrain has contributed to unusual diversity in its basic speech. Proximity to Virginia and access to southeastern and central Pennsylvania helped to create a language mixture that now is dominantly Midland and yet reflects earlier ties to Southern English. In 1990, 4,030,234 residents, or 91.1% of the population five years old or older, spoke only English at home. Other languages spoken at home, with the number of speakers,

Fort McHenry (on Baltimore's waterfront), birthplace of the national anthem.

included Spanish, 122,871; French, 39,484; and German, 26,454.

9 RELIGIONS

Maryland was founded as a haven for Roman Catholics, and they remain the state's leading religious group. As of 1990 there were 832,763 Roman Catholics in Maryland. Members of the major Protestant denominations included United Methodist Church, 310,008; Southern Baptist Convention, 131,627; Lutheran Church— Missouri Synod, 31,393; and Episcopal Church, 82,714. In 1994 there were an estimated 212,000 Jews.

10 TRANSPORTATION

As of 1998, total rail miles of track in Maryland amounted to 769 miles (1,237 kilometers), including 675 miles (1,086 kilometers) of Class I track. Amtrak operated about 70 trains through the state in 1998, carrying 1.5 million passengers from six stations. The Maryland Mass Transit Administration inaugurated Baltimore's first subway line in 1983. In 1984, the Washington, D.C., mass transit system was extended to the Maryland suburbs.

As of 1997 there were 29,872 miles (48,064 kilometers) of roadway and nearly 3.8 million motor vehicles registered in Maryland. The Port of Baltimore,

Maryland Governors: 1775–2001

Term	Governor	Party
1775–1777	Daniel of St. Thomas Jenifer	
1777–1779	Thomas Johnson	
1779–1782	Thomas S. Lee	
1782–1785	William Paca	
1785–1788	William Smallwood	
1788–1791	John Eager Howard	Federalist
1791–1792	George Plater	Federalist
1792	James Brice	Federalist
1792–1794	Thomas Sim Lee	Federalist
1794–1797	John Hoskins Stone	Federalist
1797–1798	John Henry	Federalist
1798–1801	Benjamin Ogle	Federalist
1801–1803	John Francis Mercer	Dem-Rep
1803–1806	Robert Bowie	Dem-Rep
1806–1809	Robert Wright	Dem-Rep
1809	James Butcher	Dem-Rep
1809–1811	Edward Lloyd	Dem-Rep
1811–1812	Robert Bowie	Dem-Rep
1812–1816	Levin Winder	Federalist
1816–1819	Charles Carnan Ridgely	Federalist
1819	Charles Goldsborough	Federalist
1819–1922	Samuel Sprigg	Dem-Rep
1822–1826	Samuel Stevens, Jr.	Dem-Rep
1826–1829	Joseph Kent	Dem-Rep
1829–1830	Daniel Martin	Anti–Jacksonian
1830–1831	Thomas King Carroll	Jacksonian
1831	Daniel Martin	Anti–Jacksonian
1831–1833	George Howard	Anti–Jacksonian
1833–1836	James Thomas	Anti–Jacksonian
1836–1839	Thomas Ward Veazey	Whig
1839–1842	William Grason	Democrat
1842–1845	Francis Thomas	Democrat
1845–1848	Thomas George Pratt	Whig
1848–1851	Philip Francis Thomas	Democrat
1851–1854	Enoch Louis Lowe	Democrat
1854–1858	Thomas Watkins Ligon	Democrat
1858–1862	Thomas Holliday Hicks	American
1862–1866	Augustus Williamson Bradford	Union-Rep
1866–1869	Thomas Swann	Union-Dem
1869–1872	Oden Bowie	Democrat
1872–1874	William Pinkney Whyte	Democrat
1874–1876	James Black Groome	Democrat
1876–1880	John Lee Carroll	Democrat
1880–1884	William Thomas Hamilton	Democrat
1884–1885	Robert Milligan McLane	Democrat
1885–1888	Henry Lloyd	Democrat
1888–1892	Elihu Emory Jackson	Democrat
1892–1896	Frank Brown	Democrat
1896–1900	Lloyd Lowndes, Jr.	Republican
1900–1904	John Walter Smith	Democrat
1904–1908	Edwin Warfield	Democrat
1908–1912	Austin Lane Crothers	Democrat
1912–1916	Phillips Lee Goldsborough	Republican
1916–1920	Emerson Columbus Harrington	Democrat
1920–1935	Albert Cabell Ritchie	Democrat
1935–1939	Harry Whinna Nice	Republican
1939–1947	Herbert Romulus O'Conor	Democrat
1947–1951	William Preston Lane, Jr.	Democrat
1951–1959	Theodore Roosevelt McKeldin	Republican
1959–1967	John Millard Tawes	Democrat
1967–1969	Spiro Theodore Agnew	Republican
1969–1977	Marvin Mandel	Democrat
1977–1979	Lee Blair III	Democrat
1979	Marvin Mandel	Democrat
1979–1987	Harry R. Hughes	Democrat
1987–1995	William Donald Schaefer	Democrat
1995–	Parris N. Glendening	Democrat

Democratic Republican – Dem-Rep
Union Democrat – Union-Dem
Union Republican – Union-Rep

the nation's 17th busiest, handled 40.1 million tons of cargo in 1998. In 2000, Baltimore–Washington International Airport, the major air terminal in the state, handled 19.7 million passengers.

11 HISTORY

The Indian tribes living in the region that was to become Maryland were Algonkian-speakers, including the Accomac, Susquehannock, and Piscataway. Although the Algonkian tribes hunted for much of their food, many (including the Susquehannock) also had permanent settlements where they cultivated corn (maize) and other crops. European penetration of the Chesapeake region began early in the 16th century, with the expeditions of Giovanni da Verrazano of Florence and the Spaniard Lucas Vázquez de Ayllón. Captain John Smith was the first English explorer of Chesapeake Bay (1608) and produced a map of the area that was used for years.

Twenty years later, George Calvert received from King Charles I a land grant that embraced not only present-day Maryland but also the present State of Delaware, a large part of Pennsylvania, and the valley between the north and south branches of the Potomac River. When he died in 1632, the title passed to his son Cecilius Calvert, second Baron Baltimore, who named the region Maryland after Charles I's queen, Henrietta Maria. Calvert established the first settlement two years later as a refuge for persecuted Roman Catholics.

In 1689, with Protestants in power both in England and Maryland, the British crown took control of the province away from the Catholic Calverts, and in 1692, the Church of England became Maryland's established religion. The Fourth Baron Baltimore regained full hereditary rights—but only because he had embraced the Protestant faith. Rule by the Calvert family through their legitimate heirs continued until the eve of the American Revolution.

Statehood

After some initial hesitancy, Maryland cast its lot with the Revolution and sent approximately 20,000 soldiers to fight in the war. On 28 April 1788, it became the seventh state to ratify the federal Constitution. By the early 19th century, Baltimore, founded in 1729, was already the state's major center of commerce and industry. The city and harbor were the site of extended military operations during the War of 1812. It was during the bombardment of Ft. McHenry in 1814 that Francis Scott Key, detained on the British frigate, composed "The Star-Spangled Banner," which became the US national anthem in March 1931.

After the War of 1812, Maryland history was marked by the continued growth of Baltimore and increasing division over immigration, slavery, and secession, which the Maryland house of delegates rejected in 1861. Throughout the Civil War, Maryland was largely occupied by Union troops because of its strategic location. Marylanders fought on both sides during the war, and one major battle took place on Maryland soil—the Battle of Antietam (1862), during which a Union army thwarted a Confederate thrust toward the north, but at an enormous cost to both sides.

The state's economic activity increased during Reconstruction, as Maryland, and especially Baltimore, played a major role in rebuilding the South. Maryland's economic base gradually shifted from agriculture to industry, with shipbuilding, steelmaking, and the manufacture of clothing and shoes leading the way. The decades between the Civil War and World War I were also notable for the philanthropic activities of such wealthy businessmen as Johns Hopkins and George Peabody, who endowed some of the state's most prestigious cultural and educational institutions. Democrat Albert C. Ritchie won election to the governorship in 1919 and served in that office until 1935, stressing local issues, states' rights, and opposition to prohibition.

The decades since World War II have been marked by significant population growth. The state has witnessed the passage of open housing and equal opportunity laws to protect Maryland's black citizens. It has also been rocked by political scandal in recent years. Perhaps the most significant occurrence has been the redevelopment of Baltimore, which, though still the hub of the state's economy, had fallen into decay. Much of Baltimore's downtown area and harbor were revitalized by urban renewal projects in the late 1970s and 1980s. Although Maryland's economy declined less than those of other states during the recession of the late 1980s and early 1990s, the state has suffered from reductions in the defense and technology industries.

12 STATE GOVERNMENT

The general assembly, Maryland's legislative body, consists of two branches: a 47-member senate and a 141-member house of delegates. All legislators serve four-year terms. Executives elected statewide are the governor and lieutenant governor (who run jointly), the comptroller of the Trea-

sury, and the attorney general. All serve four-year terms.

Bills passed by majority vote of both houses of the assembly become law when signed by the governor, or if left unsigned for 6 days while the legislature is in session or for 30 days if the legislature has adjourned. The only exception is the budget bill, which becomes effective immediately upon legislative passage. Gubernatorial vetoes may be overridden by three-fifths votes in both houses.

13 POLITICAL PARTIES

As of 1994, there were 2,463,010 registered voters, of whom 61% were Democrats; 29% Republicans; and 10% independents and members of minor parties. Maryland was one of the few states carried by President Jimmy Carter in the November 1980 presidential election, but four years later the state went for Presi-

Maryland Presidential Vote by Political Parties, 1948–2000

YEAR	MARYLAND WINNER	DEMOCRAT	REPUBLICAN	PROGRESSIVE	DEMOCRAT	STATE'S RIGHTS SOCIALIST
1948	Dewey (R)	286,521	294,814	9,983	2,467	2,941
1952	*Eisenhower (R)	395,337	499,424	7,313	—	—
1956	*Eisenhower (R)	372,613	559,738	—	—	—
1960	*Kennedy (D)	565,808	489,538	—	—	—
1964	*Johnson (D)	730,912	385,495	—	—	—
				AMERICAN IND.		
1968	Humphrey (D)	538,310	517,995	178,734	—	—
				AMERICAN		
1972	*Nixon (R)	505,781	829,305	18,726	—	—
1976	*Carter (D)	759,612	672,661	—	—	—
					LIBERTARIAN	
1980	Carter (D)	726,161	680,606	—	14,192	—
1984	*Reagan (R)	787,935	879,918	—	5,721	—
1988	*Bush (R)	826,304	876,167	5,115	6,748	—
						IND. (Perot)
1992	*Clinton (D)	988,571	707,094	2,786	4,715	281,414
1996	*Clinton (D)	966,207	681,530	—	8,765	115,812
					LIBERTARIAN	REFORM
2000	Gore (D)	1,144,088	813,827	53,768	5,310	4,248

* Won US presidential election.

dent Ronald Reagan in the national Republican landslide. In 2000, Maryland gave 57% of its vote to Democrat Al Gore and 40% to Republican George W. Bush.

Revelations of corruption afflicted both major parties during the 1970s. In 1973, Republican Spiro T. Agnew, then vice-president of the US, was accused of taking bribes while he was Baltimore County executive and then governor. Agnew resigned from the vice-presidency on 10 October 1973. His gubernatorial successor, Democrat Marvin Mandel, was convicted of mail fraud and racketeering in 1977. He served 20 months of a 36-month prison sentence before receiving a presidential pardon in 1981.

In 1994, the governor's race was one of the closest in Maryland history. Democrat Parris N. Glendening, three-term Prince George's county executive, defeated Ellen R. Sauerbrey, Republican leader of the Maryland House, by a mere 5,993 votes. Glendening was reelected by a comfortable margin in 1998. The two senators from Maryland, Paul S. Sarbanes and Barbara Mikulski, both Democrats, were reelected in 2000 and 1998, respectively.

As of the November 2000 elections, Maryland's congressional delegation consisted of four Democrats and four Republicans. There were 33 Democrats and 14 Republicans in the state senate and 106 Democrats and 35 Republicans in the state house.

14 LOCAL GOVERNMENT

As of 1997 there were 23 counties and 155 municipal governments in Maryland. Most counties had charter governments, with (in most cases) elected executives and county councils, and 15 had elected boards of county commissioners.

Baltimore is the only city in Maryland not contained within a county. It provides the same services as a county, and shares in state aid according to the same allocation formulas. The city (not to be confused with Baltimore County, which surrounds the city of Baltimore but has its county seat at Towson) is governed by a mayor and a nine-member city council. Other cities and towns are each governed by a mayor and a council, town commissioners, or council and a manager, depending on the local charter.

15 JUDICIAL SYSTEM

The court of appeals, the state's highest court, comprises a chief judge and six associate judges. Most criminal appeals are decided by the court of special appeals, consisting of a chief judge and 12 associate judges. District courts handle all criminal, civil, and traffic cases. Appeals are taken to one of eight judicial circuit courts. According to the FBI Crime Index for 1996, Maryland had a crime rate of 6,061.9 per 100,000 population. There were 23,067 prisoners in state and federal prisons in June 1997.

16 MIGRATION

During the 19th century, Baltimore ranked second only to New York as a port of entry for European immigrants. After the Civil War, many blacks migrated to Baltimore, both from rural Maryland and from southern states.

The "Pride of Baltimore II" under sail in Annapolis.

Since World War II, both the metropolitan area of Baltimore and the Maryland part of the metropolitan Washington, D.C., area have experienced rapid growth, while their inner cities have lost population. Overall, Maryland experienced a net loss from migration of about 36,000 between 1970 and 1980, much of it to Pennsylvania, Virginia, and Florida. The out-migration stopped during the 1980s, however, with a net gain of over 200,000 from 1980 to 1990. During 1990–98, the net loss from domestic migration was 49,000, while the net gain from international migration was 118,000. By 1990, just under 50% of all Maryland residents had been born in the state. An estimated 8% of the population was foreign-born in 1996, when Maryland admitted 15,561 immigrants. The federal government estimated that there were 44,000 illegal immigrants living in the state in 1996.

17 ECONOMY

Although manufacturing output continues to rise, the biggest growth areas in Maryland's economy are government, construction, trade, and services. Manufacturing, which has shifted towards high technology, information, and health-related products, lost 39,000 jobs between 1981 and 1991. With the expansion of federal employment in the Washington metropolitan area during the 1960s and

1970s, many US government workers settled in suburban Maryland, primarily Prince George's and Montgomery counties. Construction and services in those areas expanded accordingly. Between 1982 and 1992, the number of jobs grew 24% in Maryland, somewhat above the national average of 21% for that period. However, from 1992 to 2000, Maryland lost 17 percent of its federal employment in Washington D.C.

18 INCOME

As of 1998, Maryland ranked sixth nationwide in per capita (per person) income with $30,557. Median household income was $47,711 in 1998. An estimated 8.6% of Marylanders were living below the federal poverty level in 1998.

19 INDUSTRY

Baltimore is an important manufacturer of automobiles and parts, steel, and instruments. Value of shipments by manufacturers in 1997 was $38 billion. About one-third of all manufacturing activity takes place in the city of Baltimore, followed by Baltimore County, Montgomery County, and Prince George's County. Maryland is the headquarters of Lockheed Martin (aerospace), Marriott International (hospitality), Black and Decker (tools), and Giant Food.

20 LABOR

Maryland's civilian labor force in mid-1998 numbered 2.75 million, with an unemployment rate of 4.6%. As of 1998, 17.3% of all workers were union members.

21 AGRICULTURE

Maryland ranked 36th among the 50 states in agricultural income in 1998, with estimated receipts of $1.5 billion, about 40% of that in crops. The state had some 12,500 farms covering 2.1 million acres (850,000 hectares) in 1998. That same year, Maryland produced an estimated 9.1 million pounds of tobacco. Corn and cereal grains are grown mainly in southern Maryland. Production in 1998 included 43.6 million bushels of corn for grain, 14.2 million bushels of soybeans, and 10.7 million bushels of wheat. Greenhouse and nursery products contribute about 18% to agricultural receipts.

22 DOMESTICATED ANIMALS

About 60% of Maryland's farm income derives from livestock and livestock products. The Eastern Shore is an important dairy and poultry region. Cattle are raised in north-central and western Maryland, while the central region is notable for horse-breeding.

Maryland's broiler production in 1997 was ranked seventh among the 50 states, at 1.42 billion pounds. Also produced during 1997 were 882 million eggs valued at $800 million. Maryland farms and ranches had 86,000 dairy cows, 250,000 head of cattle, and 65,000 hogs in 1998.

23 FISHING

A leading source of oysters, clams, and crabs, Maryland had a total commercial catch in 1998 of 61.4 million pounds, valued at $67.2 million. Leading shellfish items are blue crabs, surf clams, and soft clams. Bigeye and yellowfin tuna together are the most important finfish, followed by menhaden, dogfish shark, swordfish, and sea bass.

24 FORESTRY

Maryland's 2.7 million acres (1.1 million hectares) of forestland cover 43% of the state's land area. Hardwoods predominate, with red and white oaks and yellow poplar among the leading hardwood varieties.

25 MINING

The value of nonfuel mineral production in Maryland in 1998 was about $358 million. In 1998, output of sand and gravel and crushed stone totaled about 11.7 million tons.

26 ENERGY AND POWER

In 1999, production of electricity was 48.5 billion kilowatt hours. About 60% of the state's electricity was produced by coal-fired plants. Coal reserves in 1998 were estimated at 64 million tons. The 1998 output of 16 coal mines totaled 4.06 million tons. There are two nuclear power plants in Maryland.

27 COMMERCE

Maryland had 1997 wholesale sales of $58 billion; retail sales totaled $48 billion. More than 75% of the state's retail facilities are located in the Baltimore metropolitan area and Montgomery and Prince George's counties surrounding Washington, D.C. Foreign exports of Maryland products totaled $4.7 billion in 1997. The value of imports arriving at the Port of Baltimore was $12.2 billion in 1995.

28 PUBLIC FINANCE

The outstanding state debt exceeded $9.87 billion as of 1997, or $1,938 per capita (per person). The estimated revenues for the fiscal year 1997 were $20.13 billion; expenditures were $16.2 billion.

29 TAXATION

Among the taxes levied by the state in 1996 were an individual income tax (2%); a corporate income tax (7%); a 5% sales and use tax; a state property tax; and motor vehicle use, franchise, cigarette, and alcoholic beverage taxes. All county and some local governments levy property taxes. The counties also tax personal income. Maryland's state tax burden in 1997 was $8.6 billion, or $1,689 per person (the 17th highest rate among the states). Marylanders paid $34.4 billion in federal income taxes in 1995 but received $36.8 billion in federal funding.

30 HEALTH

The death rates for heart disease and cerebrovascular diseases were both below the US average for these categories in 1998. In 1998, Maryland had 51 community hospitals, with 12,670 beds. The average expense for hospital care in 1998 was $1,199 per inpatient day, or $6,605 for an average stay. The medical school at Johns Hopkins University in Baltimore has superbly equipped research facilities. Federal health centers located in Bethesda include the National Institutes of Health and the National Naval Medical Center.

Maryland had 362 physicians per 100,000 in 1997. There were about 13,000 licensed nurses as of 1998. Some 16.6% of state residents did not have health insurance in 1998.

31 HOUSING

Maryland has sought to preserve many of its historic houses, especially in Annapolis, which has several ornate mansions. Block upon block of two-story brick row houses fill the older parts of Baltimore, and stone cottages built to withstand rough winters are still found in the western counties. There were an estimated 2.1 million year-round housing units in Maryland in 1999. In 1998, the median value of a home was $120,600. During 1998, 30,900 new housing units were authorized for construction. The median monthly cost for housing for owners with a mortgage in 1990 was $919, and $235 for owners without a mortgage. The median monthly rent throughout the state was $548 in 1990.

32 EDUCATION

As of 1998, 84.7% of all Marylanders age 25 and older had completed high school, and 31.8% had at least four years of college. There are 791 elementary and 202 secondary schools serving the state. Enrollment in fall 1997 for grades K–12 was 830,744 in public schools. The total public school enrollment for the city of Baltimore alone was 108,759. Expenditures for public elementary and secondary schools in the state amounted to $6,407 per student in 1995/96 (13th among the states).

As of 1995 there were 34 four-year and 23 two-year accredited colleges and universities in the state. The total enrollment for public four-year institutions was 261,262 in fall 1997. There are four state colleges and two state universities (Towson and Morgan); other institutions include the University of Baltimore, the University of Maryland (College Park), and Mount St. Mary's College (Emmitsburg). By far the largest is the University of Maryland. The leading private institution in Maryland is The Johns Hopkins University in Baltimore. The State Board for Community Colleges oversees 18 community and 2 regional two-year schools. There are 3 private two-year colleges in the state.

33 ARTS

Though close to the arts centers of Washington, D.C., Maryland has its own cultural attractions. Center Stage in Baltimore is the designated state theater of Maryland, and the Olney Theatre in Montgomery County is the official state summer theater. Both the Maryland Ballet Company and Maryland Dance Theater are nationally known.

The state's leading orchestra is the Baltimore Symphony. Baltimore is also the home of the Baltimore Opera Company, and its jazz clubs were the launching pads for such musical notables as Eubie Blake, Ella Fitzgerald, and Cab Calloway. The Peabody Institute of Johns Hopkins University in Baltimore is one of the nation's most distinguished music schools. In the mid-1990s, the State Arts Council supported theater productions by "Shakespeare on Wheels."

also the site of several federal libraries, including the National Agricultural Library, the National Library of Medicine, and the National Oceanic and Atmospheric Administration Library.

Of the approximately 147 museums and historic sites in the state, major institutions include the US Naval Academy Museum in Annapolis and Baltimore's Museum of Art and Maritime Museum. The latter's Peale Museum is the oldest museum building in the US. Important historic sites include Ft. McHenry National Monument and Shrine in Baltimore (inspiration for "The Star-Spangled Banner") and Antietam National Battlefield Site near Sharpsburg.

35 COMMUNICATIONS

In 1999, 95.3% of Maryland's occupied housing units had telephones. The state had 53 AM and 72 FM radio stations in 2000. Maryland Public Broadcasting operates six noncommercial television stations—in Annapolis, Baltimore, Frederick, Hagerstown, Oakland, and Salisbury. There were 14 large cable television systems in Maryland as of 1996.

36 PRESS

As of 1998, Maryland had 10 morning and 4 afternoon dailies, 8 Sunday papers, 7 semiweekly newspapers, and 88 weeklies. The most influential newspaper published in Baltimore is the *Sun* (daily, 314,033; Sunday, 478,516). The *Washington Post* is also widely read in Maryland.

Photo credit: © George Hall/Woodfin Camp.

The National Aquarium in Baltimore.

34 LIBRARIES AND MUSEUMS

Maryland's public libraries held 15.6 million volumes in 1999 and had a combined circulation of 45.5 million. The center of the state library network is the Enoch Pratt Free Library in the city of Baltimore. Founded in 1886, it has 28 branches, 2.8 million volumes, and a circulation of 1.5 million in 1999. Each county also has its own library system. The largest academic libraries are those of Johns Hopkins University in Baltimore and the University of Maryland at College Park. Maryland is

Photo credit: Maryland Tourism.

Calvert Marine Museum.

towns along Chesapeake Bay. There are 19 state parks with camping facilities and 10 recreation areas.

38 SPORTS

Maryland has two major league professional sports team: the Baltimore Orioles of Major League Baseball and the Baltimore Ravens of the National Football League. Horse-racing is a popular state pastime. The major tracks are Pimlico (Baltimore), Bowie, and Laurel. Several steeplechase events, including the prestigious Maryland Hunt Cup, are held annually. Thoroughbred horse races and trotter horse races in Maryland had 1996 attendances of about 536,000 and 396,000, respectively.

In collegiate basketball, the University of Maryland won the National Invitation Tournament in 1972, and Morgan State took the NCAA Division II title in 1974. Other popular sports are lacrosse and jousting.

37 TOURISM, TRAVEL, AND RECREATION

Although not a major tourist center, Maryland attracted 19 million visitors to its parks, historical sites, and national seashore (Assateague Island) in 1998. Among the state's attractions is Annapolis, the state capital and site of the US Naval Academy. On Baltimore's waterfront are monuments to Francis Scott Key and Edgar Allan Poe, historic Ft. McHenry, and many restaurants serving the city's famed crab cakes and other seafood specialties. Ocean City is the state's major seaside resort, and there are many resort

39 FAMOUS MARYLANDERS

Maryland has produced no US presidents; its lone vice-president was Spiro Theodore Agnew (1918–96), who served as governor of Maryland before being elected as Richard Nixon's vice-president in 1968. Reelected with Nixon in 1972, Agnew resigned the vice-presidency in October 1973 after a federal indictment had been filed against him.

Roger Brooke Taney (1777–1864) was US chief justice when the Supreme Court heard the *Dred Scott* case in 1856, ruling that Congress could not exclude slavery from any territory. As counsel for the

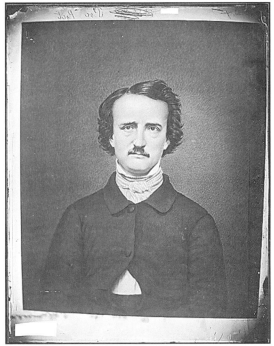

Photo credit: National Archives.

Edgar Allan Poe (1809–49) is shown here in a Civil War photograph taken by the Mathew Brady Studio for the US Army. Poe, known for his eerie short stories, died in Baltimore.

National Association for the Advancement of Colored People, Thurgood Marshall (1908–93) argued the landmark *Brown v. Board of Education* school desegregation case before the Supreme Court in 1954. President Lyndon Johnson appointed him to the Court 13 years later.

Lawyer and poet Francis Scott Key (1779–1843) wrote "The Star-Spangled Banner"—now the national anthem—in 1814. The prominent abolitionists Frederick Douglass (Frederick Augustus Washington Bailey, 1817?–95) and Harriet Tubman (1820?–1913) were born in Maryland.

Financier-philanthropist Johns Hopkins (1795–1873) was a Marylander. Peyton Rous (1879–1970) won the 1966 Nobel Prize for physiology-medicine.

Maryland's best-known modern writer was H(enry) L(ouis) Mencken (1880–1956), a Baltimore newspaper reporter who was also a gifted social commentator, political wit, and student of the American language. Edgar Allan Poe (b.Massachusetts, 1809–49), known for his poems and eerie short stories, died in Baltimore. Novelist-reformer Upton Sinclair (1878–1968) was born there, as was Emily Price Post (1873–1960), who wrote about social etiquette.

Probably the greatest baseball player of all time, George Herman "Babe" Ruth (1895–1948), was born in Baltimore. Other prominent ballplayers include Robert Moses "Lefty" Grove (1900–75) and Cal Ripken, Jr. (Calvin Edwin Ripken, Jr., b.1960).

40 BIBLIOGRAPHY

Alampi, Gary, ed. *Gale State Rankings Reporter.* Detroit: Gale Research Inc., 1994.

Aylesworth, Thomas G. *Mid-Atlantic: Delaware, Maryland, Pennsylvania.* New York: Chelsea House Publishers, 1996.

Bode, Carl. *Maryland: A Bicentennial History.* New York: Norton, 1978.

Cohen, Richard M., and Jules Witcover. *A Heartbeat Away: The Investigation and Resignation of Vice President Spiro T. Agnew.* New York: Viking, 1974.

Coleman, Brooke. *The Colony of Maryland.* New York: PowerKids Press, 1999.

Kummer, Patricia K. *Maryland.* Mankato, Minn.: Capstone Press, 1998.

Lough, Loree. *Lord Baltimore: English Politician*

and Colonist. Philadelphia: Chelsea House, 2000.

Rauth, Leslie. *Maryland*. New York: Benchmark Books, 2000.

Walsh, Richard, and William Lloyd Fox, eds. *Maryland: A History*. Baltimore: Maryland Hall of Records, 1983.

Web sites

Maryland Electronic Capital. All About Maryland. [Online] Available http://www.mec.state.md.us/ Accessed May 15, 2001.

State of Maryland Archives. Homepage. [Online] Available http://www.mdarchives.state.md.us/ Accessed May 15, 2001.

MASSACHUSETTS

Commonwealth of Massachusetts

ORIGIN OF STATE NAME: Derived from the name of the Massachusett Indian tribe that lived on Massachusetts Bay; the name is thought to mean "at or about the Great Hill."

NICKNAME: The Bay State.

CAPITAL: Boston.

ENTERED UNION: 6 February 1788 (6th).

SONG: "All Hail to Massachusetts."

FOLK SONG: "Massachusetts."

POEM: "Blue Hills of Massachusetts."

MOTTO: *Ense petit placidam sub libertate quietem* (By the sword we seek peace, but peace only under liberty).

COAT OF ARMS: On a blue shield, an Indian depicted in gold holds in his right hand a bow, in his left an arrow pointing downward. Above the bow is a five-pointed silver star. The crest shows a bent right arm holding a broadsword. Around the shield beneath the crest is a banner with the state motto in green.

FLAG: The coat of arms on a white field.

OFFICIAL SEAL: Same as the coat of arms, with the inscription *Sigillum Reipublicæ Massachusettensis* (Seal of the Republic of Massachusetts).

HEROINE: Deborah Samson.

BIRD: Chickadee.

HORSE: Morgan horse.

DOG: Boston terrier.

MARINE MAMMAL: Right whale.

FISH: Cod.

FLOWER: Mayflower (ground laurel).

TREE: American elm.

GEM: Rhodonite.

MINERAL: Babingtonite.

ROCK: Roxbury puddingstone.

HISTORICAL ROCK: Plymouth Rock.

EXPLORER ROCK: Dighton Rock.

BUILDING AND MONUMENT STONE: Granite.

FOSSIL: Theropod dinosaur tracks.

BEVERAGE: Cranberry juice.

INSECT: Ladybug.

TIME: 7 AM EST = noon GMT.

1 LOCATION AND SIZE

Located in the northeastern US, Massachusetts is the fourth largest of the six New England states. It ranks 45th in size among the 50 states. The total area of Massachusetts is 8,284 square miles (21,456 square kilometers). Massachusetts extends about 190 miles (306 kilometers) east-west; the maximum north-south extension is about 110 miles (177 kilometers). Two important islands lie south of the state's fishhook-shaped Cape Cod peninsula: Martha's Vineyard and Nantucket. The Elizabeth Islands, southwest of Cape Cod and northwest of Martha's Vineyard, consist of 16 small islands separating Buzzards Bay from Vineyard Sound. The total boundary length of Massachusetts is 515 miles (829 kilometers).

2 TOPOGRAPHY

The northern shoreline of the state is characterized by rugged high slopes, but at the southern end, along Cape Cod, the ground is flatter and covered with grassy heaths. East of the Connecticut River Valley are the eastern uplands, a ridge of heavily forested hills that is an extension of the White Mountains of New Hampshire. The Connecticut River Valley, characterized by red sandstone, curved ridges, and meadows, is the main feature of west-central Massachusetts. Found in western Massachusetts are the Taconic Range and Berkshire Hills (which extend southward from the Green Mountains of Vermont). Mt. Greylock is the highest point in the state, at 3,491 feet (1,064 meters).

There are more than 4,230 miles (6,808 kilometers) of rivers in the state. The principal ones include the Connecticut River (the longest) and the Charles, which flow into Boston harbor, and the Taunton, the Housatonic, and the Merrimack. Over 1,100 lakes dot the state. Martha's Vineyard and Nantucket Island are hilly. The Elizabeth Islands are characterized by broad, grassy plains.

Massachusetts Population Profile

Total population in 2000:	6,349,097
Population change, 1990–2000:	5.5%
Hispanic or Latino†:	6.8%
Population by race	
One race:	97.7%
White:	84.5%
Black or African American:	5.4%
American Indian/Alaska Native:	0.2%
Asian:	3.8%
Native Hawaiian/Pacific Islander:	—
Some other race:	3.7%
Two or more races:	2.3%

Population by Age Group

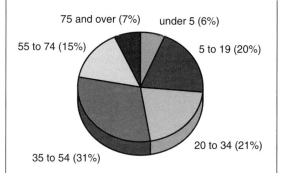

- 75 and over (7%)
- under 5 (6%)
- 55 to 74 (15%)
- 5 to 19 (20%)
- 20 to 34 (21%)
- 35 to 54 (31%)

Top Cities by Population

City	Population	% change 1990–2000
Boston	589,141	2.6
Worcester	172,648	1.7
Springfield	152,082	–3.1
Lowell	105,167	1.7
Cambridge	101,355	5.8
Brockton	94,304	1.6
New Bedford	93,768	–6.2
Fall River	91,938	–0.8
Lynn	89,050	9.6
Quincy	88,025	3.6

Notes: †A person of Hispanic or Latino origin may be of any race. NA indicates that data are not available.
Sources: U.S. Census Bureau. Public Information Office. *Demographic Profiles.* [Online] Available http://www.census.gov/Press-Release/www/2001/demoprofile.html. Accessed June 1, 2001. U.S. Census Bureau. *Census 2000: Redistricting Data.* Press release issued by the Redistricting Data Office. Washington, D.C., March, 2001.

MASSACHUSETTS

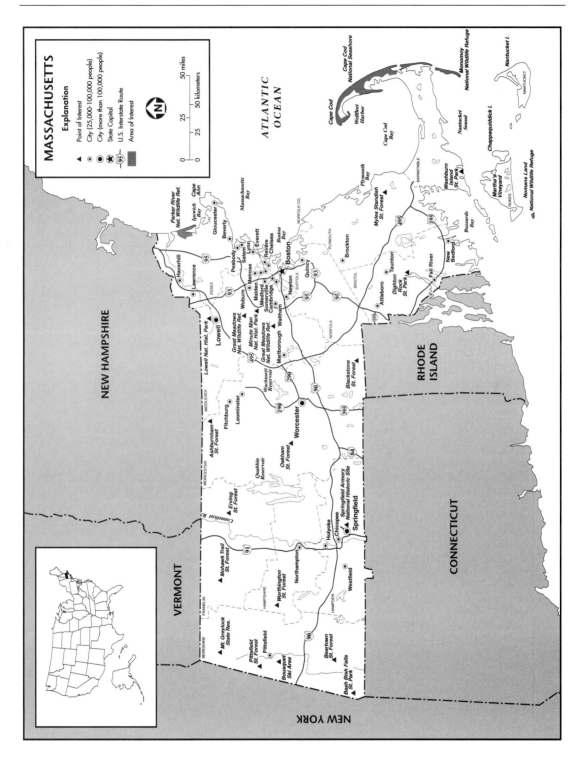

MASSACHUSETTS

Explanation

▲ Point of Interest
⊙ City (25,000-100,000 people)
◉ City (more than 100,000 people)
★ State Capital
95 U.S. Interstate Route
▨ Area of Interest

0   25   50 miles
0   25   50 kilometers

NEW HAMPSHIRE

VERMONT

NEW YORK

CONNECTICUT

RHODE ISLAND

ATLANTIC OCEAN

Cape Cod
Cape Cod National Seashore
Monomoy National Wildlife Refuge
Nantucket I.
NANTUCKET
Wellfleet Harbor
Cape Cod Bay
Nantucket Sound
Chappaquiddick I.
Martha's Vineyard
DUKES
Nomans Land National Wildlife Refuge

Plymouth Bay
Massachusetts Bay
Boston Bay
Buzzards Bay
BARNSTABLE
PLYMOUTH
NORFOLK CO.
NORFOLK
BRISTOL

Washburn Island St. Park

Myles Standish St. Forest

Brockton
New Bedford
Fall River
Dighton Rock St. Park
Taunton
Attleboro

Parker River Nat. Wildlife Ref.
Ipswich Bay
Cape Ann
Gloucester
Beverly
Salem
Peabody
Lynn
Revere
Chelsea
Everett
Melrose
Malden
Medford
Somerville
Cambridge
Boston
Quincy
Newton
Waltham
Woburn
Haverhill
Lawrence
ESSEX
MIDDLESEX
WORCESTER

Great Meadows Nat. Wildlife Ref.
Minute Man Nat. Hist. Park
Great Meadows Nat. Wildlife Ref.
Marlborough
Lowell Nat. Hist. Park
Lowell
Ashburnham St. Forest
Fitchburg
Leominster
Wachusett Reservoir
Worcester
Blackstone St. Forest

Quabbin Reservoir
Oakham St. Forest
Erving St. Forest
Connecticut R.
Holyoke
Chicopee
Springfield
Springfield Armory National Historic Site
Northampton
Westfield
HAMPSHIRE
HAMPDEN
FRANKLIN
BERKSHIRE

Mohawk Trail St. Forest
Worthington St. Forest
Mt. Greylock State Res.
Pittsfield St. Forest
Pittsfield
Bousquet Ski Area
Beartown St. Forest
Bash Bish Falls St. Park

123

3 CLIMATE

Although Massachusetts is a relatively small state, there are significant climatic differences between its eastern and western sections. The entire state has cold winters and moderately warm summers. The Berkshires in the west have both the coldest winters and the coolest summers. Normal temperatures for Pittsfield in the Berkshires are 22°F (–6°C) in January and 68°F (20°C) in July. The interior lowlands are several degrees warmer in both winter and summer. The coastal sections are the warmest areas of the state. Normal temperatures for Boston are 30°F (–1°C) in January and 74°F (23°C) in July. The record high temperature in the state was 107°F (42°C) in 1975; the record low was –35°F (–37°C) in 1981. Precipitation ranges from 39 to 46 inches (99 to 117 centimeters) annually. The average snowfall for Boston is 42 inches (107 centimeters), with the range in the Berkshires considerably higher.

4 PLANTS AND ANIMALS

Maple, birch, beech, and other species cover the Massachusetts uplands. Common shrubs include rhodora, mountain laurel, and shadbush. Various ferns grow throughout the state. Typical wild flowers include several varieties of orchid, lily, and goldenrod.

Common native mammals include the white-tailed deer, river otter, mink, and porcupine. Among the Bay State's 336 resident bird species are the mallard, ring-necked pheasant, downy woodpecker, and song sparrow. Native inland fish include brook trout, chain pickerel, and yellow perch. Common reptiles are the snapping turtle and northern water snake. The Cape Cod coasts are rich in a variety of shellfish, including clams, mussels, shrimps, and oysters. Among endangered mammals are the sperm, blue, and humpback whales.

5 ENVIRONMENTAL PROTECTION

With disposal of treated sewage sludge in Boston Harbor halted in 1991 and with improved sewage treatment, the harbor today is markedly cleaner. In the late 1980s, 10% of the flounder caught in Boston Harbor had liver tumors caused by toxic chemicals. By 1993, no flounder tested had tumors. New primary water treatment plants opened in 1994 and 1996.

With adoption of Massachusetts acid rain legislation in 1985, sulfur dioxide output from Massachusetts sources has been cut by 17%. Additional decreases, particularly from out-of-state power plants, are expected to further cut sulfur dioxide emissions. The state's solid waste recycling and composting rate was 28% in 1994. In 1998, about 49% of solid waste was incinerated. Active landfills dropped in number from 220 in 1988 to 119 in 1994. There were 31 hazardous waste sites in 1998.

Wildlife management has restored populations of wild turkeys, white-tailed deer, Atlantic salmon, and other species. Since about 1900, the Commonwealth has protected 528,400 acres (213,800 hectares) through acquisitions or restrictions. All environment-related programs

The state house in Boston.

are administered by the Executive Office of Environmental Affairs (EOEA).

6 POPULATION

Massachusetts's population, according to the 2000 federal census, was over 6.34 million (13th in the US). A decreased population of 6.31 million is projected for 2005. Despite the projected population decline, Massachusetts had an average growth rate of 5.5% between 1990 and 2000. The state's birthrate is well below the US average, and a net out-migration of 301,000 people between 1970 and 1983 was the largest drop of all New England states. Between 1990 and 1998, the state lost another 236,700 residents due to out-migration. In 1990, about 84.3% of the state was urban and 15.7% rural. A density of 809.8 persons per square mile (312.7 persons per square kilometer), making Massachusetts one of the most densely populated states. In comparison, the national average is only 79.6 persons per square mile (30.7 per square kilometer).

The state's largest city is Boston, which ranked 20th among the largest US cities in 2000 with a population of 589,141. Other large cities (with their 2000 populations) are Worcester, 172,648; Springfield, 152,082; and Lowell, 105,167. More than 70% of all state residents live in the Greater Boston area, which in 1996 had a

Massachusetts Population by Race

Census 2000 was the first national census in which the instructions to respondents said, "Mark one or more races." This table shows the number of people who are of one, two, or three or more races. For those claiming two races, the number of people belonging to the various categories is listed. The U.S. government conducts a census of the population every ten years.

	Number	Percent
Total population	6,349,097	100.0
One race	6,203,092	97.7
Two races	138,177	2.2
White *and* Black or African American	19,459	0.3
White *and* American Indian/Alaska Native	12,754	0.2
White *and* Asian	15,769	0.2
White *and* Native Hawaiian/Pacific Islander	1,664	—
White *and* some other race	48,948	0.8
Black or African American *and* American Indian/Alaska Native	3,747	0.1
Black or African American *and* Asian	1,469	—
Black or African American *and* Native Hawaiian/Pacific Islander	915	—
Black or African American *and* some other race	23,362	0.4
American Indian/Alaska Native *and* Asian	727	—
American Indian/Alaska Native *and* Native Hawaiian/Pacific Islander	68	—
American Indian/Alaska Native *and* some other race	1,330	—
Asian *and* Native Hawaiian/Pacific Islander	1,084	—
Asian *and* some other race	5,395	0.1
Native Hawaiian/Pacific Islander *and* some other race	1,486	—
Three or more races	7,828	0.1

Source: U.S. Census Bureau. *Census 2000: Redistricting Data.* Press release issued by the Redistricting Data Office. Washington, D.C., March, 2001. A dash (—) indicates that the percent is less than 0.1.

metropolitan population of 5.56 million (seventh largest in the US). Over one-quarter of the population is 19 years of age and younger, despite Massachusetts' median age being one year older than the national average of 35.3.

7 ETHNIC GROUPS

Early industrialization helped make Massachusetts a magnet for many European migrants, particularly the Irish. As late as 1990 more than half of the population identified with at least one single ancestry group, the largest being the Irish (26% of the population), English (15%), Italian (14%), French (10%), Portuguese (5%), and Polish (6%). In 1996, an estimated 9.7% of the state's population was foreign-born.

The 20th century has seen an influx of working-class blacks from southern states, and a sizable class of black professionals has developed. In 1997 there were an estimated 383,600 black Americans in Massachusetts, or 6.3% of the population. Blacks constituted more than 25% of Boston's population. The state also had 358,500 people of Hispanic ancestry, predominantly Puerto Rican and Dominican.

Greater Boston has a small, well-organized Chinatown. In the suburbs reside many business and professional Chinese, as well as those connected with the region's numerous educational institutions. The Asian and Pacific Islander population was estimated at 209,900 in 1997 (3.4%). Statewide, there were 47,245 Chinese in 1990, 12,878 Koreans, 10,662 Japanese, and 13,101 Vietnamese. Although small tribal settlements persist on Cape Cod, Massachusetts had only an estimated 14,400 Native Americans in 1997. Cape Cod also has settlements of Portuguese fishermen, as has New Bedford.

8 LANGUAGES

On the whole, Massachusetts English is classed as Northern, but early migration up the Connecticut River created special variations within the eastern half of the state. A few place-names—such as Massachusetts itself, Chicopee, and Naukeag— are borrowed from the Algonkian-speaking Native American tribes. In 1990, 84.8% of the population five years of age or older spoke only English at home. Principal other languages spoken at home, and number of speakers, were Spanish, 228,458; Portuguese, 133,373; French, 124,973; Italian, 81,987; and Chinese, 43,248.

9 RELIGIONS

As of 1990, there were 2,961,259 Roman Catholics in Massachusetts, more than half the total population. The largest Protestant denominations were: United Church of Christ, 135,983 members; Episcopal, 122,190; American Baptist (USA), 66,156; United Methodist, 71,858; Lutheran Church-Missouri Synod, 7,053; and Congregationalist, 9,931. There were also 35,787 Unitarians. Most of the state's estimated 268,000 Jewish population in 1994 lived in Boston.

Although small, the Church of Christ, Scientist is significant to Massachusetts's history. Its first house of worship was founded in 1879 in Boston by Mary Baker Eddy, who, four years earlier, had published the Christian Science textbook, *Science and Health with Key to the Scriptures*. In Boston, the church continues to publish an influential newspaper, the *Christian Science Monitor*.

10 TRANSPORTATION

As of 1998, 10 railroads transported freight through Massachusetts. Boston is the northern terminus of Amtrak's Northeast Corridor, linking New England with Washington, D.C., via New York City and Philadelphia. At the end of 1998, the state had 1,057 rail miles (1,701 kilometers) of track. In 1995/96, Amtrak operated about 30 daily trains through the state, with a total of about 1.3 million riders.

The Boston subway, which began operation in 1897, is the oldest subway system in the US. Boston also is one of the few cities in the US with an operating trolley system. About 40% of all Bostonians commute to work by public transportation, the second-highest percentage in the nation, following New York City.

In 1997, 35,024 miles (56,354 kilometers) of public roadways crisscrossed the state. The interstate highway network in Massachusetts totaled 565 miles (909 kilometers) in 1996. About $3 billion was spent by all units of government for highways in 1997. That same year, over 5 million motor vehicles were registered in the state, of which 3.8 million were automobiles, 1.2 million were trucks, and 11,363 were buses. There also were 88,800 motorcycles.

Because it is the major American city closest to Europe, Boston is an important shipping center for both domestic and foreign cargo. In 1998, 21.2 million tons of cargo passed through the Port of Boston. Other important ports are Fall River and Salem. There were 81 airports and 126 heliports in the state at the beginning of 1997. Logan International, near Boston, was the 17th-busiest airport in the nation in 1999 for passenger travel. The airport handles about 150,000 departing aircraft, boards 26 million passengers, and processes 800 million pounds of freight and mail annually.

11 HISTORY

When English settlers arrived in present-day Massachusetts, they encountered five main Algonkian tribes: the Nauset, a fishing people on Cape Cod; the Wampanoag in the southeast; the Massachusetts in the northeast; the Nipmuc in the central hills; and the Pocumtuc in the west. In the wake of John and Sebastian Cabot's voyages (1497 and following), fishermen from England, France, Portugal, and Spain began fishing off the Massachusetts coast. Within 50 years, fur trading with the Native Americans was established.

Permanent English settlement, which would ultimately destroy the Algonkian peoples, began in 1620 when a small band of Puritans left their temporary haven at Leiden in the Netherlands to start a colony in the northern part of Virginia lands, near the Hudson River. Their ship, the *Mayflower,* was blown off course by an Atlantic storm, and they landed on Cape Cod before settling in an abandoned Wampanoag village they called Plymouth. Ten years later, a much larger Puritan group settled the Massachusetts Bay Colony, to the north in Salem. Between 1630 and 1640, about 20,000 English people, chiefly Puritans, settled in Massachusetts with offshoots moving to Connecticut and Rhode Island.

Farming soon overtook fishing and fur trading in economic importance. After the trade in beaver skins was exhausted, the remaining Native American tribes were devastated in King Philip's War (1675–76). Shipbuilding and Atlantic commerce brought added prosperity to the Massachusetts Bay Colony. In 1692, Massachusetts and the colony of Plymouth were merged under a new charter.

During the 18th century, settlement spread across the entire colony. Boston, the capital, attained a population of 15,000 by 1730. Colonial government provided more advantages than drawbacks for commerce, and supply contracts during the French and Indian War enriched the colony's economy. But the postwar recession after 1763 was accompanied by a new imperial policy that put pressure on Massachusetts as well as other colonies. From 1765, when Bostonians violently protested the Stamp Act, Massachusetts was in the forefront of the resistance.

Massachusetts Governors: 1775–2001

1775–1780	Council of State	
1780–1785	John Hancock	
1785–1787	James Bowdoin	
1787	Thomas Cushing	
1787–1793	John Hancock	—
1793–1797	Samuel Adams	Dem-Rep
1797–1799	Increase Sumner	Federalist
1799–1800	Moses Gill	Federalist
1800–1807	Caleb Strong	—
1807–1808	James Sullivan	Dem-Rep
1808–1809	Levi Lincoln	Dem-Rep
1809–1810	Christopher Gore	Federalist
1810–1812	Elbridge Gerry	Dem-Rep
1812–1816	Caleb Strong	Federalist
1816–1823	John Brooks	Federalist
1823–1825	William Eustis	Republican
1825	Marcus Morton	Republican
1825–1834	Levi Lincoln, Jr.	Nat-Rep
1834–1835	John Davis	Whig
1835–1836	Samuel Turell Armstrong	Indep-Whig
1836–1840	Edward Everett	Whig
1840–1841	Marcus Morton	Democrat
1841–1843	John Davis	Whig
1843–1844	Marcus Morton	Democrat
1844–1851	George Nixon Briggs	Whig
1851–1853	George Sewel Boutwell	Democrat
1853–1854	John Henry Clifford	Whig
1854–1855	Emory Washburn	Whig
1855–1858	Henry Joseph Gardner	Know Nothing
1858–1861	Nathaniel Prentice Banks	Republican
1861–1866	John Albion Andrew	Republican
1866–1869	Alexander Hamilton Bullock	Republican
1869–1872	William Claflin	Republican
1872–1874	William Barrett Washburn	Republican
1874–1875	Thomas Talbot	Republican
1875–1876	William Gaston	Democrat
1876–1879	Alexander Hamilton Rice	Republican
1879–1880	Thomas Talbot	Republican
1880–1883	John Davis Long	Republican
1883–1884	Benjamin Franklin Butler	Dem/Green
1884–1887	George Dexter Robinson	Republican
1887–1890	Oliver Ames	Republican
1890–1891	John Quincy Adams Brackett	Republican
1891–1894	William Eustis Russell	Democrat
1894–1896	Frederic Thomas Greenhalge	Republican
1896–1900	Roger Wolcott	Republican
1900–1903	Winthrop Murray Crane	Republican
1903–1905	John Lewis Bates	Republican
1905–1906	William Lewis Douglas	Democrat
1906–1909	Curtis Guild, Jr.	Republican
1909–1911	Eben Sumner Draper	Republican
1911–1914	Eugene Noble Foss	Democrat
1914–1916	David Ignatius Walsh	Democrat
1916–1919	Samuel Walker McCall	Republican
1919–1921	John Calvin Coolidge	Republican
1921–1925	Channing Harris Cox	Republican
1925–1929	Alvan Tufts Fuller	Republican
1929–1931	Frank G. Allen	Republican
1931–1935	Joseph Buell Ely	Democrat
1935–1937	James Michael Curley	Democrat
1937–1939	Charles Francis Hurley	Democrat
1939–1945	Leverett Saltonstall	Republican
1945–1947	Maurice Joseph Tobin	Democrat
1947–1949	Robert Fiske Bradford	Republican
1949–1953	Paul Andrew Dever	Democrat
1953–1957	Christian Archibald Herter	Republican
1957–1961	Foster Furcolo	Democrat
1961–1963	John Anthony Volpe	Republican
1963–1965	Endicott Peabody	Democrat
1965–1969	John Anthony Volpe	Republican
1969–1975	Francis Williams Sargent	Republican
1975–1979	Michael Stanley Dukakis	Democrat
1979–1983	Edward J. King	Democrat
1983–1991	Michael Stanley Dukakis	Democrat
1991–1996	William Floyd Weld	Republican
1996–	Argeo Paul Cellucci	Republican

Democratic/Greenbacker – Dem/Green
Democratic Republican – Dem-Rep
National Republican – Nat-Rep

By December 1773, when East India Company tea was dumped into Boston harbor to prevent its taxation, most of the colony was committed to resistance. When Parliament retaliated for the Tea Party by closing the port of Boston in 1774, Massachusetts was ready to rebel. Battle began at Lexington and Concord on 19 April 1775. By this time, Massachusetts had the backing of the Continental Congress. For Massachusetts, the battlefield experience of the Revolution was largely confined to 1775, after which the fighting shifted southward.

Statehood

Massachusetts entered the Union on 6 February 1788. Federalist policies—supporting a strong central government—were dominant, and they were supported by the Whigs in the 1830s and the Republicans from the late 1850s. This political alignment reflected the importance to the state of national commercial and industrial development, as Massachusetts lacked the resources for strong agricultural development.

At Waltham, Lowell, and Lawrence the first large-scale factories in the US were erected. Massachusetts became a leader in industries including textiles, metalworking, shoes and leather goods, and shipbuilding. By the 1850s, steam engines and clipper ships were both Bay State products. The industrial development of Massachusetts was accompanied by a literary and intellectual flowering centered in Concord, the home of Ralph Waldo Emerson, Henry David Thoreau, and a cluster of others who became known as transcendentalists. Abolitionism found some of its chief leaders in Massachusetts.

Post–Civil War

In the years following the Civil War, Massachusetts emerged as an urban industrial state. Its population, fed by immigrants from England, Scotland, Germany, and especially Ireland, grew rapidly in the middle decades of the century. Later, between 1880 and 1920, another wave of immigrants came from French Canada, Italy, Russia, Poland, Scandinavia, Portugal, Greece, and Syria. Still later, between 1950 and 1970, black southerners and Puerto Ricans settled in the cities.

The Massachusetts economy, relatively stagnant between 1920 and 1950, revived in the second half of the 20th century through a combination of university tal-

Massachusetts Presidential Vote by Political Party, 1948–2000

YEAR	MASSACHUSETTS WINNER	DEMOCRAT	REPUBLICAN	SOCIALIST LABOR	PROGRESSIVE
1948	*Truman (D)	1,151,788	909,370	5,535	38,157
1952	*Eisenhower (R)	1,083,525	1,292,325	1,957	4,636
1956	*Eisenhower (R)	948,190	1,393,197	5,573	—
1960	*Kennedy (D)	1,487,174	976,750	3,892	—
1964	*Johnson (D)	1,786,422	549,727	4,755	—
					AMERICAN IND.
1968	Humphrey (D)	1,469,218	766,844	6,180	87,088
				SOC. WORKERS	AMERICAN
1972	McGovern (D)	1,332,540	1,112,078	10,600	2,877
1976	*Carter (D)	1,429,475	1,030,276	8,138	7,555
				LIBERTARIAN	
1980	*Reagan (R)	1,048,562	1,054,213	21,311	—
1984	*Reagan	1,239,600	1,310,936	—	—
					NEW ALLIANCE
1988	Dukakis (D)	1,401,415	1,194,635	24,251	9,561
					IND. (Perot)
1992	*Clinton (D)	1,318,639	805,039	9,021	630,731
1996	*Clinton (D)	1,571,763	718,107	20,426	227,217
				LIBERTARIAN	
2000	Gore (D)	1,616,487	878,502	16,366	173,564

*Won US presidential election.

Photo credit: Susan D. Rock.

A view of Boston from across the Charles River.

ent, investment, a skilled work force, and political clout. As the old industries and the mill cities declined, new high-technology manufacturing developed in Boston's suburbs, led by electronics and defense-related industries. White-collar employment and middle-class suburbs flourished, though run-down mill towns and Yankee dairy farms and orchards still dotted the landscape.

In the 1970s and early 1980s, a revolution in information technology and increased defense spending fueled a high-technology boom which centered on new manufacturing firms outside Boston along Route 128. Unemployment dropped from 12% in 1978 to 4% in 1987. However, with the beginnings of a nationwide recession in 1989, the Massachusetts economy declined dramatically, losing 14% of its total jobs in three years. Massachusetts's economic woes were increased by the collapse in the late 1980s of risky real estate ventures. By 1992, a number of indications suggested that recovery, slow in coming, had begun to take hold.

12 STATE GOVERNMENT

The Massachusetts constitution of 15 June 1780 is, according to the state, the oldest written constitution in the world still in effect. The legislature of Massachusetts, known as the General Court, is composed of a 40-member senate and 160-member

Photo credit: Kennedy Library

Senator Robert F. Kennedy (1925–68), born in Brookline, was killed by an assassin's bullet while campaigning for the U.S. presidency.

house of representatives, all of whom are elected every two years.

The governor and lieutenant governor are elected jointly every four years. The governor appoints all state and local judges, as well as the heads of the ten executive offices. Other elected officials include the attorney general, secretary of the commonwealth, and treasurer. Massachusetts also has an eight-member executive council with the power to review the governor's judicial appointments and pardons, and to authorize expenditures from the state treasury.

To win passage, a bill must gain a majority vote of both houses of the legislature. After a bill is passed, the governor has ten days in which to sign it, return it for reconsideration (usually with amendments), veto it, or refuse to sign it ("pocket veto"). A veto may be overridden by a two-thirds majority in both houses.

13 POLITICAL PARTIES

Democrats have, for the most part, dominated state politics in Massachusetts since 1928, when the state voted for Democratic presidential candidate Alfred E. Smith—the first time the Democrats won a majority in a Massachusetts presidential election. In 1960, John F. Kennedy, who had been a popular US senator from Massachusetts, became the first Roman Catholic president in US history. Since then the state has voted for all Democratic presidential candidates except Adlai Stevenson in 1952 and 1956, Jimmy Carter in 1980, and Walter Mondale in 1984. In 1972, it was the only state carried by Democrat George McGovern. Massachusetts chose its native son, Democratic Governor Michael Dukakis, for president in 1988 and voted again for a Democrat in 1992 and 1996 electing Bill Clinton both times and in 2000 with Al Gore.

As of 1994, there were 1,346,097 registered Democrats, or 40% of the total number of registered voters; 447,181 Republicans, or 13%; and 1,558,640 independents, or 47%. As of 2001, the governorship was held by a Republican, Argeo Paul Cellucci, and the US Senate seats were held by Democrats, Edward ("Ted") Kennedy and John Kerry. The US

House delegation in 2001 consisted of ten Democrats. The Massachusetts state senate had 34 Democrats and 6 Republicans, while the state house of representatives had 137 Democrats and only 23 Republicans.

14 LOCAL GOVERNMENT

As of 1997, Massachusetts had 12 county governments, 44 cities, and 307 towns. In all 13 counties except Suffolk County, executive authority was vested in three county commissioners. All Massachusetts cities are governed by mayors and city councils. Towns are governed by selectmen, who are usually elected to either one or two-year terms. Town meetings—a carryover from the colonial period—still take place regularly. By state law, to be designated a city, a place must have at least 12,000 residents. Towns with more than 6,000 inhabitants may hold representative town meetings that are limited to elected officials.

15 JUDICIAL SYSTEM

The supreme judicial court, composed of a chief justice and six other justices, is the highest court in the state. It has appeals jurisdiction in matters of law and also advises the governor and legislature on legal questions. The superior courts, actually the highest level of trial court, have a chief justice and 79 other justices. These courts hear law, equity, civil, and criminal cases, and make the final determination in matters of fact. The appeals court, consisting of a chief justice and nine other justices, hears appeals of decisions by district and municipal courts.

Other court systems in the state include the land court, probate and family court, housing court, and juvenile court. Massachusetts's total crime rate per 100,000 inhabitants was 3,435.9 in 1998. As of June 1999 there were 11,715 prisoners in state and federal correctional institutions in Massachusetts.

16 MIGRATION

From 1970 to 1990, Massachusetts lost nearly 400,000 residents in net migration to other states, but experienced an overall net increase from migration of 59,000 due to migration from abroad. During 1990–98, the state lost 237,000 residents to other states, while immigration from abroad added 135,000. An estimated 9.7% of the state's population was foreign-born in 1996, when 23,085 immigrants were legally admitted from abroad. The federal government estimated that there were 85,000 illegal immigrants already living in the state that year. As of 1990, 68.7% of all state residents had been born in Massachusetts. The only significant migration from other areas of the US to Massachusetts has been the influx of southern blacks since World War II. According to census estimates, Massachusetts gained 84,000 blacks between 1940 and 1975; in 1998, it had a black population of about 395,000 persons, mostly in the Boston area.

17 ECONOMY

From its beginnings as a farming and seafaring colony, Massachusetts became one of the most industrialized states in the country in the late 19th century and, more recently, a leader in the manufacture of high-technology products. Fueled in part by a dramatic increase in the Pentagon's budget that focused on sophisticated weaponry, as well as by significant advances in information technology, high-technology companies rose up around the outskirts of Boston in the 1970s and early 1980s. Wholesale and retail trade, transportation, and public utilities also prospered.

In the late 1980s, the boom ended. The minicomputer industry failed to innovate at the same pace as its competitors as the market became increasingly crowded, and defense contractors suffered from cuts in military spending. Between 1988 and 1991, jobs in both high-technology and non-high technology manufacturing declined by 17%. In addition, the early 1980s had also seen the rise of real estate ventures which collapsed at the end of the decade when the market became saturated. Unemployment rose to 9% in 1991. Since then, the economy has recovered as several banks started new lending programs; unemployment was 4% in 1997.

18 INCOME

In 1998, Massachusetts ranked fourth among the 50 states in per capita (per person) income, with $33,496. The median household income in 1998 was $42,017. Some 10.3% of all Bay Staters had incomes below the federal poverty level during 1998.

19 INDUSTRY

Massachusetts is an important manufacturing center. Significant concentrations of industrial machinery employment are in Attleboro, Wilmington, Worcester, and the Springfield area. Much of the manufacturing industry is located along Route 128. This is a superhighway that circles Boston, from Gloucester in the north to Quincy in the south, and is unique in its concentration of high-technology enterprises.

Massachusetts's future as a manufacturing center depends on its continued preeminence in the production of computers, optical equipment, and other sophisticated instruments. Among the major computer manufacturers in the state are Digital Equipment Corporation in Maynard, and Data General in Westboro.

20 LABOR

In 1998, the state's labor force numbered 3.27 million persons. The unemployed numbered 109,000 in 1998, for an unemployment rate of 3.3%. About 15.9% of all workers in the state were members of labor unions in 1998.

21 AGRICULTURE

As of 1998, there were 6,000 farms in Massachusetts, covering 570,000 acres (231,000 hectares). Farming was mostly limited to the western Massachusetts counties of Hampshire, Franklin, and Berkshire, and southern Bristol County. Total agricultural income for 1999 was estimated at $413 million (41st of the 50 states), of which crops provided 76%. Although the state is not a major farming area, it is the largest producer of cranberries in the US. Cranberry production for 1998 was 179.8 million pounds, about 33% of the US total. Output totals for other crops in 1998 were as follows: corn for silage, 429,000 tons; hay, 202,000 tons; and tobacco, 1.27 million pounds.

22 DOMESTICATED ANIMALS

Massachusetts is not a major producer of livestock. Receipts from livestock and related products totaled $103 million in 1995. As of 1999, the state had 57,000 cattle, 19,500 hogs, and 9,500 sheep. In 1997, egg production was 156 million, valued at $7.9 million. Some 26,000 dairy cows produced 429 million pounds of milk that year.

23 FISHING

The fishing ports of Gloucester and New Bedford are among the busiest in the US. The value of the commercial catch— $204.4 million—was the fifth highest in the US at 252.5 million pounds in 1998. Lobster and cod are valuable commercial species. The state's long shoreline and many rivers make sport-fishing a popular pastime for both deepsea and freshwater fishers.

24 FORESTRY

Forestry is a minor industry in the state. Forested lands cover about 3.2 million acres (1.3 million hectares). Red oak and white ash are found in the west. Specialty products include maple syrup and Christmas trees. Massachusetts has the sixth-largest state park system in the nation, with 38 state parks and 74 state forests totaling some 273,000 acres (110,000 hectares). There are no national forests in Massachusetts.

25 MINING

The value of nonfuel mineral production in Massachusetts in 1998 was estimated at $192 million. Crushed stone and construction sand and gravel are the state's two leading mineral commodities. In 1998 there were 13.1 million metric tons of crushed stone and 14 million short tons of sand and gravel produced, worth $91.7 million and $76.6 million, respectively. Other mineral commodities produced included lime, peat, and industrial sand and gravel, $11.3 million; and dimension stone, $15.1 million. Industrial minerals processed or manufactured in the state included abrasives, graphite, gypsum, perlite, and vermiculite.

26 ENERGY AND POWER

Massachusetts is highly dependent on oil for electric generation and home heating, and energy costs in the state are among the highest in the US. During the early 1980s, as much as 81% of the state's electric power output was generated from oil. In 1998, about 26 billion kilowatt hours of electric power were produced. Approximately 33% of this electricity was for residential use, 44% commercial, 21% industrial, and 2% for other purposes. Massachusetts has no proven oil or coal reserves. There is one nuclear power plant.

The state consumes but does not produce natural gas. In 1998, about 320.3 billion cubic feet (9 billion cubic meters) of natural gas were delivered.

Photo credit: Susan D. Rock.

A seafood vendor at Haymarket.

27 COMMERCE

Massachusetts's machinery and electrical goods industries are important components of the state's wholesale trade, along with motor vehicle and automotive equipment, and paper and paper products. State wholesale sales totaled $116 billion in 1997; retail sales were $63 billion. Foreign exports of Massachusetts products totaled $16 billion in 1997 (11th in the US).

28 PUBLIC FINANCE

The total debt of state and local governments as of 1997 was more than $29.39 billion, or $4,803 per capita (per person), the 5th highest ratio of state public debt per person among the states.

The estimated revenues for the 1997 fiscal year were $26.58 billion; expenses were $25.79 billion.

29 TAXATION

Massachusetts's tax burden on a per capita (per person) basis as of 1997 was $2,175 (6th among the states). Total tax revenues received in 1997 were $13.5 billion. As of 1997, the state levied a flat tax rate of 5.95% on income. The corporate income tax rate was 9.5%. There is also a sales tax, estate taxes, a cigarette tax, a gasoline tax, and a motor vehicle excise tax of $25 for every $1,000 of valuation. Bay Staters paid federal income taxes totaling $18.69 billion in 1995, but received $35.82 billion in federal funding—or, for every $1 paid to the federal government the state got back $1.91.

30 HEALTH

The death rate from cancer in 1996 was above the US average. The Division of Drug Rehabilitation administers drug treatment from a statewide network of hospital agencies and self-help groups.

Massachusetts had 82 community hospitals, with 16,493 beds in 1998. Among the best-known institutions are Massachusetts General Hospital, a leading research and treatment center, and the Massachusetts Eye and Ear Infirmary, a Boston clinic. In 1998, there were 402 physicians per 100,000. That same year, full-time registered nurses numbered over 15,000. Prominent medical schools located in the state include Harvard Medical School and Tufts University School of Medicine. The average cost per inpatient day for hospital care was $1,390 in 1998, or $7,662 for an average cost per stay.

31 HOUSING

Massachusetts's housing stock, much older than the US average, reflects the state's colonial heritage and its ties to English architectural traditions. Two major styles are common: colonial, typified by a wood frame, two stories, center hall entry, and center chimney; and Cape Cod, one-story houses built by fishermen, with shingled roofs, clapboard fronts, and unpainted shingled sides. Many new houses are also built in these styles.

As of 1999, there were an estimated 2.56 million housing units in the state. In 1998, 19,300 new housing units were authorized, with a value of over $2.5 billion. Monthly cost for owners with a mortgage in 1990 was $985 and $298 for those without a mortgage; median monthly rent was $580. In 1998, the median value of a home in Massachusetts was $212,600.

32 EDUCATION

Massachusetts has a long history of support for education. The Boston Latin School opened in 1635 as the first public school in the colonies. Harvard College—the first college in the US—was founded the following year. Today the state boasts some of the most highly regarded private secondary schools and colleges in the country.

As of 1998, 85.6% of state residents age 25 or older were high school graduates and 31% had completed four or more years of college. As of fall 1997, there were 949,006 students enrolled in public schools. Expenditures for public elementary and secondary schools amounted to $7,387 per student in 1999/00. Private preparatory schools include such prestigious institutions as Andover, Deerfield, and Groton. Enrollment in private schools in fall 1997 totaled 127,165.

There are 116 colleges and universities in the state. The major public university system is the University of Massachusetts, with campuses at Amherst, Boston, Dartmouth, Lowell, and a medical school at Worcester. Harvard University is one of the country's premier institutions; its 1999/00 student population was about 19,000. Also located in Cambridge are Radcliffe College (whose enrollment is included in Harvard's) and the Massachusetts Institute of Technology, or MIT (1861), with about 10,000 students in 1999/00.

Mount Holyoke College, the first US college for women, was founded in 1837. Other prominent private schools include Amherst College, Boston College, Boston University, Brandeis University, the New England Conservatory of Music, Northeastern University, Smith College, Tufts University, and Wellesley College.

33 ARTS

Boston is the center of artistic activity in Massachusetts, and Cape Cod and the Berkshires are areas of significant seasonal artistic activity. Boston is the home of several small theaters, some of which offer previews of shows bound for Broadway. Of the regional theaters scattered throughout the state, the Williamstown Theater in the Berkshires and the Provincetown Theater on Cape Cod are especially noteworthy.

The Boston Symphony, one of the major orchestras in the US, was founded in 1881. During the summer, the symphony is the main attraction of the Berkshire Music Festival at Tanglewood in Lenox. An off-shoot of the Boston Symphony, the Boston Pops Orchestra, gained fame under the conductorship of Arthur Fiedler. Boston is also the headquarters of the Opera Company of Boston. The Boston Ballet Company is the state's major dancing troupe. The Massachusetts Cultural Council provides grants and services to support public programs in the arts, sciences, and the humanities.

34 LIBRARIES AND MUSEUMS

The first public library in the US was established in Boston in 1653. Six regional library systems served 351 towns and cities. The major city libraries are in Boston, Worcester, and Springfield. Statewide in 1999 there were 38 million volumes in all public libraries.

The Boston Athenaeum, with 650,000 volumes, is the most noteworthy private library in the state. Harvard University's library system is one of the largest in the world, with 14.3 million volumes in 1999. Other major academic libraries are those of Boston University, the University of Massachusetts (Amherst), Smith College, and Boston College.

Boston houses a number of important museums, among them the Museum of Fine Arts with vast holdings of artwork. These include extensive Far East and French impressionist collections and American art and furniture, the Isabella Stewart Gardner Museum, and the Museum of Science. Plymouth Plantation in Plymouth is a re-creation of life in the 17th century, and Old Sturbridge Village, a working historical farm, displays 18th- and 19th-century artifacts. The state had over 344 museums in 2000.

35 COMMUNICATIONS

The first American post office was established in Boston in 1639. As of 1999, 95.4% of the state's occupied housing units had telephones. The state had 73 AM stations and 111 FM stations in 2000, when 28 television stations were also in operation. Boston's WGBH is a major producer of programming for the Public Broadcasting Service. In 1996 there were 21 large cable television systems. In 2000, Massachusetts had 239,358 Internet domain name registrations, ranking seventh among the 50 states.

36 PRESS

Publishing milestones that occurred in the state include the first book printed in the English colonies (Cambridge, 1640) and the first regularly issued American newspaper, the *Boston News-Letter* (1704). As of 1998 there were 33 daily newspapers in the state (including 11 morning, 22 evening). The *Boston Globe,* the most widely read newspaper in the state, has won numerous awards for journalistic

Photo credit: Susan D. Rock.

A young spectator waits for the St. Patrick's Day parade to start. In 1990, over 25% of the population claimed Irish ancestry.

excellence on the local and national levels. The *Christian Science Monitor* is highly respected for its coverage of national and international news.

Major newspapers and their average daily circulations in 1998 were the *Boston Globe* (470,825); the *Boston Herald* (271,425); and the *Christian Science Monitor* (71,924). *The Atlantic,* which began publishing in 1857, *Harvard Law Review, Harvard Business Review,* and *New England Journal of Medicine* are other influential publications. Massachusetts is also a center of book publishing, with more than 100 publishing houses, including Little, Brown and Company, Houghton Mifflin, Merriam-Webster, and Harvard University Press.

37 TOURISM, TRAVEL, AND RECREATION

Massachusetts beaches are a popular destination for summer travelers, but other areas have their own attractions. In 1997, tourists spent more than $10.8 billion in the state. The largest number of visitor-days are spent in Barnstable County (Cape Cod). The Cape Cod National Seashore drew 5 million visitors in 1996. Among its many attractions are beaches, fishing, good dining spots, artists' colonies, and summer theaters. Beaches, fishing, and quaint villages are also among the charms of Nantucket and Martha's Vineyard.

Boston is the second most popular area for tourists. A trip to the city might include visits to such old landmarks as Faneuil Hall, Old North Church, the USS *Constitution,* and Paul Revere's House, and such newer attractions as the John Hancock Observatory and the sky walk above the Prudential Tower. Boston Common is one of the oldest public parks in the country.

The Berkshires are the summer home of the Berkshire Music Festival at Tanglewood and the Jacob's Pillow Dance Festival in Lee, and during the winter also provide recreation for cross-country and downhill skiers. In Concord are the homes of Henry David Thoreau, Ralph Waldo Emerson, and Louisa May Alcott. Norfolk County, south of Boston, has the homes of three US presidents: John Adams and John

Sculptor Nancy Schon of Newton created this depiction of Mrs. Mallard and her ducklings to celebrate the 150th anniversary of Boston Public Garden in 1987. The sculpture is based on the Caldecott Medal winning book Make Way for Ducklings (1941) *by Robert McCloskey.*

Quincy Adams in Quincy, and John F. Kennedy in Brookline.

38 SPORTS

There are five major league professional sports teams in Massachusetts: the Boston Red Sox of Major League Baseball, the New England Patriots of the National Football League, the Boston Celtics of the National Basketball Association, the Boston Bruins of the National Hockey League, and the New England Revolution of Major League Soccer.

Probably the most famous amateur athletic event in the state is the Boston Marathon, a race of more than 26 miles (42 kilometers) held every Patriots' Day (third Monday in April). During the summer, a number of boat races are held, and rowing is also popular. Each October the traditional sport is celebrated in a regatta on the Charles River among college students from across the Northeast. Suffolk Downs in East Boston features thoroughbred horse-racing.

39 FAMOUS BAY STATERS

Massachusetts has produced an extraordinary collection of public figures and leaders of thought. Its four US presidents were John Adams (1735–1826), a signer of the Declaration of Independence; his son John Quincy Adams (1767–1848); John Fitzgerald Kennedy (1917–63), and George Herbert Walker Bush (b. 1924).

Massachusetts's great jurists include US Supreme Court Justices Joseph Story (1779–1845); Oliver Wendell Holmes, Jr. (1841–1935); Louis D. Brandeis (b.Kentucky, 1856–1941); and Felix Frankfurter (b.Austria, 1882–1965). David Souter (b.1939), was appointed as a Supreme Court justice in 1990. Stephen Breyer (b. California, 1939), a Supreme Court justice, was first a Circuit Court of Appeals judge in Boston before his appointment in 1994.

Literary genius has flourished in Massachusetts. In the 17th century, the colony was the home of poets Anne Bradstreet (1612–72) and Edward Taylor (1645–1729) and of the theologian Cotton Mather (1663–1728). During the 1800s, Massachusetts was the home of novelists Nathaniel Hawthorne (1804–64), Louisa May Alcott (b.Pennsylvania, 1832–88), and Henry James (b.New York, 1843–1916); essayists Ralph Waldo Emerson (1803–82) and Henry David Thoreau (1817–62); and poets Henry Wadsworth Longfellow (b.Maine, 1807–82) and Emily Dickinson (1830–86). Among 20th-century notables are novelist and short-story writer John Cheever (1912–82); and poets Robert

Photo credit: EPD Photos.

Women's rights activist Susan B. Anthony lived in Massachusetts.

Lowell (1917–77), Anne Sexton (1928–74), and Sylvia Plath (1932–63). Henry James's elder brother, William (b.New York, 1842–1910), pioneered psychology; and George Santayana (b.Spain, 1863–1952), philosopher and author, grew up in Boston. Mary Baker Eddy (b.New Hampshire, 1821–1910) founded the Church of Christ, Scientist, during the 1870s.

Reformers have abounded in Massachusetts, especially in the 19th century. William Lloyd Garrison (1805–79) was an outstanding abolitionist. Margaret Fuller (1810–50), and Susan Brownell Anthony

(1820–1906) were leading advocates of women's rights. Horace Mann (1796–1859) led the fight for public education; and Mary Lyon (1797–1849) founded Mount Holyoke, the first women's college in the US. The 20th century reformer and National Association for the Advancement of Colored People (NAACP) leader William Edward Burghardt (W.E.B.) Du Bois (1868–1963) was born in Great Barrington.

Leonard Bernstein (1918–90) was a composer and conductor of worldwide fame. Arthur Fiedler (1894–79) was the celebrated conductor of the Boston Pops Orchestra. Composers include William Billings (1746–1800) and Alan Hovhaness (b.1911). Louis Henri Sullivan (1856–1924) was an important architect. Painters include John Singleton Copley (1738–1815), James Whistler (1834–1903), and Winslow Homer (1836–1910).

Among the notable scientists associated with Massachusetts are Samuel F. B. Morse (1791–1872), inventor of the telegraph; Elias Howe (1819–67), inventor of the sewing machine; and Robert Hutchins Goddard (1882–1945), a physicist and rocketry pioneer.

40 BIBLIOGRAPHY

Aylesworth, Thomas G. *Southern New England: Connecticut, Massachusetts, Rhode Island.* New York: Chelsea House, 1996.

Deetz, James. *The Times of Their Lives: Life, Love, and Death in Plymouth Colony.* New York: W.H. Freeman, 2000.

Leotta, Joan. *Massachusetts.* New York: Children's Press, 2001.

LeVert, Suzanne. *Massachusetts.* New York: Benchmark Books, 2000.

Whitehall, Walter M., and Norman Kotker. *Massachusetts: A Pictorial History.* New York: Scribner, 1981.

Whitehurst, Susan. *The Colony of Massachusetts.* New York: PowerKids Press, 2000.

Web sites

Commonwealth of Massachusetts. Official Website. [Online] Available http://www.state.ma.us/ Accessed May 15, 2001.

Weber Publications. Massachusetts. [Online] Available http://www.50states.com/ massachu.htm Accessed May 15, 2001.

MICHIGAN

State of Michigan

ORIGIN OF STATE NAME: Possibly derived from the Fox Indian word *mesikami*, meaning "large lake."

NICKNAME: The Wolverine State.

CAPITAL: Lansing.

ENTERED UNION: 26 January 1837 (26th).

SONG: "Michigan, My Michigan" (unofficial).

MOTTO: *Si quaeris peninsulam amoenam circumspice* (If you seek a pleasant peninsula, look about you).

COAT OF ARMS: In the center, a shield depicts a peninsula on which a man stands, at sunrise, holding a rifle. At the top of the shield is the word "Tuebor" (I will defend), beneath it the state motto. Supporting the shield are an elk on the left and a moose on the right. Over the whole, on a crest, is an American eagle beneath the US motto, *E pluribus unum.*

FLAG: The coat of arms centered on a dark blue field, fringed on three sides.

OFFICIAL SEAL: The coat of arms surrounded by the words "The Great Seal of the State of Michigan" and the date "A.D. MDCCCXXXV." (1835, the year the state constitution was adopted).

BIRD: Robin.

FISH: Trout.

FLOWER: Apple blossom.

TREE: White pine.

GEM: Isle Royale Greenstone (Chlorastrolite).

STONE: Petoskey stone.

TIME: 7 AM EST = noon GMT; 6 AM CST = noon GMT.

1 LOCATION AND SIZE

Located in the eastern north-central US, Michigan is the third-largest state east of the Mississippi River and ranks 23d in size among the 50 states. The total area of Michigan (excluding Great Lakes waters) is 58,527 square miles (151,585 square kilometers). The state consists of the upper peninsula adjoining three of the Great Lakes—Superior, Huron, and Michigan—and the lower peninsula, projecting northward between Lakes Michigan, Erie, and Huron. Michigan has islands in Lakes Superior, Huron, and Michigan, and also in the St. Mary's and Detroit Rivers. The state's total boundary length is 1,673 miles (2,692 kilometers).

2 TOPOGRAPHY

Michigan's two peninsulas are generally level land masses, including flat lowlands in the eastern portion of both peninsulas, higher land in the western part of the lower peninsula, and hilly uplands in the upper peninsula, attaining elevations of 1,800 feet (550 meters). The state's highest point, at 1,979 feet (603 meters), is Mt. Arvon, in Baraga County.

Michigan's political boundaries extend into four of the five Great Lakes (all but Lake Ontario), giving the state jurisdiction over portions of these lakes. In addition, Michigan has about 35,000 inland lakes and ponds. The state's leading river is the Grand, flowing through the lower peninsula into Lake Michigan. Other major rivers of the lower peninsula include the Kalamazoo, Muskegon, Saginaw, and Huron. Most major rivers in the upper peninsula (including the longest, the Menominee) flow southward into Lake Michigan. Most of the many islands belonging to Michigan are located in northern Lake Michigan and in Lake Huron.

3 CLIMATE

Michigan has a temperate climate with well-defined seasons. The warmest temperatures and longest frost-free period are found most generally in the southern part of the lower peninsula. Detroit's temperatures range from 23°F (−5°C) in January to 72°F (22°C) in July. Colder temperatures and a shorter growing season prevail in the more northerly regions. Sault Ste. Marie ranges from 13°F (−11°C) in January to 64°F (18°C) in July. The coldest temperature ever recorded in the state (in 1934) is −51°F (−46°C). The all-time high of 112°F (44°C) was recorded in 1936.

Detroit has an average annual precipitation of 31 inches (79 centimeters). Rainfall tends to decrease as one moves

Michigan Population Profile

Total population in 2000:	9,938,444
Population change, 1990–2000:	6.9%
Hispanic or Latino†:	3.3%
Population by race	
One race:	98.1%
White:	80.2%
Black or African American:	14.2%
American Indian/Alaska Native:	0.6%
Asian:	1.8%
Native Hawaiian/Pacific Islander:	—
Some other race:	1.3%
Two or more races:	1.9%

Population by Age Group

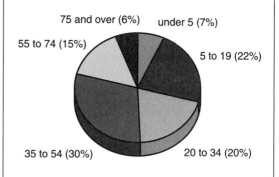

Top Cities by Population

City	Population	% change 1990–2000
Detroit	951,270	−7.5
Grand Rapids	197,800	4.6
Warren	138,247	−4.6
Flint	124,943	−11.2
Sterling Heights	124,471	5.7
Lansing	119,128	−6.4
Ann Arbor	114,024	4.0
Livonia	100,545	−0.3
Dearborn	97,775	9.5
Westland	86,602	2.2

Notes: †A person of Hispanic or Latino origin may be of any race. NA indicates that data are not available.
Sources: U.S. Census Bureau. Public Information Office. *Demographic Profiles.* [Online] Available http://www.census.gov/PressRelease/www/2001/demoprofile.html. Accessed June 1, 2001. U.S. Census Bureau. *Census 2000: Redistricting Data.* Press release issued by the Redistricting Data Office. Washington, D.C., March, 2001.

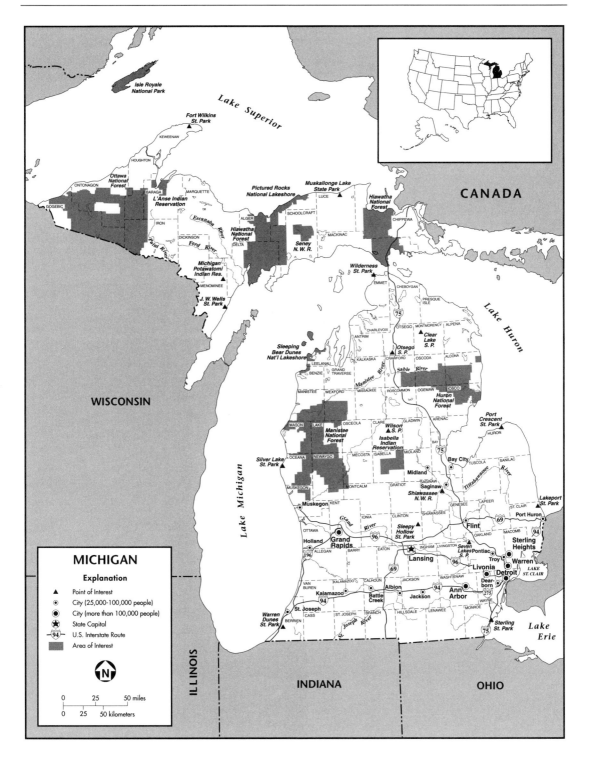

MICHIGAN

Isle Royale
National Park

Lake Superior

Fort Wilkins
St. Park

KEWEENAW

HOUGHTON

Ottawa National
Forest

ONTONAGON

BARAGA

MARQUETTE

Pictured Rocks
National Lakeshore

Muskallonge Lake
State Park

LUCE

CANADA

L'Anse Indian
Reservation

GOGEBIC

ALGER

SCHOOLCRAFT

Hiawatha
National
Forest

CHIPPEWA

IRON

Escanaba River

DICKINSON

Ford River

DELTA

Hiawatha
National
Forest

Seney
N. W. R.

MACKINAC

Michigan
Potawatomi
Indian Res.

MENOMINEE

Wilderness
St. Park

EMMET

CHEBOYGAN

PRESQUE
ISLE

Lake Huron

J. W. Wells
St. Park

75

CHARLEVOIX

OTSEGO

MONTMORENCY

ALPENA

Sleeping
Bear Dunes
Nat'l Lakeshore

ANTRIM

Clear
Lake
S. P.

LEELANAU

GRAND
TRAVERSE

KALKASKA

CRAWFORD

OSCODA

Otsego
S. P.

Sable River

ALCONA

WISCONSIN

BENZIE

Manistee River

MISSAUKEE

ROSCOMMON

OGEMAW

IOSCO

MANISTEE

WEXFORD

Huron
National
Forest

Port
Crescent
St. Park

MASON

LAKE

OSCEOLA

CLARE

GLADWIN

ARENAC

HURON

Manistee
National
Forest

Wilson
S. P.

MECOSTA

Isabella
Indian
Reservation

MIDLAND

BAY

75

Bay City

TUSCOLA

SANILAC

Silver Lake
St. Park

OCEANA

NEWAYGO

ISABELLA

Midland

Lake Michigan

MONTCALM

GRATIOT

SAGINAW

Saginaw

Tittabawassee River

Lakeport
St. Park

MUSKEGON

KENT

IONIA

CLINTON

Shiawassee
N. W. R.

SHIAWASSEE

GENESEE

LAPEER

ST. CLAIR

Port Huron

Muskegon

69

Grand River

Sleepy
Hollow
St. Park

Flint

OAKLAND

MACOMB

94

Holland

Grand
Rapids

96

OTTAWA

ALLEGAN

BARRY

EATON

INGHAM

LIVINGSTON

Seven
Lakes
S. P.

Pontiac

Sterling
Heights

196

Lansing

Troy

Warren

96

Livonia

Detroit

LAKE
ST. CLAIR

69

Dear-
born

VAN
BUREN

KALAMAZOO

CALHOUN

JACKSON

WASHTENAW

WAYNE

Kalamazoo

94

Albion

Battle
Creek

Jackson

Ann
Arbor

94

MONROE

Warren
Dunes
St. Park

St. Joseph

CASS

ST. JOSEPH

BRANCH

HILLSDALE

LENAWEE

BERRIEN

St. Joseph River

Sterling
St. Park

75

Lake
Erie

ILLINOIS

INDIANA

OHIO

MICHIGAN

Explanation

▲ Point of Interest
⊙ City (25,000-100,000 people)
● City (more than 100,000 people)
★ State Capital
94 U.S. Interstate Route
▮ Area of Interest

N

0   25   50 miles
0   25   50 kilometers

northward. The greatest snowfall is found in the extreme northern areas.

4 PLANTS AND ANIMALS

Maple, birch, hemlock, aspen, spruce, and fir predominate in the upper peninsula. Maple, birch, aspen, pine, and beech are common in the lower. Elms have largely disappeared because of the ravages of disease, while the white pine (the state tree) and red pine have been replaced in cutover lands by aspen and birch.

Strawberries, raspberries, blueberries, and cranberries are among the fruit-bearing plants and shrubs that grow wild in many areas of the state, as do mushrooms and wild asparagus. The state flower is the apple blossom. Wild flowers also abound, with as many as 400 varieties found in a single county. Protected plants include all members of the orchid, trillium, and gentian families.

Despite intensive hunting, the deer population remains high. Other game animals include the common cottontail, snowshoe hare, and raccoon. In addition to the raccoon, important native furbearers are the river otter and the beaver. More than 300 types of birds have been observed. The robin is the state bird. Ruffed grouse, bob-white quail, and various ducks and geese are hunted extensively. Reptiles include the massasauga, the state's only poisonous snake.

Whitefish, perch, and lake trout (the state fish) are native to the Great Lakes, while perch, bass, and pike are found in inland waters. Rainbow and brown trout have been introduced, and in the late 1960s, the state enjoyed its most spectacular success with the introduction of several species of salmon.

The Michigan list of threatened or endangered animals includes the gray wolf, Kirtland's water snake, blue pike, and five species of cisco.

5 ENVIRONMENTAL PROTECTION

The environmental protection program area encompasses five divisions: air quality; environmental response; surface water quality; underground storage tanks; and waste management. The Michigan Department of Natural Resources (DNR) is the state's fourth largest department.

The Environmental Response Act provides for the identification of sites of environmental contamination throughout the state and an appropriation procedure to support their cleanup. The Solid Waste Management Act and the Hazardous Waste Management Act provide the legal basis for the separate management of hazardous wastes under a detailed regulatory program. There were 71 hazardous waste sites in Michigan as of 1998. The DNR also seeks to provide quality recreational opportunities to the people of Michigan through the effective management of state recreational lands and parks, boating facilities, and fish and wildlife.

6 POPULATION

Michigan ranked eighth among the 50 states in the 2000 census, with a population of over 9.9 million. Population density for the entire state the same year was 175 persons per square mile (67.6 persons

Michigan Population by Race

Census 2000 was the first national census in which the instructions to respondents said, "Mark one or more races." This table shows the number of people who are of one, two, or three or more races. For those claiming two races, the number of people belonging to the various categories is listed. The U.S. government conducts a census of the population every ten years.

	Number	Percent
Total population	9,938,444	100.0
One race	9,746,028	98.1
Two races	180,824	1.8
White *and* Black or African American	35,461	0.4
White *and* American Indian/Alaska Native	47,122	0.5
White *and* Asian	20,599	0.2
White *and* Native Hawaiian/Pacific Islander	1,497	—
White *and* some other race	51,880	0.5
Black or African American *and* American Indian/Alaska Native	8,436	0.1
Black or African American *and* Asian	2,360	—
Black or African American *and* Native Hawaiian/Pacific Islander	453	—
Black or African American *and* some other race	6,138	0.1
American Indian/Alaska Native *and* Asian	954	—
American Indian/Alaska Native *and* Native Hawaiian/Pacific Islander	83	—
American Indian/Alaska Native *and* some other race	1,062	—
Asian *and* Native Hawaiian/Pacific Islander	936	—
Asian *and* some other race	3,625	—
Native Hawaiian/Pacific Islander *and* some other race	218	—
Three or more races	11,592	0.1

Source: U.S. Census Bureau. *Census 2000: Redistricting Data.* Press release issued by the Redistricting Data Office. Washington, D.C., March, 2001. A dash (—) indicates that the percent is less than 0.1.

per square kilometer). Over half the population was concentrated in the Detroit metropolitan area.

Since 1950, Detroit has lost population, dropping to 951,270 in 2000, when it held tenth place among U.S. cities. As Detroit lost population, however, many of its suburban areas grew at an even greater rate and the Detroit metropolitan area population totaled 5.28 million in 1996, up from 3.95 million in 1960.

Other Michigan cities with their 2000 populations include: Grand Rapids, 197,800; Warren, 138,247; Flint, 124,943; Sterling Heights, 124,471; Lansing (the capital), 119,128; and Ann Arbor, 114,024. Like Indiana and Alabama, 29% of Michigan's population is 19 years of age and younger.

7 ETHNIC GROUPS

The black population of Michigan in 1997 was estimated at 1.39 million, 14.2% of the state's total population. Nearly two-thirds lived in Detroit, where they made up over 75% of the population, the highest percentage in any US city of one million or more.

There were about 253,800 persons of Hispanic origin living in the state in 1997, predominantly of Mexican descent. The state's Asian population has been increasing: as of 1997 there were an estimated 150,800 (1.5%), primarily Asian Indians, Koreans, Chinese, Filipinos, Japanese, and Vietnamese. The 1997 federal estimate included about 59,700 Native Americans. The Ottawa, Ojibwa, and Potawatomi were the principal groups with active tribal organizations.

8 LANGUAGES

Except for the huge industrial area in southeastern Michigan, English in the state is remarkably uniform in its retention of the major Northern dialect features of upper New York and western New England. Southern blacks have introduced into the southeastern automotive manufacturing areas a regional variety of English that has become a controversial educational concern.

In 1990, only 6.6% of the state's population five years old or older spoke a language other than English at home. Other languages spoken at home, with the number of speakers, included Spanish, 137,490; Polish, 64,527; German, 57,328; and Italian, 38,023.

9 RELIGIONS

Michigan had 2,338,608 Roman Catholics in 1990, and an estimated 107,116 Jews. Among Protestant denominations, a census taken in 1990 showed various Lutheran groups with a combined total of 421,029 members and Methodist groups with 252,129 members. Among other major denominations, the Presbyterian Church had 126,326 members; the Episcopal Church, 71,727, and the Reformed Church in America, 100,680. The Seventh

Day Adventists, who had their world headquarters in Battle Creek from 1855 to 1903, numbered 37,949 in 1980; the Salvation Army, 7,896; and the Church of Jesus Christ of Latter-day Saints (Mormon), 23,475.

10 TRANSPORTATION

Because of Michigan's location, its inhabitants have always depended heavily on the Great Lakes for transportation. Although extensive networks of railroads and highways now reach into all parts of the state, the Great Lakes remain major avenues of commerce.

There were 3,820 rail miles (6,146 kilometers) of track in 1995. Most railroad passenger service is provided by Amtrak, which operates five trains through the state and carried 534,668 Michigan passengers in 1995/96.

As of 1997, the state had 89,549 miles (144,084 kilometers) of rural roads and 29,634 miles (47,681 kilometers) of urban roads. There were 1,239 miles (1,994 kilometers) of interstate highway open to traffic in 1996. There were over 5.1 million registered passenger cars, nearly 2.9 million trucks, 24,771 buses, and 154,335 motorcycles in 1997.

The opening of the St. Lawrence Seaway in 1959 made it possible for a large number of oceangoing vessels to dock at Michigan ports. In 1998, the port of Detroit handled over 19.4 million tons of cargo. The major airport is Detroit Metropolitan Wayne County Airport, which in 1996 boarded 14.1 million passengers and handled 170,980 aircraft departures.

Photo credit: Courtesy Michigan Travel Bureau.

A cargo ship passes through the Soo Locks at Sault Ste. Marie. The locks enable cargo ships to travel between Lake Superior and Lake Huron.

11 HISTORY

In the early 17th century, when European exploration began, Michigan's lower peninsula was practically uninhabited. The Algonkian-speaking Ojibwa and Menomini inhabited portions of the upper peninsula. Other groups, including the Winnebago, Sioux, and Huron, later settled in the area. For two centuries after the first Europeans came to Michigan, the Native Americans remained a vital force in the area's development, providing furs for trade and serving as potential allies in wars between rival colonial powers. However, after the War of 1812, when the fur trade declined and the possibility of war receded, the value of the Indians to the white settlers diminished. Between 1795 and 1842, tribal lands in Michigan were ceded to the federal government, and the Huron, Miami, and many Potawatomi were removed from the area.

The first European explorer known to have reached Michigan was a Frenchman, Etienne Brulé, who explored the Sault Ste. Marie area around 1620. Missionary and fur trading posts—and, later, military forts—were established at Sault Ste. Marie by Father Jacques Marquette in 1668. In 1701, Antoine Laumet de la Mothe Cadillac founded a permanent settlement at the site of present-day Detroit.

Following France's defeat in the French and Indian War, and an unsuccessful Native American rebellion, the British were in firm control of the area by 1764 and continued to occupy it until 13 years after the American Revolution, in which the need to protect the fur trade from encroachment by American farmers had placed the people of Michigan solidly on the British side.

Statehood

After occupation by the British in the War of 1812, the Michigan territory was finally returned to American authority under the terms of the Treaty of Ghent at the end of 1814. With the opening in 1825 of the Erie Canal, settlers for the first time pushed into the interior of southern Michigan. By 1833, Michigan had attained a population of 60,000 qualifying it for statehood. After the settlement of boundary disputes with Indiana and Ohio—including the so-called Toledo War, in which no one was killed—Michigan became part of the Union on 26 January 1837.

In July 1854, antislavery Democrats joined with members of the Whig and Free-Soil parties to organize Michigan's Republican Party, which swept into office that year and, with rare exceptions, controlled the state until the 1930s. Approximately 90,000 Michigan men served in the Union army, taking part in all major actions of the Civil War.

Michigan grew rapidly in economic importance. Agriculture sparked the initial growth of the new state and was responsible for its rapid increase in population. By 1850, the southern half of the lower peninsula was filling up. Less than two decades later, exploitation of vast pine forests in northern Michigan had made the state the top lumber producer in the US. Settlers were also attracted to the area by the discovery of rich mineral deposits.

Industrialization

Toward the end of the 19th century, new opportunities in manufacturing opened up. The sudden popularity of Ransom E. Olds's Oldsmobile inspired a host of Michiganians to produce similar practical, relatively inexpensive automobiles. By 1904, Detroit's Cadillac (initially a cheap car), the first Fords, and the Oldsmobile made Michigan the leading automobile producer in the country—and, later, in the world.

Industrialization brought with it urbanization; the census of 1920 for the first time showed a majority of Michiganians living in towns and cities. Nearly all industrial development was concentrated in the southern third of the state, particularly the southeastern Detroit area. The northern two-thirds of the state, where nothing took up the slack left by the decline in lumber and mining output, steadily lost population and became increasingly troubled economically.

The onset of the depression of the 1930s had devastating effects in Michigan. The market for automobiles collapsed; by 1932, half of Michigan's industrial workers were unemployed. The ineffectiveness of the Republican state and federal gov-

Michigan Governors: 1835–2001

Years	Governor	Party	Years	Governor	Party
1835–1840	Stevens Thomson Mason	Democrat	1897–1900	Hazen Stuart Pingree	Republican
1840–1841	William Woodbridge	Whig	1901–1904	Aaron Thomas Bliss	Republican
1841	James Wright Gordon	Whig	1905–1910	Fred Maltby Warner	Republican
1842–1846	John Stewart Barry	Democrat	1911–1912	Chase Salmon Osborn	Republican
1846–1847	Alpheus Felch	Democrat	1913–1916	Woodbridge Nathan Ferris	Democrat
1847	William L. Greenly	Democrat	1917–1920	Albert Edson Sleeper	Republican
1848–1850	Epaphroditus Ransom	Democrat	1921–1926	Alexander Joseph Groesbeck	Republican
1850–1851	John Stewart Barry	Democrat	1927–1930	Fred Warren Green	Republican
1852–1853	Robert McClelland	Democrat	1931–1932	Wilber Marion Brucker	Republican
1853–1854	Andrew Parsons	Democrat	1933–1934	William Alfred Comstock	Democrat
1855–1858	Kinsley Scott Bingham	Republican	1935–1936	Frank Dwight Fitzgerald	Republican
1859–1860	Moses Wisner	Republican	1937–1938	Francis William Murphy	Democrat
1861–1864	Austin Blair	Republican	1939	Frank Dwight Fitzgerald	Republican
1865–1868	Henry Howland Crapo	Republican	1939–1940	Luren Dudley Dickenson	Republican
1869–1872	Henry Porter Baldwin	Republican	1941–1942	Murray Delos Van Wagoner	Democrat
1873–1876	John Judson Bagley	Republican	1943–1946	Harry Francis Kelly	Republican
1877–1880	Charles Miller Croswell	Republican	1947–1948	Kim Sigler	Republican
1881–1882	David Howell Jerome	Republican	1949–1960	Gerhard Mennen Williams	Democrat
1883–1884	Josiah William Begole	Fusion	1961–1962	John Burley Swainson	Democrat
1885–1886	Russell Alexander Alger	Republican	1963–1969	George Wilcken Romney	Republican
1887–1890	Cyrus Gray Luce	Republican	1969–1983	William Grawn Milliken	Republican
1891–1892	Edward Baruch Winans	Democrat	1983–1991	James Johnston Blanchard	Democrat
1893–1896	John Tyler Rich	Republican	1991–	John Engler	Republican

ernments during the crisis led to a landslide victory for the Democrats. Factory workers, driven by the desire for greater job security, joined the recruiting campaign launched by the new Congress of Industrial Organizations (CIO). By 1941, the United Automobile Workers (UAW) had organized the entire auto industry, and Michigan had been converted to a strongly pro-union state.

By the mid-1950s, the Democrats controlled practically all statewide elective offices. However, Republicans maintained their control of the legislature and frustrated the efforts of Democratic administrations to institute social reforms. In the 1960s, as a result of US Supreme Court rulings, the legislature was reapportioned. This shifted a majority of legislative seats into urban areas and enabled the Democrats generally to control the legislature since that time.

1980s–1990s

The nationwide recession of the early 1980s hit Michigan harder than most other states because of its effect on the auto industry. Auto makers had already suffered heavy losses as a result of their inability to foresee the decline of the big luxury cars and because of the increasing share of the American auto market captured by foreign, mostly Japanese, manufacturers. During the late 1970s and the first two years of the 1980s, US automakers were forced to lay off hundreds of thousands of workers, tens of thousands of whom left the state. Many smaller businesses, dependent on the auto industry, closed their doors, adding to the unemployment problem.

When Governor James J. Blanchard took office in 1983, he was faced with the immediate tasks of saving Michigan from bankruptcy and reducing the unemployment rate, which had averaged more than 15% in 1982 (60% above the US average). The new governor was forced to institute budget cuts totaling $225 million and to lay off thousands of government workers. Also, at his urging, the state legislature increased Michigan's income tax by 38%.

By May 1984, Michigan's unemployment rate dropped to 11.3%, but the state faced the difficult task of restructuring its economy to lessen its dependence on the auto industry. By the late 1980s, there were signs of success. Less than 25% of wage earners worked in factories in 1988, a drop from 30% in 1978. Despite continued layoffs and plant closings by auto manufacturers between 1982 and 1988, Michigan added half a million more jobs than it lost. The state established a $100 million job-retraining program to upgrade the skills of displaced factory workers, and contributed $5 million to a joint job-training program created by General Motors and the United Automobile Workers.

12 STATE GOVERNMENT

The legislature consists of a senate of 38 members, elected for terms of four years, and a house of representatives of 110 members, elected for two-year terms. Legislation may be adopted by a majority of

Michigan Presidential Vote by Political Parties, 1948–2000

YEAR	MICHIGAN WINNER	DEMOCRAT	REPUBLICAN	PROGRESSIVE	SOCIALIST	PROHIBITION
1948	Dewey (R)	1,003,448	1,038,595	46,515	6,063	13,052
					SOC. WORKERS	
1952	*Eisenhower (R)	1,230,657	1,551,529	3,922	655	10,331
1956	*Eisenhower (R)	1,359,898	1,713,647	—	—	6,923
				SOC. LABOR		
1960	*Kennedy (D)	1,687,269	1,620,428	1,718	4,347	2,029
1964	*Johnson (D)	2,136,615	1,060,152	1,704	3,817	
						AMERICAN IND.
1968	Humphrey (D)	1,593,082	1,370,665	1,762	4,099	331,968
						AMERICAN
1972	*Nixon (R)	1,459,435	1,961,721	2,437	1,603	63,321
				PEOPLE'S		LIBERTARIAN
1976	Ford (R)	1,696,714	1,893,742	3,504	1,804	5,406
				CITIZENS	COMMUNIST	
1980	*Reagan (R)	1,661,532	1,915,225	11,930	3,262	41,597
1984	*Reagan (R)	1,529,638	2,251,571	1,191	—	10,055
				NEW ALLIANCE	WORKERS LEAGUE	
1988	*Bush (R)	1,675,783	1,965,486	2,513	1,958	18,336
				IND. (Perot)	TISCH IND. CITIZENS	
1992	*Clinton (D)	1,871,182	1,554,940	824,813	8,263	10,175
1996	*Clinton (D)	1,989,653	1,481,212	336,670	—	27,670
					LIBERTARIAN	CONSTITUTIONAL
2000	Gore (D)	2,170,418	1,953,139	84,165	16,711	3,791

*Won US presidential election

each house, but to override a governor's veto, a two-thirds vote of the members of each house is required. Elected executive officials include the governor and lieutenant governor (who run jointly), secretary of state, and attorney general, all serving four-year terms.

Legislative action is completed when a bill has been passed by both houses of the legislature and signed by the governor. A bill also becomes law if not signed by the governor after a 14-day period when the legislature is in session. The governor may stop passage of a bill by vetoing it or, if the legislature adjourns before the 14-day period expires, by refusing to sign it.

13 POLITICAL PARTIES

From its birth in 1854 through 1932, the Republican Party dominated state politics. The problems caused by the economic depression of the 1930s revitalized the Democratic Party and made Michigan a strong two-party state. Most labor organizations, led by the powerful United Automobile Workers union, have generally supported the Democratic Party since the 1930s. But in recent years, moderate Republicans have had considerable success in attracting support among previously Democratic voters.

Ronald Reagan won 49% of the state's popular vote in 1980 and 59% in 1984. Michigan elected Republican George Bush in 1988, but voted for Democrat Bill Clinton in 1992 and 1996 and Al Gore in 2000. In the latter election, Gore received 51% of the vote, Republican George W. Bush trailed with 46% of the vote. In the 1998 mid-term elections, Republican gov-

Photo credit: EPD Photos/LBJ Presidential Library

Gerald R. Ford, the 38th US president, was appointed to the vice-presidency by Richard M. Nixon in 1973 upon the resignation of Vice-President Spiro T. Agnew. When Nixon resigned on 9 August 1974, Ford became president. He is shown here giving his address to the nation in which he granted Nixon a full pardon. A difficult and unpopular decision at the time, The Kennedy Library cited the decision as a "profile in courage" during an awards ceremony in May 2001.

ernor John Engler was reelected. The state's Senators are Democrat Carl Levin and Republican Spencer Abraham. In 2001, the state's 16-member US House delegation consisted of nine Democrats and seven Republicans. There were 22 Republicans and 14 Democrats in the Michigan state senate (with 2 vacancies), and 51 Democrats and 59 Republicans in the state house.

14 LOCAL GOVERNMENT

In 1997 there were 2,775 separate units of local government in Michigan, including 83 counties, 534 municipal governments, and 1,242 townships. Each county is administered by a county board of commissioners. Executive authority is vested in five officers elected for four-year terms: the sheriff, prosecuting attorney, treasurer, clerk, and registrar of deeds. An increasing number of counties are placing overall administrative responsibility in the hands of a county manager or administrator.

Most cities establish their own form of government under an adopted charter. Some charters provide for the election of a mayor; other cities have chosen the council-manager system. Township government, its powers strictly limited by state law, consists of a supervisor, clerk, treasurer, and up to four trustees.

15 JUDICIAL SYSTEM

Michigan's highest court is the state supreme court, consisting of seven justices elected for eight-year terms. The chief justice is elected by the members of the court. The high court hears cases on appeal from lower state courts and also administers the state's entire court system. Unless the supreme court agrees to review a court of appeals ruling, the latter's decision is final.

The major trial courts in the state as of 1997 were the 57 circuit courts. The circuit courts have original jurisdiction in all felony criminal cases, civil cases involving sums of more than $10,000, and divorces. A special division of the circuit court was created in 1998 to better serve families and individuals. Circuit courts also hear appeals from lower courts and state administrative agencies. Probate courts have original jurisdiction in cases involving juveniles and dependents, and also handle wills and estates, adoptions, and commitments of the mentally ill.

Michigan had an overall 1998 crime rate of 4,682.9 per 100,000 population. There were 46,253 prisoners in state or federal correctional facilities in June 1999.

16 MIGRATION

After World War II, many Europeans immigrated to Michigan. Smaller groups of Mexicans, Spanish-speaking peoples from Latin America, and Arabic-speaking peoples, who by the late 1970s were more numerous in Detroit than in any other US city, also arrived. Between 1940 and 1970, a net total of 518,000 migrants were drawn to Michigan. The economic problems of the auto industry in the 1970s and 1980s caused a significant reversal of this trend, with the state suffering a net loss of over 460,000 in the 1980s. During 1990–98, Michigan lost over 190,000 residents to other states, while gaining about 87,000 in migration from abroad. An estimated 5% of the state's population was foreign-born in 1996. In 1998, 13,943 immigrants from abroad were legally admitted into the state. The total number of illegal immigrants living in Michigan was estimated at 37,000 in 1996.

Most parts of northern Michigan have suffered a loss of population since the early years of this century as a result of rural-to-urban migration. However, since 1950, the central cities have experienced a steady loss of population to the suburbs, in part caused by the migration of whites from areas that were becoming increasingly black. By 1998, the black population numbered 1.4 million, the majority of whom lived in the Detroit-Ann Arbor-Flint metropolitan area.

17 ECONOMY

Michigan's dependence on automobile production has caused grave and persistent economic problems since the 1950s. Michigan's unemployment rates in times of recession have far exceeded the national average, since auto sales are among the hardest hit in such periods. Although the state was relatively prosperous during the record automotive production years of the 1960s and 1970s, the high cost of gasoline and the encroachment of imports on domestic car sales had disastrous effects by 1980. At that time it became apparent that the state's future economic health required greater diversification of industry.

Employment in car manufacturing dropped 16.5% between 1981 and 1991, and manufacturing employment as a whole dropped 6% in those years. Jobs in the nonmanufacturing sector, on the other hand, increased 59.9%. Service jobs increased 5% and wholesale and retail trade grew 3%. By the early 1990s, both the trade and service sectors employed more people than the manufacturing industry. By the mid-1990s, private goods producing industries accounted for 35% of the state's economic output, private services-producing industries contributed 54%, and government accounted for 11%.

18 INCOME

In 1998, Michigan had a per capita (per person) income of $26,885 (19th among the states). The median household income was $40,639 in 1998. Some 10.8% of the population lived below the federal poverty level in 1998.

19 INDUSTRY

The rise of the auto industry in the early 20th century completed the transformation of Michigan into one of the most important manufacturing areas in the world. In 1997, the total value of shipments totaled $218 billion.

Motor vehicles and equipment dominate the state's economy. The value of shipments by automotive manufacturers was $85.1 billion, or 41% of the total. Michigan's 19 auto production facilities account for about 23% of US car and truck production in 1998. Production of nonelectrical machinery and metal products was directly related to automobile production. The Detroit metropolitan area is the major industrial region: this area includes not only a heavy concentration of auto-related plants, but also major steel, chemical, and pharmaceutical industries, among others. In 1997, Michigan was the headquarters of 14 Fortune 500 companies, including General Motors (first in revenues), Ford (second), and Chrysler (ninth). In 1998 Chrysler merged with Germany's Daimler Benz to become DaimlerChrysler.

20 LABOR

Michigan's civilian labor force in mid-1998 included 5.02 million workers. Of

The harbor at Mackinac Island.

these, about 194,000, or 3.9%, were unemployed.

Michigan has 18 national labor unions operating in its borders. Its most powerful and influential industrial union since the 1930s has been the United Automobile Workers (UAW), with nearly 751,000 members nationwide in 1995. Its national headquarters is in Detroit. Some 22.6% of all workers in the state were union members in 1998.

21 AGRICULTURE

In 1998, Michigan had 52,000 farms occupying 10.4 million acres (4.2 million hectares). In 1999, Michigan's agricultural income was estimated at nearly $3.5 bil-

lion, placing Michigan 23rd among the 50 states. About 62% came from crops and the rest from livestock and livestock products. Dairy products, cattle, corn, and soybeans were the principal commodities. In 1998, the state ranked first in output of tart cherries; third in apples; and fourth in prunes and plums.

The southern half of the lower peninsula is the principal agricultural region, and the area along Lake Michigan is a leader in fruit-growing. Leading field crops in 1998 included 227.5 million bushels of corn for grain, 73.7 million bushels of soybeans, and 30.7 million bushels of wheat. Output of commercial apples totaled 930 million pounds (422 million kilograms).

22 DOMESTICATED ANIMALS

The same areas of southern Michigan that lead in crop production also lead in livestock and livestock products. In 1999 there were 1.05 million cattle in the state, valued at $808.5 million, and 1.12 million hogs, valued at $53.8 million. In 1997, milk production from 306,000 dairy cows was 5.4 million pounds (2.4 million kilograms). Mink pelts are also marketed.

23 FISHING

Commercial fishing, once an important factor in the state's economy, is relatively minor today. The commercial catch in 1998 was 14.8 million pounds (6.7 million kilograms) valued at $8.8 million. Principal species landed are silver salmon and alewives. Sport fishing continues to flourish and is one of the state's major tourist attractions. A state salmon-planting program, begun in the mid-1960s, has made salmon the most popular game fish for Great Lakes sport-fishers.

24 FORESTRY

Michigan's forestland covered 19.3 million acres (7.8 million hectares), or more than half the state's total land area in 1997. The major wooded regions are in the northern two-thirds of the state, where great pine forests enabled Michigan to become the leading lumber-producing state in the last four decades of the 19th century. State and national forests cover 6.9 million acres (2.8 million hectares).

25 MINING

Nonfuel mineral production was valued at $1.75 billion in 1998 in Michigan. Michigan continued to lead the nation in the quantity and value of crude iron oxide pigments, and magnesium chloride produced. Michigan ranked second in the nation in the production of bromine, iron ore, and peat. In 1998, the production of 5.9 million metric tons of cement was worth $448 million. Over 61.7 million metric tons of construction sand and gravel were valued at $229 million. Crushed stone, production, at 42 million metric tons, was worth $158 million.

26 ENERGY AND POWER

In 1997, energy consumption per capita (per person) totaled 333.1 million Btu (83.6 million kilocalories). Coal is the principal source of fuel used in generating electric power, while natural gas is the major fuel used for other energy needs. In 1999, electric energy production totaled 85.1 billion kilowatt hours. Hydroelectric plants, which had produced more than 10% of the state's electric energy in 1947, yielded less than 0.5% in 1998. Coal-fired steam units produced 81%; nuclear-powered units, 15%; and other units, about 4%.

Michigan is dependent on outside sources for most of its fuel needs. Petroleum production in 1999 totaled 7.8 million barrels, and natural gas output was 238.2 billion cubic feet (6.7 billion cubic meters), less than one-fourth the natural gas consumed in the state. Proven petroleum reserves were 44 million barrels at the end of 1998; natural gas reserves, 2.3 trillion cubic feet (66 billion cubic meters). The state has five nuclear power plants.

27 COMMERCE

Michigan had 1997 wholesale sales of $165 billion. Leading categories were motor vehicles and automobile parts and supplies (accounting for nearly one-fifth of all sales by value), groceries, metals and minerals, and machinery. Retail sales totaled $97 billion, seventh among the states. The Detroit/Ann Arbor/Flint area accounted for about half of Michigan's retail sales. With its ports open to ocean-going vessels through the St. Lawrence Seaway, Michigan is a major exporting and importing state for foreign as well as domestic markets. Exports of Michigan's manufactured goods totaled $29 billion in 1998, fifth in the US.

28 PUBLIC FINANCE

The state constitution requires the governor to submit a budget proposal to the legislature each year. The revenues for 1997 were $45.51 billion; expenditures were $36.09 billion.

The total state debt in 1997 was $14.43 billion, or $1,476 per capita (per person).

29 TAXATION

Sales and income taxes are the main sources of state revenues. Property taxes are reserved entirely to local governments. In 1994, Michigan's school system eliminated the use of property taxes for its funds. In 1997/98, Michigan's state tax burden was over $21.6 billion, or $2,209 per person.

Other state taxes and fees are levied on inheritances, corporate and financial-insti-tution income, cigarettes, alcoholic beverages, parimutuel wagering, and gasoline and other fuels. Michigan's share of the federal tax burden in 1995 was $48.3 billion.

30 HEALTH

Major causes of death in 1998 included heart disease, cerebrovascular diseases, accidents, (of which motor vehicle accidents accounted for 50%), and suicide. In 1998, Michigan had 151 community hospitals, with 27,168 beds. The average expense of hospital care was $1,189 per inpatient day, or $6,759 for an average cost per stay. Michigan had 218 physicians per 100,000 in 1997. Licensed nurses numbered over 28,000 in 1998. Roughly 13.2% of state residents did not have health insurance in 1998.

31 HOUSING

In 1999 there were an estimated 4.2 million housing units in Michigan. During the 1980s, the housing stock increased by only 7%. In 1998, 54,500 new privately owned housing units were authorized for construction, valued at $5.9 billion. A limited amount of state aid for low-income housing is available through the State Housing Development Authority.

32 EDUCATION

Historically, Michigan has strongly supported public education, which helps account for the fact that the percentage of students attending public schools is one of the highest in the US. But the cost of maintaining this extensive public educational system has become a major problem in recent years because of the declining school-age population.

In 1998, 76.4% of persons 25 years and over had completed four years of high school, and 19.8% had received a bachelor's degree or higher. In 1995 there were 2,496 public elementary schools and 776 public secondary schools. Public school enrollment totaled 1.7 million in fall 1997. Expenditures for public elementary and secondary schools amounted to $7,483 per student in 1999/00. That same year there were 192,422 pupils in private schools. The largest number of these were enrolled in Catholic schools.

In the fall of 1997, Michigan had 71 colleges and universities and 30 community colleges with a combined enrollment of 549,742. The oldest state school is the University of Michigan, founded at its Ann Arbor campus in 1837. Other public universities are Michigan State and Wayne State. Michigan also has 54 independent, nonprofit colleges and universities with a total enrollment of 85,412. Among the state's private colleges and universities, are the University of Detroit, Kalamazoo College, and Albion College (1835).

33 ARTS

Michigan's major center of arts and cultural activities is the Detroit area. Orchestra Hall is the home of the Detroit Symphony Orchestra; the Music Hall and the Masonic Auditorium present a variety of musical productions; and the Fisher Theater is the major home for Broadway productions. Nearby Meadow Brook, in Rochester, has a prestigious summer music program.

The University of Michigan, Michigan State, Wayne State, and Eastern Michigan University have notable art schools. The Cranbrook Academy of Arts, which was created by the architect Eliel Saarinen, is a significant art center, and the Ann Arbor Art Fair, begun in 1959, is one of the largest and most prestigious summer outdoor art shows in the country.

The Meadow Brook Theater at Rochester is perhaps the largest professional theater company. Detroit also has a number of little theater groups. Successful summer theaters include the Cherry County Playhouse at Traverse City and the Star Theater in Flint.

The Detroit Symphony Orchestra is nationally known. Grand Rapids and Kalamazoo have regional orchestras. The National Music Camp at Interlochen is a major center for young musicians throughout the country. There are local ballet and opera groups in Detroit and in a few other communities.

Michigan's best-known contribution to popular music was that of Berry Gordy, Jr., whose Motown recording company in the 1960s popularized the "Detroit sound" and featured such artists as Diana Ross and the Supremes, Smokey Robinson and the Miracles, the Four Tops, the Temptations, and Stevie Wonder.

34 LIBRARIES AND MUSEUMS

In 1996, Michigan had 380 public libraries, 109 academic libraries, and numerous special libraries. In 1999, public libraries in the state had a total of nearly 26 million volumes and a circulation exceeding 50

Photo credit: Courtesy Michigan Travel Bureau.

Mackinac Bridge, Mackinaw City.

million. The largest public library is the Detroit Public Library, with 2.5 million volumes in 1995. Among academic libraries, the University of Michigan at Ann Arbor had 6.2 million volumes and 656,663 periodical subscriptions in 1999. In 1980, the Gerald R. Ford Presidential Library was opened on the university campus.

The Detroit Institute of Arts is the largest art museum in the state and has an outstanding collection of African art. The Kalamazoo Institute of Art, the Flint Institute of Art, the Grand Rapids Art Museum, and the Hackley Art Gallery in Muskegon are important art museums.

The Detroit Historical Museum heads the more than 229 museums in the state. In Dearborn, the privately run Henry Ford Museum and Greenfield Village are leading tourist attractions.The major historical sites open to the public include the late-18th-century fort on Mackinac Island and the reconstructed early-18th-century fort at Mackinaw City.

35 COMMUNICATIONS

In 1999, 94.2% of occupied housing units in the state had telephones. Michigan had 137 AM radio stations and 261 FM stations in 2000. As of 2000 there were 57 television stations in the state. By

2000, a total of 145,596 Internet domain names had been registered in Michigan.

36 PRESS

In 1998 there were 49 daily newspapers in Michigan. In addition, 26 Sunday editions were published in the state and there were also 331 weekly or other non-daily newspapers. The number of daily papers has declined in recent decades. Since 1959, Detroit has been the only Michigan city with more than one daily. In 1989, its two leading newspapers entered a joint operating agreement. Leading daily newspapers in Michigan with average daily circulation in 1998 are the *Detroit Free Press* and the *Detroit News* (699,786); the *Grand Rapids Press* (139,703); and the *Flint Journal* (93,603).

37 TOURISM, TRAVEL, AND RECREATION

Tourism has been an important source of economic activity in Michigan since the 19th century and now rivals agriculture as the second most important segment of the state's economy.

The opportunities offered by Michigan's water resources are the number one attraction. No part of the state is more than 85 miles (137 kilometers) from one of the Great Lakes, and most of the population lives only a few miles away from one of the thousands of inland lakes and streams.

Historic attractions have been heavily promoted in recent years, following the success of Dearborn's Henry Ford Museum and Greenfield Village, which attract about 1.5 million paying visitors each year. Tours of Detroit automobile factories and other industrial sites, such as Battle Creek's breakfast-food plants, are also important attractions.

Camping and recreational facilities are provided by the federal government at three national forests, comprising 2.8 million acres (1.1 million hectares). Three facilities are operated by the National Park Service (Isle Royale National Park, the Pictured Rocks National Lakeshore, and Sleeping Bear Dunes National Lakeshore). There are also several federally-operated wildlife sanctuaries. State-operated facilities include 64 parks and recreational areas with 172,343 acres (69,747 hectares), and state forests and wildlife areas totaling 4.25 million acres (1.72 million hectares).

38 SPORTS

Michigan has five major league professional sports teams, all of them centered in Detroit: the Tigers of Major League Baseball, the Lions of the National Football League, the Pistons of the National Basketball Association, the Shock of the Women's National Basketball Association, and the Red Wings of the National Hockey League.

Horse-racing, Michigan's oldest organized spectator sport, is controlled by the state racing commissioner, who regulates thoroughbred and harness-racing seasons at tracks in the Detroit area and at Jackson. Thoroughbred and harness-racing drew attendances of 469,000 and 1.4 million, respectively, in 1996. Auto-racing is also popular in Michigan. The state hosts three major races, the Detroit Grand Prix, the US 500 Indy car race, and Michigan 500 stock-car race.

Interest in college sports centers on the football and basketball teams of the University of Michigan and Michigan State University, which usually are among the top-ranked teams in the country. The University of Michigan's football stadium, seating 104,001, is the largest college-owned stadium in the country. The Michigan State basketball team won the NCAA tournament in 2000.

39 FAMOUS MICHIGANIANS

Only one Michiganian has held the offices of US president and vice-president: Gerald R. Ford (Leslie King, Jr., b.Nebraska, 1913), the 38th US president, who was appointed to the vice-presidency by Richard M. Nixon in 1973 upon the resignation of Vice-President Spiro T. Agnew. When Nixon resigned on 9 August 1974, Ford became president, the first to hold that post without having been elected to high national office.

Two Michiganians have served as associate justices of the Supreme Court: Henry B. Brown (b.Massachusetts, 1836–1913), author of the 1896 segregationist decision in *Plessy v. Ferguson;* and Frank Murphy (1890–1949), who also served as US attorney general and was a notable defender of minority rights during his years on the court. Another justice, Potter Stewart (1915–85), was born in Jackson but appointed to the court from Ohio.

Other Michiganians who have held high federal office include Robert S. McNamara

(b.California, 1916), secretary of defense; and W. Michael Blumenthal (b.Germany, 1926), secretary of the treasury. Detroit's first black mayor, Coleman A. Young (b.Alabama, 1918–97), promoted programs to revive the city's tarnished image while in office during 1974–93.

The most famous figure in the early development of Michigan is Jacques Marquette (b.France, 1637–75). Laura Haviland (b.Canada, 1808–98) was a noted leader in the fight against slavery and for black rights, while Lucinda Hinsdale Stone (b.Vermont, 1814–1900) and Anna Howard Shaw (b.England, 1847–1919) were important in the women's rights movement.

Nobel laureates from Michigan include diplomat Ralph J. Bunche (1904–71), winner of the Nobel Peace Prize in 1950; and Glenn T. Seaborg (b.1912–99), Nobel Prize winner in chemistry in 1951, and for whom element 106, seaborgium, is named.

In the business world, William C. Durant (b.Massachusetts, 1861–1947), Henry Ford (1863–1947), and Ransom E. Olds (b.Ohio 1864–1950) are the three most important figures in making Michigan the center of the American auto industry. Ford's grandson, Henry Ford II (1917–87), was the dominant personality in the auto industry from 1945 through 1979. Two brothers, John Harvey Kellogg (1852–1943) and Will K. Kellogg (1860–1951), helped make Battle Creek the center of the breakfast-food industry. Pioneer aviator Charles A. Lindbergh (1902–74) was born in Detroit.

Photo credit: EPD Photos/Library of Congress.

Industrialist Henry Ford (1863–1947) helped usher in the age of the automobile.

Among prominent labor leaders in Michigan were Walter Reuther (b.West Virginia, 1907–70), president of the United Automobile Workers, and his controversial contemporary, James Hoffa (b.Indiana, 1913–75?), president of the Teamsters Union, whose disappearance and presumed murder remain a mystery.

The best-known literary figures who were either native or adopted Michiganians include Ring Lardner (1885–1933), master of the short story; Edna Ferber (1885–1968), best-selling novelist; Howard Mumford Jones (1892–1980), critic and scholar; and Bruce Catton (1899–1978), Civil War historian.

Other prominent Michiganians past and present include Frederick Stuart Church (1842–1924), painter; Albert Kahn (b.Germany, 1869–1942), innovator in factory design; and (Gottlieb) Eliel Saarinen (b.Finland, 1873–1950), architect and creator of the Cranbrook School of Art. Malcolm X (Malcolm Little, b.Nebraska, 1925–65) developed his black separatist beliefs while living in Lansing.

Popular entertainers born in Michigan include Danny Thomas (Amos Jacobs, 1914–91); Ed McMahon (b.1923); Julie Harris (b.1925); Ellen Burstyn (Edna Rae Gilhooley, b.1932); Della Reese (Dellareese Patricia Early, b.1932); William "Smokey" Robinson (b.1940); Diana Ross (b.1944); Bob Seger (b.1945); Stevie Wonder (Stevland Morris, b.1950); and Madonna (Madonna Louise Ciccone, b.1959); along with film director Francis Ford Coppola (b.1939).

Among sports figures who had notable careers in the state were Joe Louis (Joseph Louis Barrow, b.Alabama, 1914–81); heavyweight boxing champion from 1937 to 1949; "Sugar Ray" Robinson (1921–89), who held at various times the welterweight and middleweight boxing titles; and baseball Hall of Famer Al Kaline (b.Maryland, 1934), a Detroit Tigers star. Basketball star Earvin "Magic" Johnson (b. 1959), who broke Oscar Robertson's record for most assists, was born in Lansing.

40 BIBLIOGRAPHY

Aylesworth, Thomas G. *Eastern Great Lakes: Indiana, Michigan, Ohio.* New York: Chelsea House, 1996.

Brill, Marlene Targ. *Michigan.* New York: Benchmark, 1998.

McAuliffe, Emily. *Michigan Facts and Symbols.* Mankato, Minn.: Hilltop Books, 1999.

Wills, Charles. *A Historical Album of Michigan.* Brookfield, Conn.: Millbrook Press, 1996.

Wittenberg, Eric J., ed. *One of Custer's Wolverines: the Civil War Letters of Brevet Brigadier General James H. Kidd, 6th Michigan Infantry.* Kent, Ohio: Kent State University Press, 2000.

Web sites

Library of Michigan. Michigan In Brief. [Online] Available http://www.libofmich.lib.mi.us Accessed May 16, 2001.

State of Michigan. Michigan State Government – Governor John Engler. [Online] Available http://www.migov.state.mi.us/ Accessed May 16, 2001.

MINNESOTA

State of Minnesota

ORIGIN OF STATE NAME: Derived from the Sioux Indian word *minisota,* meaning "sky-tinted waters."

NICKNAME: The North Star State.

CAPITAL: St. Paul.

ENTERED UNION: 11 May 1858 (32d).

SONG: "Hail! Minnesota."

MOTTO: *L'Etoile du Nord* (The North Star).

FLAG: On a blue field bordered on three sides by a gold fringe, a version of the state seal is surrounded by a wreath with the statehood year (1858), the year of the establishment of Ft. Snelling (1819), and the year the flag was adopted (1893). Five clusters of gold stars and the word "Minnesota" fill the outer circle.

OFFICIAL SEAL: A farmer, with a powder horn and musket nearby, plows a field in the foreground, while in the background, before a rising sun, an Indian on horseback crosses the plains; pine trees and a waterfall represent the state's natural resources. The state motto is above, and the whole is surrounded by the words "The Great Seal of the State of Minnesota 1858." Another version of the seal in common use shows a cowboy riding across the plains.

BIRD: Common loon.

FISH: Walleye.

FLOWER: Pink and white lady slipper.

TREE: Red (Norway) pine.

GEM: Lake Superior agate.

GRAIN: Wild rice.

MUSHROOM: Morel or sponge mushroom.

DRINK: Milk.

TIME: 6 AM CST = noon GMT.

1 LOCATION AND SIZE

Situated in the western north-central US, Minnesota is the largest midwestern state and ranks 12th in size among the 50 states, with a total area of 84,402 square miles (218,601 square kilometers). The state extends 406 miles (653 kilometers) north-south and 358 miles (576 kilometers) east-west. Its boundary length totals 1,783 miles (2,870 kilometers).

A small peninsula known as the Northwest Angle is separated from Minnesota and the United States by the Lake of the Woods. The area covers about 120 square miles (311 square kilometers) and only borders Canada's province of Manitoba.

2 TOPOGRAPHY

Minnesota consists mainly of flat prairie. There are rolling hills and deep river valleys in the southeast. The northeast, known as Arrowhead Country, is more rugged and includes the Vermilion Range and the Mesabi Range. Eagle Mountain, in the extreme northeast, rises to a height of 2,301 feet (701 meters), the highest point in the state.

With more than 15,000 lakes and extensive wetlands, rivers, and streams, Minnesota has more inland water than any other state except Alaska. A total of 2,212 square miles (5,729 square kilometers) of Lake Superior lies within Minnesota's jurisdiction. The Mississippi River drains about three-fifths of the state. Other rivers include the Minnesota and the Red River.

3 CLIMATE

Minnesota has a continental climate, with cold, often frigid winters and warm summers. Normal daily mean temperatures range from 11°F (–12°C) in January to 73°F (23°C) in July in the Twin Cities of Minneapolis–St. Paul. The lowest temperature recorded in the state of Minnesota was –60°F (–51°C) in 1996; the highest, 114°F (46°C) in 1936.

Mean annual precipitation ranges from 19 inches (48 centimeters) in the northwest to 32 inches (81 centimeters) in the southeast. Heavy snowfalls occur from November to April, averaging between 30 inches (76 centimeters) and 70 inches (178 centimeters) annually. Blizzards hit Minnesota twice each winter on the average.

Minnesota Population Profile

Total population in 2000:	4,919,479
Population change, 1990–2000:	12.4%
Hispanic or Latino†:	2.9%
Population by race	
One race:	98.3%
White:	89.4%
Black or African American:	3.5%
American Indian/Alaska Native:	1.1%
Asian:	2.9%
Native Hawaiian/Pacific Islander:	—
Some other race:	1.3%
Two or more races:	1.7%

Population by Age Group

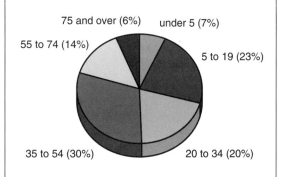

75 and over (6%) under 5 (7%)
55 to 74 (14%)
5 to 19 (23%)
35 to 54 (30%)
20 to 34 (20%)

Top Cities by Population

City	Population	% change 1990–2000
Minneapolis	382,618	3.9
St. Paul	287,151	5.5
Duluth	86,918	1.7
Rochester	85,806	21.3
Bloomington	85,172	–1.3
Brooklyn Park	67,388	19.5
Plymouth	65,894	29.5
Eagan	63,557	34.1
Coon Rapids	61,607	16.3
Burnsville	60,220	17.4

Notes: †A person of Hispanic or Latino origin may be of any race. NA indicates that data are not available.
Sources: U.S. Census Bureau. Public Information Office. *Demographic Profiles.* [Online] Available http://www.census.gov/Press-Release/www/2001/demoprofile.html. Accessed June 1, 2001. U.S. Census Bureau. *Census 2000: Redistricting Data.* Press release issued by the Redistricting Data Office. Washington, D.C., March, 2001.

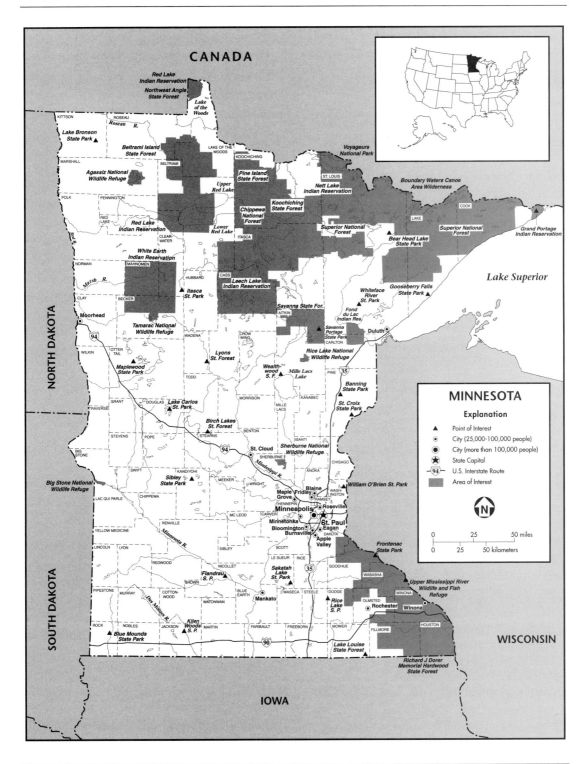

MINNESOTA

CANADA

Red Lake
Indian Reservation
Northwest Angle
State Forest

Lake
of the
Woods

KITTSON

ROSEAU
Roseau R.

Lake Bronson
State Park

MARSHALL

Beltrami Island
State Forest

LAKE OF THE
WOODS

KOOCHICHING

Voyageurs
National Park

Agassiz National
Wildlife Refuge

Pine Island
State Forest

ST. LOUIS

Boundary Waters Canoe
Area Wilderness

POLK

PENNINGTON

Upper
Red Lake

Nett Lake
Indian Reservation

RED
LAKE

Chippewa
National
Forest

Koochiching
State Forest

Superior National
Forest

COOK

Red Lake
Indian Reservation

Lower
Red Lake

Superior National
Forest

Grand Portage
Indian Reservation

CLEAR-
WATER

ITASCA

LAKE

Bear Head Lake
State Park

NORMAN

White Earth
Indian Reservation

HUBBARD

CASS

Lake Superior

CLAY

MAHNOMEN

Itasca
St. Park

Leech Lake
Indian Reservation

Whiteface
River
St. Park

Gooseberry Falls
State Park

BECKER

Moorhead

Marsh R.

Savanna State For.

Fond
du Lac
Indian Res.

94

Tamarac National
Wildlife Refuge

WADENA

AITKIN

Savanna
Portage
State Park

Duluth

WILKIN

CROW
WING

CARLTON

OTTER
TAIL

Lyons
St. Forest

Rice Lake National
Wildlife Refuge

Maplewood
State Park

TODD

Wealth-
wood
S. F.

Mille Lacs
Lake

PINE

35

Banning
State Park

GRANT

DOUGLAS

Lake Carlos
St. Park

MORRISON

MILLE
LACS

KANABEC

St. Croix
State Park

TRAVERSE

Birch Lakes
St. Forest

BENTON

STEVENS

POPE

STEARNS

ISANTI

Sherburne National
Wildlife Refuge

BIG
STONE

94

St. Cloud

SHERBURNE

CHISAGO

SWIFT

KANDIYOHI

Mississippi R.

ANOKA

William O'Brien St. Park

Big Stone National
Wildlife Refuge

Sibley
State Park

MEEKER

WRIGHT

Blaine

WASH-
INGTON

MINNESOTA

Explanation

▲ Point of Interest

⊙ City (25,000-100,000 people)

◉ City (more than 100,000 people)

★ State Capital

—94— U.S. Interstate Route

▨ Area of Interest

LAC QUI PARLE

CHIPPEWA

Maple
Grove

Fridley

RAMSEY

Minneapolis

Roseville

MC LEOD

CARVER

Minnetonka

St. Paul

RENVILLE

Bloomington

Eagan

Burnsville

DAKOTA

YELLOW MEDICINE

Minnesota R.

SIBLEY

Apple
Valley

Frontenac
State Park

LINCOLN

LYON

REDWOOD

SCOTT

LE SUEUR

RICE

35

GOODHUE

WABASHA

0   25   50 miles
0   25   50 kilometers

Flandrau
S. P.

NICOLLET

Sakatah
Lake
St. Park

Upper Mississippi River
Wildlife and Fish
Refuge

PIPESTONE

MURRAY

COTTON-
WOOD

BROWN

BLUE
EARTH

WATONWAN

Mankato

WASECA

STEELE

DODGE

OLMSTED

WINONA

Rice
Lake
S. P.

Rochester

Winona

ROCK

NOBLES

JACKSON

Kilen
Woods
S. P.

MARTIN

FARIBAULT

FREEBORN

MOWER

FILLMORE

HOUSTON

Blue Mounds
State Park

90

Lake Louise
State Forest

WISCONSIN

Richard J Dorer
Memorial Hardwood
State Forest

NORTH DAKOTA

SOUTH DAKOTA

Des Moines R.

IOWA

4 PLANTS AND ANIMALS

Minnesota is divided into three main life zones: the wooded lake regions of the north and east, the prairie lands of the west and southwest, and a transition zone in between. Oak, maple, elm, birch, pine, ash, and poplar still thrive, although much of the state's woodland has been cut down since the 1850s. Common shrubs include thimbleberry, sweetfern, and several varieties of honeysuckle. Familiar among some 1,500 native flowering plants are prairie phlox and blazing star. Pink and white lady's-slipper is the state flower.

Among Minnesota's common mammals are the opossum, raccoon, and white-tailed deer. The western meadowlark, Brewer's blackbird, and Carolina wren are among some 240 resident bird species. Minnesota's many lakes are filled with such game fishes as walleyed pike, northern pike, and rainbow trout. Endangered species include the gray (timber) wolf, trumpeter swan, and American peregrine falcon.

Photo credit: ©Minnesota Office of Tourism.

The headwaters of the Mississippi River at Itasca State Park.

5 ENVIRONMENTAL PROTECTION

The state's northern forests have been greatly depleted by fires, lumbering, and farming, but efforts to replenish them began as early as 1876, with the formation of the state's first forestry association. The present Department of Natural Resources is responsible for the management of forests, fish and game, public lands, minerals, and state parks and waters. A separate Pollution Control Agency enforces air and water quality standards and oversees solid waste disposal and pollution-related land-use planning.

Minnesotans dump 4,400 tons of waste a year (one ton per person) into 53 municipal landfills. There were 27 hazardous waste sites in the state in 1998. To control the state's solid waste, Minnesotans have established 488 curbside recycling programs. During the early 1980s, the state's Pollution Control Agency approved plans by FMC, a munitions maker, to clean up a hazardous waste site at Fridley (near Minneapolis), which the Environmental Protection Agency claimed was the country's most dangerous hazardous waste area.

Minnesota Population by Race

Census 2000 was the first national census in which the instructions to respondents said, "Mark one or more races." This table shows the number of people who are of one, two, or three or more races. For those claiming two races, the number of people belonging to the various categories is listed. The U.S. government conducts a census of the population every ten years.

	Number	Percent
Total population	4,919,479	100.0
One race	4,836,737	98.3
Two races	77,732	1.6
White *and* Black or African American	17,700	0.4
White *and* American Indian/Alaska Native	18,793	0.4
White *and* Asian	11,966	0.2
White *and* Native Hawaiian/Pacific Islander	852	—
White *and* some other race	12,015	0.2
Black or African American *and* American Indian/Alaska Native	2,413	—
Black or African American *and* Asian	1,057	—
Black or African American *and* Native Hawaiian/Pacific Islander	191	—
Black or African American *and* some other race	6,054	0.1
American Indian/Alaska Native *and* Asian	812	—
American Indian/Alaska Native *and* Native Hawaiian/Pacific Islander	50	—
American Indian/Alaska Native *and* some other race	675	—
Asian *and* Native Hawaiian/Pacific Islander	1,920	—
Asian *and* some other race	3,091	0.1
Native Hawaiian/Pacific Islander *and* some other race	143	—
Three or more races	5,010	0.1

Source: U.S. Census Bureau. *Census 2000: Redistricting Data.* Press release issued by the Redistricting Data Office. Washington, D.C., March, 2001. A dash (—) indicates that the percent is less than 0.1.

6 POPULATION

The 2000 census gave Minnesota a population of over 4.9 million. It ranked 21st among the 50 states, falling behind Arizona.

In 1990, two out of three Minnesotans lived in metropolitan areas. The Minneapolis-St. Paul metropolitan area was the country's 15th largest in 1996, with a population of over 2.76 million. Minneapolis itself had 382,618 residents in 2000, while St. Paul ranked second with 287,151. The 2000 estimates for other leading cities were as follows: Duluth, 86,918; Rochester, 85,806; Bloomington, 85,172; and Brooklyn Park, 67,388. Approximately 30% of the population was 19 years of age and younger, and one-fifth were 55 years and older. The state's population density of 61.8 persons per square mile (23.9 per square kilometer) was just under the national average of 79.6 persons per square mile (30.7 per square kilometer).

7 ETHNIC GROUPS

Minnesota has more ethnic Norwegians than any other state, and is second in number of ethnic Swedes, behind California. The other ethnic groups are concentrated in Minneapolis–St. Paul or in the iron country of the Mesabi Range.

As of 1997, there were an estimated 57,100 Native Americans in Minnesota. Besides those living in seven small reservations and four villages, a cluster of urban dwellers (chiefly Ojibwa) lived in St. Paul. In 1997, blacks were estimated at 133,100, or 2.8% of the total population. In 1997 there were an estimated 117,900 Asian and Pacific peoples, mostly Hmong, Korean, and Vietnamese. There also were 80,700 people with Hispanic origins.

8 LANGUAGES

English in the state is basically Northern, with minor infiltrations of Midland terms. Among older residents, traces of Scandinavian and Eastern European pronunciation persist. Minnesotans call the grass strip between street and sidewalk the *boulevard* and a rubber band a *rubber binder,* and many *cook coffee* when they brew it. In 1990, 3,811,700 Minnesotans five years old or older spoke only English at home. Other leading languages spoken at home were German, 45,409; Spanish, 42,362; French, 13,693; and various Scandinavian languages, 25,758.

9 RELIGIONS

As of 1990, there were 1,693,568 known Protestants, including 1,069,703 Lutherans, 142,771 United Methodists, 66,715 Presbyterians, 55,497 members of the United Church of Christ, and 31,980 Episcopalians. Roman Catholics numbered 1,110,071 in 1990. The estimated Jewish population was 42,000 in 1994.

10 TRANSPORTATION

In 1998, Minnesota had a total of 4,493 rail miles (7,229 kilometers) of track, over 85% of which was Class I track. Amtrak serves Minneapolis–St. Paul en route from Chicago to Seattle. The total number of Minnesota riders in 1995/96 came to 126,967. Minnesota had 130,815 miles (210,481 kilometers) of state and local roads and streets in 1997. In 1997 there were 2.31 million registered automobiles, 1.59 million trucks, and 13,817 buses.

The port of Duluth-Superior, at the western terminus of the Great Lakes–St. Lawrence Seaway, is the 19th busiest US port, handling over 42 million tons of domestic and international cargo in 1998. The ports of Minneapolis and St. Paul together handled more than 6.3 million tons of cargo that year. As of 1997, the state had 370 airports and 70 seaplane bases. Minneapolis–St. Paul International Airport handled 154,956 departing flights, boarding 12.6 million passengers.

11 HISTORY

At the time of European penetration in the 17th and early 18th centuries, the two principal Native American nations were the Dakota and, after 1700, the Ojibwa. The first Europeans whose travels through the region have been documented were Pierre Esprit Radisson and his brother-in-law, Médart Chouart, Sieur de Groseilliers, who probably reached the interior of northern Minnesota in the 1650s. In 1679, Daniel Greysolon, Sieur Duluth, formally claimed the region for King Louis XIV of France.

In the two centuries before statehood, French, English, and American explorers, fur traders, and missionaries came to Minnesota. Competition for control of the upper Mississippi Valley ended with the British victory in the French and Indian War, which placed the portion of Minnesota east of the Mississippi under British control. The land west of the Mississippi was ceded by France to Spain in 1762. Although the Spanish paid little attention to their northern territory, the British immediately sent in fur traders and explorers.

US Claims

There was little activity in the region during the Revolutionary War, and for a few decades afterward, the British continued to pursue their interests there. After the War of 1812, the US Congress passed an act curbing British participation in the fur trade. Under the Northwest Ordinance of 1787, Minnesota east of the Mississippi became part of the Northwest Territory. Most of western Minnesota was acquired by the US as part of the Louisiana Purchase of 1803. The Red River Valley became a secure part of the US after an agreement with England on the northern boundary was reached in 1818.

In 1819, a military post was established on land acquired from the Dakota by Lieutenant Zebulon Pike, on a bluff overlooking the junction of the Mississippi and Minnesota rivers. For three decades, Ft. Snelling served as the principal center of civilization in Minnesota and the key frontier outpost in the northwest.

Beginning in 1837, a series of treaties with the Dakota and Ojibwa transferred large areas of tribal land to the US government, cutting off the profitable relationship between fur traders and Native Americans and opening the land for lumbering, farming, and settlement. In 1849, the Minnesota Territory was established, and in 1851 the legislature named St. Paul as the capital. As lumbering grew and additional treaties opened up more land, the population boomed, reaching a total of more than 150,000 by 1857.

Statehood

On 11 May 1858, Minnesota officially became the 32d state. In the first presidential election in which Minnesota participated, Abraham Lincoln, the Republican candidate, easily carried the state. When the Civil War broke out, Minnesota was the first state to answer Lincoln's call for troops. In all, Minnesota supplied more than 20,000 men to fight for the Union.

More challenging to the defense of Minnesota was the Dakota uprising of 1862, led by chief Little Crow, in which more than 300 whites and an unknown number of Native Americans were killed. In the aftermath, 38 Dakota captives were hanged and the Dakota remaining in Minnesota were removed to reservations in Nebraska. Also during 1862, Minnesota's first railroad joined St. Anthony (Minneapolis) and St. Paul with 10 miles (16 kilometers) of track.

The railroads soon ushered in an era of large-scale commercial farming. Wheat provided the biggest cash crop, as exports

Minnesota Governors: 1858–2001

1858–1860	Henry Hastings Sibley	Democrat	1925–1931	Theodore Christianson	Republican
1860–1863	Alexander Ramsey	Republican	1931–1936	Floyd Bjornstjerne Olson	Farmer Laborite
1863–1864	Henry Adoniram Swift	Republican	1936–1937	Hjalmar Petersen	Farmer Laborite
1864–1866	Stephen Miller	Republican	1937–1939	Elmer Austin Benson	Farmer Laborite
1866–1870	William Rogerson Marshall	Republican	1939–1943	Harold Edward Stassen	Republican
1870–1874	Horace Austin	Republican	1943–1947	Edward John Thye	Republican
1874–1876	Cushman Kellogg Davis	Republican	1947–1951	Luther Wallace Youngdahl	Republican
1876–1882	John Sargent Pillsbury	Republican	1951–1955	Clyde Elmer Anderson	Republican
1882–1887	Lucius Frederick Hubbard	Republican	1955–1961	Orville Lothrop Freeman	D.F.L.
1887–1889	Andrew Ryan McGill	Republican	1961–1963	Elmer Lee Andersen	Republican
1889–1893	William Rush Merriam	Republican	1963–1967	Karl Fritjof Rolvaag	D.F.L.
1893–1895	Knute Nelson	Republican	1967–1971	Harold LeVander	Republican
1895–1899	David Marston Clough	Republican	1971–1976	Wendell Richard Anderson	D.F.L.
1899–1901	John Lind	Popularist Democrat	1976–1979	Rudolph George Perpich	D.F.L.
1901–1905	Samuel Rinnah Van Sant	Republican	1979–1983	Albert Harold Quie	Independent Republican
1905–1909	John Albert Johnson	Democrat	1983–1991	Rudolph George Perpich	D.F.L.
1909–1915	Adolph Olson Eberhart	Republican	1991–1999	Arne Carlson	Republican
1915	Winfield Scott Hammond	Democrat	1999–	Jesse Ventura	Reform
1915–1921	Joseph Alfred Arner Burnquist	Republican			
1921–1925	Jacob Aall Ottesen Preus	Republican		Democrat Farmer Labor – D.F.L.

rose from 2 million bushels in 1860 to 95 million in 1890. Meanwhile, the falls of St. Anthony (Minneapolis) became the major US flour-milling center. By 1880, 27 Minneapolis mills were producing more than 2 million barrels of flour annually. Despite these signs of prosperity, discontent grew among Minnesota farmers, who were plagued by high railroad rates and damaging droughts. The first national farmers' movement, the National Grange of the Patrons of Husbandry, was founded in 1867 by a Minnesotan, Oliver H. Kelley, and spread more rapidly in Minnesota than in any other state.

Industrialization

Most immigrants during the 1860s and 1870s settled on the rich farmland of the north and west, but after 1880 the cities and industries grew more rapidly. When iron ore was discovered in the 1880s in the sparsely settled northeast, even that part of the state attracted settlers, many of them immigrants from eastern and southern Europe. Before the turn of the century, Duluth had become a major lake port, and by the eve of World War I, Minnesota had become a national iron-mining center.

The economic picture changed after the war. Facing the depletion of their forests and an agricultural depression, Minnesotans adapted to the new realities in various ways. Farmers planted corn, soybeans, and sugar beets along with wheat, and new food-processing industries developed. In 1948, for the first time, the dollar value of all manufactured products exceeded total cash farm receipts. Later were added business machines, electronics, computers, and other high-technology industries.

Economic disruption and the growth of cities and industries encouraged challenges to the Republican leadership from Democrats and third parties. John Johnson, a progressive Democratic governor first elected in 1904, was especially active in securing legislation to regulate the insurance industry. His successor, Republican Adolph Eberhart, promoted numerous progressive measures, including one establishing direct primary elections. The Farmer-Labor Party had many electoral successes in the 1920s and reached its peak with the election of Floyd B. Olson to the governorship in 1930. Olson introduced a graduated income tax and other progressive measures, but his death in office in 1936 was a crippling blow to the party.

In 1938, the Republicans recaptured the governorship with the election of Harold E. Stassen. However, a successful merger of the Farmer-Labor and Democratic parties was engineered in 1943–44. After World War II, Hubert Humphrey (later a US vice-president) and his colleagues Orville Freeman, Eugene McCarthy, and Eugenie Anderson emerged as leaders of this new coalition. Their political heir, Walter Mondale, was vice-president in 1977–81 but, as the Democratic presidential candidate in 1984, lost the election in a Republican landslide, carrying only his native state and the District of Columbia.

In March 1998, Rep. Collin Peterson, whose legislative district includes the

Minnesota Presidential Vote by Political Parties, 1948–2000

YEAR	MINNESOTA WINNER	DEMOCRAT(1)	REPUBLICAN(2)	PROGRESSIVE	SOCIALIST	SOCIALIST LABOR(3)
1948	*Truman (D)	692,966	483,617	27,866	4,646	2,525
1952	*Eisenhower (R)	608,458	763,211	2,666	—	2,383
					SOC. WORKERS	
1956	*Eisenhower (R)	617,525	719,302	—	1,098	2,080
1960	*Kennedy (D)	779,933	757,915	—	3,077	962
1964	*Johnson (D)	991,117	559,624	—	1,177	2,544
						AMERICAN IND.
1968	Humphrey (D)	857,738	658,643	—	—	68,931
				PEOPLE'S		AMERICAN
1972	*Nixon (R)	802,346	898,269	2,805	4,261	31,407
				LIBERTARIAN		
1976	*Carter (D)	1,070,440	819,395	3,529	4,149	13,592
					CITIZENS	
1980	Carter (D)	954,173	873,268	31,593	8,406	6,136
1984	Mondale (D)	1,036,364	1,032,603	2,996	1,219	—
				MINN. PROG.	SOCIALIST WORKERS	
1988	Dukakis (D)	1,109,471	962,337	5,109	5,403	2,155
				IND. (Perot)	CONSTITUTION	
1992	*Clinton (D)	1,020,997	747,841	3,373	562,506	3,363
					GREEN (Nader)	
1996	*Clinton (D)	1,120,438	766,476	8,271	257,704	24,908
				REFORM		
2000	Gore (D)	1,168,266	1,109,659	126,696	22,166	1,022

*Won US presidential election.
1 Called Democratic-Farmer-Labor Party in Minnesota.
2 Since 1976, called Independent-Republican in Minnesota.
3 Appeared as Industrial Government Party on the ballot.

Northwest Angle's population of about 100, proposed an amendment to the US Constitution. The proposal would allow the residents to vote on the possibility of secession from the United States in order to join Canada. Sport fishing is the Northwest Angle's only significant business. Fishing restrictions imposed by nearby Ontario on non-Canadian fishers have impaired business at the ten Northwest Angle fishing resorts so much that its people are considering joining Canada rather than lose their livelihood. The proposal marked the first time since the 1860s that a portion of any state had earnestly tried to secede.

12 STATE GOVERNMENT

The Minnesota legislature consists of a 67-member senate and a 134-member house of representatives. Senators serve four years and representatives two years. The governor and lieutenant governor are jointly elected for four-year terms. Other constitutional officers are the secretary of state, auditor, treasurer, and attorney general, all serving for four years.

Once a bill is passed by a majority of both houses, the governor may sign it, veto it in whole or in part, or pocket-veto it by failing to act within 14 days of adjournment. A two-thirds vote of both houses is sufficient to override a veto. Constitutional amendments require the approval of a majority of both houses of the legislature and are subject to ratification by the electorate.

13 POLITICAL PARTIES

The two major political parties are the Democratic-Farmer-Labor Party (DFL) and the Independent-Republican Party (IR), as Minnesota's Republican Party is now officially called. The Republican Party dominated Minnesota politics from the 1860s through the 1920s, except for a period around the turn of the century. The DFL, formed in 1944 by merger between the Democratic Party and the Farmer-Labor Party, rose to prominence in the 1950s under US Senator Hubert Humphrey.

Minnesota is famous as a breeding ground for presidential candidates, who include Republican Governor Harold Stassen (1948, 1952, and later years); and Democrats Vice-President Hubert Humphrey (1968), US Senator Eugene McCarthy (1968, 1976), and Walter Mondale (1976, 1980, 1984). Mondale was chosen in 1976 by Jimmy Carter as his vice-presidential running mate; he again ran with Carter in 1980, when the two lost their bid for reelection. In the 1984 election, Minnesota was the only state to favor the Walter Mondale-Geraldine Ferraro ticket. In the 2000 elections Democrat Al Gore carried the state with 48% of the vote. Republican George W. Bush earned 46%.

In 1990, after serving four terms, Democrat Rudy Perpich lost the governorship to Independent-Republican Arne Carlson, who was reelected in 1994. Minnesota's voters stunned the nation in 1998 when they elected Independent Jesse Ventura, a former professional wrestler, as governor. In 1999, the two US Senate seats were held by Democrat Paul Wellstone and Republican Rod Grahams, while the Democrats controlled the state's congressional delegation. In 2001, there were 39 members of the DFL party serving in the Minnesota state senate, and 27 Independent-Republicans. Party representation in the state house consisted of 65 Democratic-Farmer-Labor members and 69 Independent-Republicans.

14 LOCAL GOVERNMENT

Minnesota is divided into 87 counties and 13 regional administrations. As of 1997, the state had 1,796 townships (more than any other state) and 855 municipal governments. Each of Minnesota's counties is governed by a board of commissioners. Other elected officials include the auditor, treasurer, recorder, and sheriff. Regional development commissions, or RDCs, prepare and adopt regional development plans and review applications for loans and grants. The mayor-council system is the most common form of city government. Townships are governed by a board of three supervisors and other officials.

15 JUDICIAL SYSTEM

Minnesota's highest court is the supreme court, consisting of a chief justice and six associate justices. The district court, divided into ten judicial districts, is the principal court of original jurisdiction. County courts, operating in all counties of the state except two, exercise civil jurisdiction in cases where the amount in contention is $5,000 or less, and criminal jurisdiction in preliminary hearings and misdemeanors. They also hear cases involving family disputes, and have joint jurisdiction with the district court in

Photo credit: © Minnesota Office of Tourism.

The Split Rock Lighthouse shines a welcome to ships on Lake Superior.

divorces, adoptions, and certain other proceedings.

The probate division of the county court system presides over guardianship and incompetency proceedings and all cases relating to the disposing of estates. Crime rates are generally below the national average. In 1998, Minnesota's total crime rate per 100,000 was 4,046.5. Federal and state correctional institutions had a total population of 5,753 in June 1999. That year, Minnesota had 121 prisoners per 100,000 state residents.

16 MIGRATION

Especially since 1920, new arrivals from other states and countries have been relatively few. The state experienced a net loss from migration of 80,000 between 1970 and 1980, but nearly halted the trend in the 1980s when immigration nearly equaled emigration. As of 1990, 73.6% of all Minnesota residents were native-born. During 1990–98, Minnesota had a net gain of 71,000 in interstate migration and 47,000 in migration from abroad. Within the state, there has been a long-term movement to metropolitan areas and especially to the suburbs of major cities. From 1980 to 1996, the population of the Minneapolis-St. Paul metropolitan area grew by almost 25%.

17 ECONOMY

Furs, wheat, pine lumber, and high-grade iron ore were once the basis of Minnesota's economy. As these resources diminished, however, the state turned to wood pulp, dairy products, corn and soybeans, taconite, and manufacturing, often in such food-related industries as meat-packing, canning, and the processing of dairy products.

The leading sources of income in Minnesota have shifted again in recent years. Manufacturing remains central to the state's economy, but finance, real estate, and insurance have also come to play a dominant role. Government and trade activities rose significantly between the late 1960s and early 1980s, while the role played by manufacturing and construction declined. By the mid-1990s, private goods-producing industries accounted for 28% of the state's economic output, while private services-producing industries contributed 61%. Government accounted for 11%.

18 INCOME

In 1998, Minnesota ranked eleventh among the 50 states in personal income per capita (per person) at $29,263. The median household income in 1998 was $44,579. In 1998, 9.9% of all state residents lived below the poverty level.

19 INDUSTRY

In the early 20th century, canning and meat-packing were among the state's largest industries. While food and food products remain important, the state's economy has diversified significantly from its early beginnings. Minnesota now has high-technology industries such as computer-manufacturing, scientific instruments, and medical products as well as resource-based industries such as food products and wood products.

The total value of shipments by manufacturers in 1997 exceeded $78 billion, with food products accounting for about one-fifth. Industry is concentrated in the state's southeast region, especially in the Twin Cities (Minneapolis-St. Paul) area. Among the well-known national firms with headquarters in Minnesota are 3M (Minnesota Mining and Manufacturing), General Mills, Honeywell, and Hormel Foods.

Photo credit: © Nathan Benn/Woodfin Camp.

A broker is working in the trading pit of Minneapolis Grain Exchange.

20 LABOR

About one-third of the state's labor force is employed in agriculture or agriculture-related industries, most notably food processing. In 1998, the civilian labor force totaled 2.68 million persons, of whom 2.5% were unemployed. Some 18.8% of all workers were union members in 1998.

21 AGRICULTURE

Cash receipts from farm marketings totaled $7 billion in 1999, placing Minnesota sixth among the 50 states. For 1998, Minnesota ranked first in the production of sugar beets, and sweet corn and green peas for processing; second in flaxseed; and third in oats and soybeans, and spring wheat. As of 1998, the state had 80,000 farms, covering 28.9 million acres (11.7 million hectares), or 57% of the state's total land area. Just under 5% of the population lives on a farm.

The main farming areas are in the south and southwest, where corn, soybeans, and oats are important, and in the Red River Valley along the western border, where oats, wheat, sugar beets, and potatoes are among the chief crops. The following table shows selected major crops in 1998:

CROP	PRODUCTION	
Soybeans	285 million	bushels
Corn for grain	1 billion	bushels
Wheat	80.4 million	bushels
Oats	9.53 million	bushels
Sugar beets	8.25 million	tons

22 DOMESTICATED ANIMALS

Excluding the northeast, livestock-raising is dispersed throughout the state. In 1999, Minnesota had 2.5 million cattle and 5.7 million hogs (third in the US).

During 1997, milk production ranked fifth among the states, at 9.1 billion pounds (4.1 billion kilograms). Minnesota produced more turkey in 1997 than any other state except North Carolina; 1.01 billion pounds (460 million kilograms), valued at $395.7 million.

23 FISHING

Commercial fishers in 1998 landed 427,000 pounds (194,000 kilograms) of fish, valued at $224,000. The catch

Photo credit: ©Minnesota Office of Tourism.

Dancers at the Red Lake Native American Pow Wow. The two historic nations in Minnesota were the Dakota and the Ojibwa, or Chippewa.

included herring and smelts from Lake Superior, whitefish and yellow pike from large inland lakes, and carp and catfish from the Mississippi and Minnesota rivers. Sport-fishing attracts some 1.5 million anglers annually to the state's 2.6. million acres (1.1 million hectares) of fishing lakes and 7,000 miles (11,000 kilometers) of fishing streams. These are stocked with trout, bass, pike, muskie, and other fish.

24 FORESTRY

Forests, which originally occupied two-thirds of Minnesota's land area, have been depleted by lumbering, farming, and forest fires. Forestland covered 16.8 million acres (5.9 million hectares), or 36% of the state's total area, in 1997. Over half the timber that is harvested is used in paper products; 10% is used in furniture; and 30% is used in wood products. Mills that process raw logs account for half of forest and forest-product employment in Minnesota.

The state's two national forests—Superior and Chippewa—together cover 2.7 million acres (1.1 million hectares). More than 3 million acres (1.2 million hectares) are planted each year—more than enough to replace those harvested or destroyed by fire, insects, or disease.

25 MINING

The value of nonfuel mineral production in Minnesota in 1998 was estimated to be about $1.73 billion. Iron ore, Minnesota's leading mineral commodity, accounted for 85% ($1.47 billion) of the state's total mineral value. The combined value of construction sand and gravel, and crushed stone—the two other leading mineral commodities produced—accounted for 12% of Minnesota's mineral value in 1998. Minnesota ranked first nationally in the production of iron ore.

26 ENERGY AND POWER

Minnesota produced 44 billion kilowatt hours of electricity in 1998. Steam-generating plants accounted for 78% of total installed capacity; most plants were coal-fired. There are three nuclear reactors. Minnesota's 7 million acres (2.8 million hectares) of peat lands, the state's only known fossil fuel resource, constitute nearly half of the US total (excluding Alaska).

27 COMMERCE

Access to the Great Lakes, the St. Lawrence Seaway, and the Atlantic Ocean, as well as to the Mississippi River and the Gulf of Mexico, helps make Minnesota a major marketing and distribution center for the upper Midwest. The state's wholesale sales totaled $103 billion in 1997; retail sales were $49 billion. The Minneapolis–St. Paul area accounted for 63% of the state's retail sales. Exports to foreign countries amounted to $9.1 billion in 1998.

28 PUBLIC FINANCE

Revenues for 1997 were $22.88 billion; expenditures were $18.44 billion. As of 1997, the state's outstanding debt totaled $4.86 billion, or $1,037 per capita (per person).

29 TAXATION

Minnesota ranked fourth among the 50 states in 1997 in state taxes collected per person ($2,395). Corporate profits and individual income are taxed at graduated rates. There is also a 6.5% state sales tax, a gasoline tax, and a cigarette tax. Gift and inheritance taxes were repealed in 1980.

Minnesota has an estate tax, generally only on amounts above $200,000, with an additional $250,000 exemption for a surviving spouse. Commercial, industrial, and residential property is subject to property tax, the principal source of revenue for local governing units. Minnesota paid out more than $24.3 billion in federal taxes in 1995 and received $19 billion in federal expenditures—or, for every $1 paid to the federal government it received 78¢ in federal funding.

30 HEALTH

The death rates in 1998 per 100,000 population for two leading causes, heart disease and cerebrovascular disease, were 198.3 and 60.5, respectively. In 1998, the overall death rate of 787.1 per 100,000 was below the national rate of 864.7. In 1998, Minnesota had 136 community hospitals, with 16,486 beds. The average hospital expense in 1998 was $768 per inpatient day, or $6,390 for an average cost per stay. Minnesota had 247 physicians per 100,000 in 1997. In 1998, licensed full-time nurses numbered about 11,000. Some 9.3% of state residents did not have health insurance in 1998.

The Mayo Clinic, developed by Drs. Charles H. and William J. Mayo in the 1890s and early 1900s, was the first private clinic in the US and became a world-renowned center for surgery.

31 HOUSING

According to a 1999 estimate based on the 1990 census, Minnesota had 2 million year-round housing units. The median valuation of an owner-occupied house in 1998 was $128,000. In 1998, 30,400 new units valued at $3.5 billion were authorized for construction. The median monthly cost for an owner with a mortgage was $724 in 1990, and $186 for an owner without a mortgage. Renters paid a median amount of $422 per month in 1990.

32 EDUCATION

In 1998, according to state data, 89.4% of Minnesotans aged 25 or older were high school graduates. In fall 1997, Minnesota had an estimated 853,621 public school students, and 48,400 teachers. Expenditures for public elementary and secondary schools amounted to $7,326 per student in 1999/00. There were 90,400 students enrolled in private elementary and secondary schools in fall 1997. The state has four major systems of public postsecondary education. The state's 48 public and private four-year colleges and universities had an enrollment of 269,887 in fall 1997.

The University of Minnesota had 59,185 students in fall 2000, and there were 26 private colleges, including Carleton College, a notable independent institution.

33 ARTS

The Ordway Music Theater in St. Paul is the home of the Minnesota Opera Company and of the St. Paul Chamber Orchestra. The Minnesota Orchestra enlisted Eiji Ouie as musical director in 1995; Hugh Wolf became music director of the St. Paul Chamber Orchestra in 1992. Bobby McFerrin became creative chair of the St. Paul Chamber Orchestra in 1994. The Minnesota Opera, conducted by Phillip Brunelle, and the St. Olaf College Choir, at Northfield, also have national reputations. The Tyrone Guthrie Theater, founded in Minneapolis in 1963, is one of the nation's most prestigious repertory companies.

The Walker Art Center in Minneapolis is an innovative museum with an outstanding contemporary collection, while the Minneapolis Institute of Arts exhibits more traditional works. The Weisman Art Museum of the University of Minnesota is in Minneapolis, and the Minnesota Museum of Art is in St. Paul.

34 LIBRARIES AND MUSEUMS

Minnesota has 361 public libraries. The total number of books and audiovisual items exceeded 16.6 million in 1999, when the state's public library circulation reached 43.5 million. The largest single public library system is the Minneapolis Public Library and Information Center; the leading academic library, with over 2.5

million volumes, is maintained by the University of Minnesota at Minneapolis. There are 164 museums and historic sites. In addition to several noted museums of the visual arts, Minnesota is home to the Mayo Medical Museum at the Mayo Clinic in Rochester. Historic sites include the boyhood home of Charles Lindbergh in Little Falls and the Sauk Centre home of Sinclair Lewis.

35 COMMUNICATIONS

As of 1999, 96.9% of Minnesota's occupied housing units had telephones. Commercial broadcasting began with the opening of the first radio station in 1922. As of 2000 there were 303 radio stations—101 AM and 202 FM—and 35 television stations. As of 1996, nine major cable television systems served the state. In 2000, a total of 116,792 Internet domain names had been registered in Minnesota.

36 PRESS

In April 1982, Minneapolis's only daily newspapers were merged into the *Minneapolis Star and Tribune.* As of 1998, the state had 14 morning dailies, 11 evening dailies, and 14 Sunday papers. The leading dailies, with their daily circulations in 1998 are the *Minneapolis Star and Tribune* (334,751); the *St. Paul Pioneer Press* (199,119); and the *Duluth News-Tribune* (51,223). As of 1997, 337 weekly newspapers and 176 periodicals were being published in Minnesota.

37 TOURISM, TRAVEL, AND RECREATION

With its lakes and parks, ski trails and campsites, and historical and cultural attractions, Minnesota provides ample recreational opportunities for residents and visitors alike.

Besides the museums, sports stadiums, and concert halls in the big cities, Minnesota's attractions include the 220,000-acre (80,000-hectare) Voyageurs National Park, near the Canadian border; Grand Portage National Monument, in Arrowhead Country, a former fur-trading center with a restored trading post; and Lumbertown USA, a restored 1870s lumber community.

The state maintains and operates 66 parks, 9,240 miles (14,870 kilometers) of trails, 10 scenic and natural areas, 5 recreation areas, and 18 canoe and boating routes. Minnesota also has 288 primary wildlife refuges. An estimated 723,000 people enjoy boating each year on Minnesota's scenic waterways. Winter sports have gained in popularity, and many parks are now used heavily all year round.

38 SPORTS

There are four major league professional teams in Minnesota: the Minnesota Twins of Major League Baseball, the Minnesota Vikings of the National Football League, the Minnesota Timberwolves of the National Basketball Association, and the Minnesota Wild of the National Hockey League. The Minnesota North Stars of the National Hockey League moved to Dallas in 1993. In collegiate sports, the University of Minnesota Golden Gophers are a

Big Ten football team. The university is probably best known for its ice hockey team, which supplied the coach, Herb Brooks, and many of the players for the gold medal–winning US team in the 1980 Winter Olympics.

39 FAMOUS MINNESOTANS

No Minnesotan has been elected to the US presidency, but several have sought the office, including two who served as vice-president. Hubert Horatio Humphrey (b.South Dakota, 1911–78) was vice-president under Lyndon Johnson and a serious contender for the presidency in 1960, 1968, and 1972. Humphrey's protégé, Walter Frederick "Fritz" Mondale (b.1928)—after serving as vice-president under Jimmy Carter (and as Carter's running mate in his unsuccessful bid for reelection in 1980)—won the Democratic presidential nomination in 1984. Warren Earl Burger (1907–95) of St. Paul was named chief justice of the US Supreme Court in 1969. Three other Minnesotans have served on the court: Pierce Butler (1866–1939); William O. Douglas (1898–1980); and Harry A. Blackmun (b.Illinois, 1908–97).

The first woman ambassador in US history was Eugenie M. Anderson (b.Iowa, 1909–97).

The Mayo Clinic was founded in Minnesota by Dr. William W. Mayo (b.England, 1819–1911) and developed through the efforts of his sons, Drs. William H. (1861–1939) and Charles H. (1865–1939) Mayo. Oil magnate J. Paul Getty (1892–1976) was a Minnesota native, as was Richard W. Sears (1863–1914), founder of Sears, Roebuck.

The first US citizen ever to be awarded the Nobel Prize for literature was Sinclair Lewis (1885–1951), whose novel *Main Street* (1920) was modeled on life in his hometown of Sauk Centre. Prominent literary figures besides Sinclair Lewis include F. Scott Fitzgerald (1896–1940), well known for his classic novel *The Great Gatsby*.

Minnesota-born entertainers include Judy Garland (Frances Gumm, 1922–69), Bob Dylan (Robert Zimmerman, b.1941), and Jessica Lange (b.1949). In 1961 Minnesotan Roger Maris (1934–85) set the record for the most home runs hit in a baseball season; his record stood until 1998.

40 BIBLIOGRAPHY

Aylesworth, Thomas G. *Western Great Lakes: Illinois, Iowa, Minnesota, Wisconsin.* New York: Chelsea House, 1996.

Hazard, Evan B. *The Mammals of Minnesota.* Minneapolis: University of Minnesota Press, 1982.

Hintz, Martin. *Minnesota.* New York: Children's Press, 2000.

Lass, William E. *Minnesota: A Bicentennial History.* New York: Norton, 1977.

Sateren, Shelley Swanson, ed. *A Civil War Drummer Boy: the Diary of William Bircher, 1861–1865.* Mankato, Minn.: Blue Earth Books, 2000.

Uschan, Michael V. *Jesse Ventura.* San Diego: Lucent Books, 2001.

Web sites

State of Minnesota. All About Minnesota. [Online] Available http://www.state.mn.us/aam Accessed May 16, 2001.

State of Minnesota. North Star: Minnesota Government Information and Services. [Online] Available http://www.state.mn.us/ Accessed May 16, 2001.

MISSISSIPPI

State of Mississippi

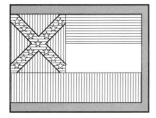

ORIGIN OF STATE NAME: Derived from the Ojibwa Indian words *misi sipi,* meaning great river.

NICKNAME: The Magnolia State.

CAPITAL: Jackson.

ENTERED UNION: 10 December 1817 (20th).

SONG: "Go, Mississippi."

MOTTO: *Virtute et armis* (By valor and arms).

COAT OF ARMS: An American eagle clutches an olive branch and a quiver of arrows in its talons.

FLAG: Crossed blue bars, on a red field, bordered with white and emblazoned with 13 white stars—the motif of the Confederate battle flag—cover the upper left corner. The field consists of three stripes of equal width, blue, white, and red.

OFFICIAL SEAL: The seal consists of the coat of arms surrounded by the words "The Great Seal of the State of Mississippi."

MAMMAL: White-tailed deer.

WATER MAMMAL: Porpoise.

BIRD: Mockingbird.

WATERFOWL: Wood duck.

FISH: Largemouth or black bass.

INSECT: Honeybee.

FOSSIL: Prehistoric whale.

FLOWER: Magnolia.

TREE: Magnolia.

STONE: Petrified wood.

BEVERAGE: Milk.

TIME: 6 AM CST = noon GMT.

1 LOCATION AND SIZE

Located in the eastern south-central US, Mississippi ranks 32d in size among the 50 states. The total area of Mississippi is 47,233 square miles (122,333 square kilometers). Mississippi's maximum east-west extension is 188 miles (303 kilometers); its greatest north-south distance is 352 miles (566 kilometers). The total boundary length of Mississippi is 1,015 miles (1,634 kilometers). Several small islands lie off the coast.

2 TOPOGRAPHY

Mississippi lies entirely within two lowland plains: the Mississippi Alluvial Plain (popularly known as the Delta), extending eastward from the Mississippi, and the Gulf Coastal Plain, covering the rest of the state. Mississippi's maximum elevation is

806 feet (246 meters) at Woodall Mountain in the north.

The state's largest lakes—Grenada, Sardis, Enid, and Arkabutla—are all artificial. Mississippi's longest inland river, the Pearl, flows about 490 miles (790 kilometers) from the eastern center of the state to the Gulf of Mexico.

3 CLIMATE

Mississippi has short winters and long, humid summers. Summer temperatures vary little from one part of the state to another, averaging around 80°F (27°C). During the winter, however, because of the temperate influence of the Gulf of Mexico, the southern coast is much warmer than the north. In January, Biloxi averages 52°F (11°C) to Oxford's 41°F (5°C). The lowest temperature ever recorded in Mississippi was –19°F (–28°C) in 1966; the highest, 115°F (46°C), was set in 1930. The north-central region averages 53 inches (135 centimeters) of precipitation a year; the coastal region, 62 inches (157 centimeters). Mississippi lies in the path of hurricanes moving northward from the Gulf of Mexico during the late summer and fall.

4 PLANTS AND ANIMALS

Post and white oaks, hickory, and magnolia grow in the forests of the uplands. Various willows and gums (including the tupelo) are in the Delta; and longleaf pine is in the Piney Woods. Wildflowers include the black-eyed Susan and Cherokee rose. Common among the state's mammals are the opossum, armadillo, and coyote. Birds include varieties of wren, thrush, and hawk, along with numerous waterfowl

Mississippi Population Profile

Total population in 2000:	2,844,658
Population change, 1990–2000:	10.5%
Hispanic or Latino†:	1.4%
Population by race	
One race:	99.3%
White:	61.4%
Black or African American:	36.3%
American Indian/Alaska Native:	0.4%
Asian:	0.7%
Native Hawaiian/Pacific Islander:	—
Some other race:	0.5%
Two or more races:	0.7%

Population by Age Group

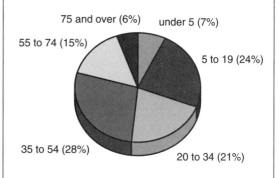

75 and over (6%)
under 5 (7%)
55 to 74 (15%)
5 to 19 (24%)
35 to 54 (28%)
20 to 34 (21%)

Top Cities by Population

City	Population	% change 1990–2000
Jackson	184,256	–6.3
Gulfport	71,127	74.4
Biloxi	50,644	9.3
Hattiesburg	44,779	6.9
Greenville	41,633	–7.9
Meridian	39,968	–2.6
Tupelo	34,211	11.5
Southhaven	28,977	61.4
Vicksburg	26,407	26.3
Pascagoula	26,200	1.2

Notes: †A person of Hispanic or Latino origin may be of any race. NA indicates that data are not available.
Sources: U.S. Census Bureau. Public Information Office. *Demographic Profiles.* [Online] Available http://www.census.gov/Press-Release/www/2001/demoprofile.html. Accessed June 1, 2001. U.S. Census Bureau. *Census 2000: Redistricting Data.* Press release issued by the Redistricting Data Office. Washington, D.C., March, 2001.

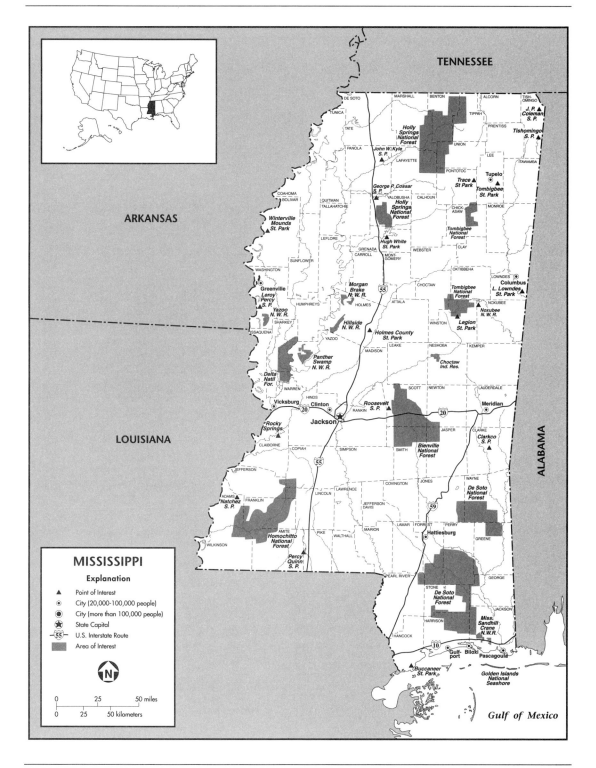

and seabirds. Black bass, perch, and mullet are common freshwater fish. The Florida panther and gray bat are among the state's endangered species.

5 ENVIRONMENTAL PROTECTION

The Mississippi Department of Environmental Quality (MDEQ) is responsible for most environmental regulatory programs in the state. The agency implements one of the premier pollution prevention programs in the nation. As of 1998, Mississippi had three hazardous waste sites.

6 POPULATION

With a 2000 census population of 2.84 million, Mississippi ranked 31st among the 50 states. The same year, the population density was 60.6 persons per square mile (23.4 persons per square kilometer), comparable to the density of Minnesota. Mississippi is one of the most rural states in the US. Mississippi's largest city, Jackson, had a 2000 population of 184,256. Gulfport had a population of 71,127; Biloxi, 50,644; and Hattiesburg, 44,779. Over 30% of the population in 2000 was 19 years of age and younger.

7 ETHNIC GROUPS

Since 1860, blacks have constituted a larger proportion of the population of Mississippi than of any other state (although the District of Columbia does have a higher proportion). Because of out-migration, the proportion of black Mississippians declined to an estimated 36.4% in 1997, when the state had 1.7 million whites, 993,400 blacks, 18,500 Asians and Pacific Islanders, and 9,900 Native Americans. Of the total population, 21,600 (0.8%) were of Hispanic origin.

8 LANGUAGES

English in the state is largely Southern, with some South Midland speech in northern and eastern Mississippi because of population drift from Tennessee. In 1990, 97.2% of Mississippi residents five years old and older spoke only English in the home. Other languages spoken at home, and the number of people who spoke them, included Spanish, 25,061, and French, 13,215.

9 RELIGIONS

Protestants have dominated Mississippi since the late 18th century. During 1990, membership in the two principal Protestant denominations was: Southern Baptist Convention, 869,942 known members; and United Methodist Church, 240,325. There were 94,948 Roman Catholics and an estimated 2,466 Jews in 1990.

10 TRANSPORTATION

In 1998, there were 2,593 rail miles (4,172 kilometers) of track in the state. Amtrak operated two long-distance trains through Mississippi, with stops at 13 stations in the state. The total number of Mississippi riders was 94,930 in 1996.

Mississippi had 73,150 miles (117,698 kilometers) of roads at the end of 1997, including 685 miles (1,102 kilometers) of interstate highways. In 1997 there were 2.23 million registered motor vehicles, including 1.26 million automobiles and 960,747 trucks. Mississippi has two deep-

Mississippi Population by Race

Census 2000 was the first national census in which the instructions to respondents said, "Mark one or more races." This table shows the number of people who are of one, two, or three or more races. For those claiming two races, the number of people belonging to the various categories is listed. The U.S. government conducts a census of the population every ten years.

	Number	Percent
Total population	2,844,658	100.0
One race	2,824,637	99.3
Two races	18,382	0.6
White *and* Black or African American	3,462	0.1
White *and* American Indian/Alaska Native	5,259	0.2
White *and* Asian	2,402	0.1
White *and* Native Hawaiian/Pacific Islander	287	—
White *and* some other race	2,885	0.1
Black or African American *and* American Indian/Alaska Native	1,372	—
Black or African American *and* Asian	802	—
Black or African American *and* Native Hawaiian/Pacific Islander	230	—
Black or African American *and* some other race	785	—
American Indian/Alaska Native *and* Asian	131	—
American Indian/Alaska Native *and* Native Hawaiian/Pacific Islander	13	—
American Indian/Alaska Native *and* some other race	186	—
Asian *and* Native Hawaiian/Pacific Islander	169	—
Asian *and* some other race	344	—
Native Hawaiian/Pacific Islander *and* some other race	55	—
Three or more races	1,639	0.1

Source: U.S. Census Bureau. *Census 2000: Redistricting Data.* Press release issued by the Redistricting Data Office. Washington, D.C., March, 2001. A dash (—) indicates that the percent is less than 0.1.

water seaports, Gulfport and Pascagoula. The Tennessee-Tombigbee Waterway links the Ohio River and the Gulf Coast. The Yazoo is also open to river traffic. The most important airfield, Allen C. Thompson Field (near Jackson) boarded 375,604 passengers in 1996.

11 HISTORY

Upon the appearance of the first Spanish explorers in the early 16th century, Mississippi's Native Americans numbered some 30,000 and were divided into 15 tribes. Soon after the French settled in 1699, however, only three large tribes remained: the Choctaw, the Chickasaw, and the Natchez. The French destroyed the Natchez in 1729–30 in retaliation for the massacre of a French settlement.

Spaniards, of whom Hernando de Soto in 1540–41 was the most notable, explored the area that is now Mississippi in the first half of the 16th century. The French explorer Robert Cavelier, Sieur de la Salle, entered the lower Mississippi Valley in 1682 and named the entire area Louisiana in honor of the French King, Louis XIV. Soon the French opened settlements at Biloxi Bay (1699), Mobile (1702), Natchez (1716), and finally New Orleans (1718). After losing the French and Indian War, France ceded Louisiana to Spain, which ceded the portion of the colony east

Vicksburg National Military Park. Vicksburg was the site of a major battle during the Civil War.

of the Mississippi to England, which governed the new lands as West Florida.

During the Revolutionary War, Spain once again seized West Florida, which it continued to rule almost to the end of the century, although the US claimed the region after 1783. The US Congress organized the Mississippi Territory in 1798. The territory's large size convinced Congress to organize the eastern half as the Alabama Territory in 1817. Congress then offered admission to the western half, which became the nation's 20th state—Mississippi—on 10 December.

State Development

After the opening of fertile Choctaw and Chickasaw lands for sale and settlement in the 1820s, cotton agriculture increased. Slavery was used to make farming profitable. As the profitability and number of slaves increased, so did attempts by ruling white Mississippians to justify slavery morally, socially, and economically. After Lincoln's election to the US presidency, Mississippi became, on 9 January 1861, the second southern state to secede. Union forces maneuvered before Vicksburg for more than a year before Grant besieged the city and forced its surrender on 4 July 1863. Along with Vicksburg went the western half of Mississippi. Of the 78,000 Mississippians who fought in the Civil War, nearly 30,000 died.

Reconstruction was a tumultuous period during which the Republican Party

Mississippi Governors: 1817–2001

1817–1820	David Holmes	Dem-Rep		1896–1900	Anselm Joseph McLaurin	Democrat
1820–1822	George Poindexter	Dem-Rep		1900–1904	Andrew Houston Longino	Democrat
1822–1825	Walter Leake	Republican		1904–1908	James Kimble Vardaman	Democrat
1825–1826	Gerard Chittoque Brandon	Jacksonian		1908–1912	Edmond Favor Noel	Democrat
1826	David Holmes	Dem-Rep		1912–1916	Earl LeRoy Brewer	Democrat
1826–1832	Gerard Chittoque Brandon	Jacksonian		1916–1920	Theodore Gilmore Bilbo	Democrat
1832–1833	Abram Marshall Scott	Nat-Rep		1920–1924	Lee Maurice Russell	Democrat
1833	Charles Lynch	Whig		1924–1927	Henry Lewis Whitfield	Democrat
1833–1835	Hiram George Runnels	Jacksonian		1927–1928	Heron Dennis Murphree	Democrat
1835–1836	John Anthony Quitman	Democrat		1928–1932	Theodore Gilmore Bilbo	Democrat
1836–1838	Charles Lynch	Whig		1932–1936	Martin Sennett Conner	Democrat
1838–1842	Alexander Gallatin McNutt	Democrat		1936–1940	Hugh Lawson White	Democrat
1842–1844	Tilghman Mayfield Tucker	Democrat		1940–1943	Paul Burney Johnson	Democrat
1844–1848	Albert Gallatin Brown	Democrat		1943–1944	Herron Dennis Murphree	Democrat
1848–1850	Joseph W. Matthews	Democrat		1944–1946	Thomas Lowry Bailey	Democrat
1850–1851	John Anthony Quitman	Democrat		1946–1952	Fielding Lewis Wright	Democrat
1851	John Isaac Guion	Democrat		1952–1956	Hugh Lawson White	Democrat
1851–1852	James Whitfield	Democrat		1956–1960	James Plemon Coleman	Democrat
1852–1854	Henry Stuart Foote	Democrat		1960–1964	Ross Robert Barnett	Democrat
1854	John Jones Pettus	Democrat		1964–1968	Paul Burney Johnson, Jr.	Democrat
1854–1857	John Jones McRae	Democrat		1968–1972	John Bell Williams	Democrat
1857–1859	William McWillie	Democrat		1972–1976	William Lowe Waller	Democrat
1859–1863	John Jones Pettus	Democrat		1976–1980	Charles Clifton Finch	Democrat
1863–1865	Charles Clark	Democrat		1980–1984	William Forrest Winter	Democrat
1865	William Lewis Sharkey	Provisional		1984–1988	William A. Allain	Democrat
1865–1868	Benjamin Grubb Humphreys	Democrat		1988–1992	Ray Mabus, Jr.	Democrat
1868–1870	Adelbert Ames	Military		1992–1999	Kirk Fordice	Republican
1870–1871	James Lusk Alcorn	Republican		1999-	Ronnie Musgrove	Democrat
1871–1874	Ridgley Ceylon Powers	Republican				
1874–1876	Adelbert Ames	Republican				
1876–1882	John Marshall Stone	Democrat			Democratic Republican – Dem-Rep	
1882–1890	Robert Lowry	Democrat			National Republican – Nat-Rep	
1890–1896	John Marshall Stone	Democrat				

encouraged blacks to vote and hold political office, while the native white Democrats resisted full freedom for their former slaves. The era from the end of Reconstruction (1875) to World War II was a period of economic, political, and social stagnation for Mississippi. White Mississippians discriminated against blacks through segregation laws and customs and a new state constitution that removed the last vestiges of their political rights. Mississippi's agricultural economy, dominated by cotton and tenant farming, provided little economic opportunity for landless black farmworkers. According to the Tuskegee Institute, 538 blacks were lynched in Mississippi between 1883 and 1959, more than in any other state.

The Great Depression of the 1930s drove the state's agricultural economy to the brink of disaster. In 1932, cotton sank to five cents a pound, and one-fourth of the state's farmland was forfeited for nonpayment of taxes. World War II brought the first prosperity in a century to Mississippi. The war stimulated industrial growth and agricultural mechanization. By the early 1980s, Mississippi had become an industrial state.

Post-War Politics

Politics in Mississippi have also changed considerably since World War II. Within little more than a generation, legal segregation was destroyed, and black people exercised full political rights for the first time since Reconstruction. However, the "Mississippi Summer" campaign that helped win these rights also resulted in the abduction and murder of three civil rights activists in June 1964, in Philadelphia, Mississippi.

In 1987, Mississippi elected a young reformist governor, Ray Mabus, who enacted the nation's largest teacher pay increase in 1988. As of 1990, the Mississippi Legislature was nearly 23% black in a state in which blacks constitute 33% of the population.

12 STATE GOVERNMENT

Mississippi's two-chamber legislature includes a 52-member senate and a 122-member house of representatives. All state legislators are elected to four-year terms. The governor, lieutenant governor, secretary of state, attorney general, and state treasurer are independently elected for four-year terms.

13 POLITICAL PARTIES

Mississippi has traditionally been a Democratic state during most of the period since the end of Reconstruction. However, its Democratic Party has periodically been splintered along racial lines. During the 1950s and early 1960s, the segregationist White Citizens' Councils were so widespread and influential in the

Mississippi Presidential Vote by Political Parties, 1948–2000

YEAR	MISSISSIPPI WINNER	DEMOCRAT	REPUBLICAN	STATES' RIGHTS DEMOCRAT	SOCIALIST WORKERS	LIBERTARIAN
1948	Thurmond (SRD)	19,384	4,995	167,538	—	—
1952	Stevenson (D)	172,553	112,966	—	—	—
1956	Stevenson (D)	144,453	60,683	INDEPENDENT 42,961	—	—
1960	Byrd**	108,362	73,561	UNPLEDGED 116,248	—	—
1964	Goldwater (R)	52,616	356,512	—	—	—
1968	Wallace (AI)	150,644	88,516	AMERICAN IND. 415,349	—	—
1972	*Nixon (R)	126,782	505,125	AMERICAN 11,598	2,458	—
1976	*Carter (D)	381,309	366,846	6,678	2,805	2,788
1980	*Reagan (R)	429,281	441,089	WORKERS' WORLD 2,402	2,240	4,702
1984	*Reagan (R)	352,192	582,377	—	—	2,336
1988	*Bush (R)	363,921	557,890			3,329
1992	Bush (R)	400,258	487,793	IND. (Perot) 85,626	NEW ALLIANCE 2,625	2,154
1996	Dole (R)	394,022	439,838	52,222	—	2,809
2000	*Bush (R)	404,614	572,844	Progressive (Nader) 8,122	613	2,009

* Won US presidential election.
** Unpledged electors won plurality of votes and cast Mississippi's electoral votes for Senator Harry F. Byrd of Virginia.

state as to rival the major parties in political importance.

In 1980, Ronald Reagan edged Jimmy Carter by a plurality of fewer than 12,000 votes. In 1984, however, Reagan won the state by a landslide, polling 62% of the vote. In the 2000 election, Republican George W. Bush won 58% of the vote and Democrat Al Gore received 41%.

In 1995, Mississippi's governor, Kirk Fordice, was a Republican as were its two senators, Thad Cochran and Trent Lott (who was reelected in 2000). In 2001, the U.S. Representatives consisted of 3 Democrats and 2 Republicans. Mike Parker, the Democratic Representative from the southwest and central parts of the state, switched to the Republican Party in 1995.

Photo credit: EPD Photos/National Archives

Jefferson Davis (b.Kentucky, 1808–89), was president of the Confederacy from 1861 until the defeat of the South in 1865.

14 LOCAL GOVERNMENT

Each of Mississippi's 82 counties is divided into five districts, each of which elects a member to the county board of supervisors. As of 1997, Mississippi had 295 municipal governments. Most cities, including most of the larger ones, have a mayor and city council.

15 JUDICIAL SYSTEM

The Mississippi supreme court consists of a chief justice, two presiding justices, and six associate justices. The principal trial courts are 20 chancery courts, which try civil cases, and 22 circuit courts, which try both civil and criminal cases. Small-claims courts are presided over by justices of the peace, who need not be lawyers.

In 1998, Mississippi had a total FBI Crime Index rate of 4,384 per 100,000 population. There were 17,858 prisoners in state and federal prisons in Mississippi as of June 1999.

16 MIGRATION

Out-migration from Mississippi was heavy during the 1940s and 1950s, when at least 720,000 people, nearly three-quarters of them black, left the state. Black out-migration slowed considerably during the 1970s, and more whites settled in the state than left. Also during the 1970s, there was considerable intrastate migration to Hinds

Cotton fields in the Mississippi Delta. In 1994, Mississippi ranked third in the nation in cotton production.

County (Jackson) and the Gulf Coast. Between 1980 and 1990, Mississippi had a net loss from migration of 144,128 (38% whites). During 1990–98, the state had a net gain of about 43,000 from interstate migration, and 6,000 from international migration.

17 ECONOMY

Once the social turmoil of the 1950s and early 1960s had subsided, the impressive industrial growth of the immediate post-war years resumed. By the mid-1960s, manufacturing—attracted to the state, in part, because of low wage rates and a weak labor movement—surpassed farming as a source of jobs. During the following decade, the balance of industrial growth changed somewhat. The relatively low-paying garment, textile, and wood-products industries, based on cotton and timber, grew less rapidly than a number of heavy industries, including transportation equipment and electric and electronic goods. Still, Mississippi remains a poor state.

18 INCOME

As it has for much of this century, Mississippi ranked last among the 50 states in per capita (per person) personal income in 1998, at $19,776. However, a rapid rise in per person income has been closing the gap between the state's low income level and the national average. As of 1998, 18.3% of all state residents lived below the federal poverty level.

19 INDUSTRY

In 1997, the value of shipments totaled $41 billion. Food and kindred products contributed the largest amount of the 1995 total, 11%. The state's biggest manufacturing concern is Litton Industries' Ingalls shipyard at Pascagoula. In addition to merchant vessels, this yard builds US Navy ships, including nuclear-powered submarines.

20 LABOR

Data for 1998 showed a civilian labor force of approximately 1.27 million in Mississippi. The unemployment rate was 5.4%. As of 1998, 9.7% of all workers in the state were union members.

21 AGRICULTURE

In 1999, Mississippi ranked 25th among the states in income from agriculture, with marketings of over $3.1 billion. Crops accounted for $1 billion and livestock and livestock products $2.1 billion. From the 1830s through World War II, cotton was Mississippi's principal cash crop. During the postwar period, however, as mechanized farming replaced the sharecropper system, agriculture became more diversified. In 1995 Mississippi ranked third in cotton production and fifth in rice production. About 1.45 million bales of cotton worth $441 million were harvested in 1998. Soybean output in 1998 totaled 48 million bushels, worth $290 million. Rice

production was estimated at 15.5 million pounds in 1998, with a value of $99.6 million.

22 DOMESTICATED ANIMALS

Cattle are raised throughout the state, though principally in the west. In 1999, there were 1.16 million cattle and calves, valued at $533.6 million. Hogs and pigs numbered 2.75 million, worth $13.2 million. Mississippi is a leading producer of broilers, ranking fifth in 1997, when 3.3 billion pounds (1.5 billion kilograms) of chickens and broilers, worth over $1.23 billion, were produced.

23 FISHING

In 1998, Mississippi ranked eighth among the 50 states in the size of its commercial fish landings. These totaled 210.8 million pounds (95.6 million kilograms), with a value of $48.8 million. Shrimp and blue crab made up the bulk of the commercial landings. The saltwater catch also includes mullet and red snapper; the freshwater catch is dominated by buffalo fish, carp, and catfish. As of 1998, Mississippi ranked first among the states in catfish farming, mostly from ponds in the Yazoo River basin; 396 catfish farms covered about 104,250 acres (47,288 hectares) of water surface.

24 FORESTRY

Mississippi had approximately 18.6 million acres (7.5 million hectares) of commercial forested land, 62% of the total land area of the state, in 1997. Six national forests extend over 1.1 million acres (445,000 hectares). Timber production was valued at $1.1 billion in 1996.

25 MINING

Mississippi's nonfuel mineral production in 1998 was valued at $190 million. In 1998, 513,000 metric tons of clay were produced for a value of $3.53 million. About 15.6 million metric tons of sand and gravel produced were worth $73.3 million. A quantity of 4.9 million metric tons of crushed stone was worth $29.4 million.

26 ENERGY AND POWER

Mississippi generated a total of 26.4 billion kilowatt hours of electricity in 1995. Mississippi is a major petroleum producer, and its 1999 crude production totaled 17.9 million barrels. Mississippi produced 108 billion cubic feet (3 billion cubic meters) of natural gas during 1998.

27 COMMERCE

Mississippi had 1997 wholesale sales of $20 billion and retail sales of $21 billion. Exports of goods produced in Mississippi totaled $2.3 billion in 1998.

28 PUBLIC FINANCE

As of 1997, the state's outstanding debt was $2.45 billion, or $898 per capita (per person).

Total revenues for 1997 were $9.4 billion; total expenditures were $9 billion.

29 TAXATION

In 1997, Mississippi collected slightly more than $4 billion in state taxes, or $1,471 per person. The state taxes individual and corporate income and also imposes taxes on oil, natural gas, and timber. A 7% retail sales tax is levied, along with taxes on inheritance, gasoline, tobacco, beer, wine, and other items. In 1995, Mississippians paid $6 billion in federal taxes and received $14.2 billion in federal funding.

30 HEALTH

In 1998, Mississippi's death rates from heart disease and cerebrovascular diseases exceeded national rates. In 1995, there were 51.33 traffic fatalities per 100,000 licensed drivers, higher than in any other state. Mississippi had 96 community hospitals, with 13,005 beds, in 1998. The average hospital cost per inpatient stay was $4,965. The 1997 ratio of 156 physicians per 100,000 civilian population was the lowest among the states. Mississippi had over 12,000 full-time licensed nurses in 1998. About 20% of state residents did not have health insurance in 1998.

31 HOUSING

In 1999, Mississippi had 1.1 million year-round housing units. In 1998, 12,900 new housing units worth $890 million were authorized for construction. In 1990, Mississippi had the lowest median home value of any state except South Dakota, at $45,600. The median monthly costs for owners (with a mortgage) and renters in 1990 were $511 and $309, respectively. Both costs were lower than in any other state but West Virginia.

Photo credit: Courtesy of Mississippi Division of Tourism.

Jackson, the state capital of Mississippi.

32 EDUCATION

Only 77.3% of adult Mississippians 25 and older had completed high school in 1998. As of the fall of 1997, there were 504,792 students enrolled in public schools in Mississippi. Of these, 365,061 were elementary (including kindergarten), and 139,731 were secondary. Expenditures for public elementary and secondary schools amounted to $3,912 per student in 1995/96 (50th among the states). In 1997, there were 40 institutions of higher education with a total enrollment of 130,561. Eight were public universities, 15 were public junior colleges, and 17 (including 4 Bible colleges and theological seminaries) were private institutions. Important institutions of higher learning include The University of Mississippi, Mississippi State University, and Southern Mississippi University. Historically black institutions include Tougaloo College and Jackson State University.

33 ARTS

Jackson has two ballet companies, a symphony orchestra, and two opera companies. Opera South, an integrated but predominantly black company, mounts two major productions yearly. There are local symphony orchestras in Meridian, Starkville, Tupelo, and Greenville. The established professional theaters in the state are the Sheffield Ensemble in Biloxi and the New Stage in Jackson. The

Greater Gulf Coast Arts Center has been very active in bringing arts programs into the coastal area.

A distinctive contribution to US culture is the music of black sharecroppers from the Delta, known as "the blues." The Delta Blues Museum in Clarksdale has an extensive collection documenting blues history.

34 LIBRARIES AND MUSEUMS

There were 47 county or multicounty (regional) public libraries in 1999. There were 6.5 million volumes in Mississippi libraries, and total public library circulation was over 9 million. In the Vicksburg-Warren County Public Library are collections on the Civil War, state history, and oral history. Tougaloo College has special collections of African materials, civil rights papers, and oral history.

There are 65 museums, including the distinguished Mississippi State Historical Museum at Jackson, the Mississippi Blues Museum at Clarksdale, and the Lauren-Rogers Museum of Art in Laurel. Beauvoir, Jefferson Davis's home at Biloxi, is a state shrine and includes a museum. The Mississippi governor's mansion, said to be the second-oldest executive residence in the US, is a National Historical Landmark.

35 COMMUNICATIONS

In 1999, only 88% of the state's occupied housing units had telephones (up 6.8% from 1984), the lowest rate in the US. In 2000, the state had 260 operating radio stations (97 AM, 163 FM) and 32 television stations. Four large cable television systems also served Mississippi. A total of 17,234 Internet domain names had been registered in Mississippi by the year 2000.

36 PRESS

In 1998, Mississippi had 23 daily newspapers which included 9 morning dailies and 14 evening dailies. In addition there were 18 Sunday papers in the state. The state's leading newspaper is in Jackson: the *Clarion–Ledger* has a daily circulation of 105,382 (125,847 Sunday). A monthly, *Mississippi Magazine,* is published in Jackson; and a bimonthly, *Mississippi: A View of the Magnolia State,* in Jackson.

37 TOURISM, TRAVEL, AND RECREATION

Among Mississippi's major tourist attractions are its mansions and plantations, many of them in the Natchez area. At Greenwood is the Florewood River Plantation, a museum re-creating 19th-century plantation life. The Natchez Trace Parkway, Gulf Islands National Seashore, and Vicksburg National Military Park attract the most visitors annually. There are also 6 national forests and 27 state parks.

38 SPORTS

There are no major league professional teams in Mississippi. Jackson has a minor league baseball team in the Texas League. The University of Mississippi has long been prominent in college football. The Dixie National Livestock Show and Rodeo is held in Jackson in January.

39 FAMOUS MISSISSIPPIANS

Mississippi's most famous political figure, Jefferson Davis (b.Kentucky, 1808–89), was president of the Confederacy from 1861 until the defeat of the South in 1865. Imprisoned for two years after the Civil War (though never tried), Davis lived the last years of his life at Beauvoir, an estate on the Mississippi Gulf Coast. Lucius Quintus Cincinnatus Lamar (b.Georgia, 1825–93), who served as Confederate minister to Russia, was appointed secretary of the interior in 1885 and later named to the US Supreme Court.

Some of the foremost authors of 20th-century America had their origins in Mississippi. Supreme among them is William Faulkner (Falkner, 1897–1962), whose novels include such classics as *The Sound and the Fury* (1929) and *Light in August* (1932). Faulkner received two Pulitzer Prizes and in 1949 was awarded the Nobel Prize for literature. Richard Wright (1908–60), a powerful writer and leading spokesperson for the black Americans of his generation, is best remembered for his novel *Native Son* (1940) and for *Black Boy* (1945), an autobiographical account of his Mississippi childhood.

Other native Mississippians of literary renown (and Pulitzer Prize winners) are Eudora Welty (b.1909); Tennessee Williams (Thomas Lanier Williams, 1911–83); and playwright Beth Henley (b.1952). Other Mississippi authors are Shelby Foote (b.1916); Walker Percy (b.Alabama, 1916–90); and Willie Morris (b.1934).

Photo credit: EPD Photos/CSU Archives.

Leontyne Price (Mary Violet Leontine Price, b.1927), a distinguished opera soprano, was born in Laurel, Mississippi.

Among the state's numerous musicians are Leontyne Price (Mary Violet Leontine Price, b.1927), a distinguished opera soprano born in Laurel, Mississippi; famous blues singers Muddy Waters (McKinley Morganfield, 1915–83); John Lee Hooker (b.1917); and Riley "B. B." King (b.1925). Mississippi's contributions to music also include Jimmie Rodgers (1897–1933), Bo Diddley (Ellas McDaniels, b.1928), Conway Twitty (1933–94), and Jimmy Buffet (b.1946). Elvis Presley (1935–77), born in Tupelo, was one of the most popular singers in US history. Other entertainers from Mississippi include Jim Henson (1936–90) and Oprah Winfrey (b.1954).

40 BIBLIOGRAPHY

Ballard, Michael B. *Civil War Mississippi: A Guide.* Jackson: University Press of Mississippi, 2000.

Gibson, Karen Bush. *Mississippi Facts and Symbols.* Mankato, Minn.: Hilltop Books, 2001.

Harmon, Daniel E. *La Salle and the Exploration of the Mississippi.* Philadelphia: Chelsea House, 2000.

Isaacs, Sally Senzell. *Life on a Southern Plantation.* Chicago: Heinemann, 2001.

Lourie, Peter. *Mississippi River: A Journey Down the Father of Waters.* Honesdale, Pa.: Boyds Mills Press, 2000.

Mudd-Ruth, Maria. *The Mississippi River.* New York: Benchmark Books, 2001.

Siebert, Diane. *Mississippi.* New York: HarperCollins Publishers, 2001.

Web sites

State of Mississippi. Official Web Site. [Online] Available http://www.state.ms.us/ Accessed May 16, 2001.

Weber Publications. Mississippi, the South's Warmest Welcome. [Online] Available http://www.50states.com/mississi.htm Accessed May 16, 2001.

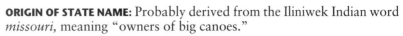

State of Missouri

ORIGIN OF STATE NAME: Probably derived from the Iliniwek Indian word *missouri,* meaning "owners of big canoes."

NICKNAME: The Show Me State.

CAPITAL: Jefferson City.

ENTERED UNION: 10 August 1821 (24th).

SONG: "Missouri Waltz."

MOTTO: *Salus populi suprema lex esto* (The welfare of the people shall be the supreme law).

COAT OF ARMS: Two grizzly bears stand on a scroll inscribed with the state motto and support a shield portraying an American eagle and a constellation of stars, a grizzly bear on all fours, and a crescent moon, all encircled by the words "United We Stand, Divided We Fall." Above are a six-barred helmet and 24 stars; below is the roman numeral MDCCCXX (1820), when Missouri's first constitution was adopted.

FLAG: Three horizontal stripes of red, white, and blue, with the coat of arms encircled by 24 white stars on a blue band in the center.

OFFICIAL SEAL: The coat of arms is surrounded by the words "The Great Seal of the State of Missouri."

BIRD: Bluebird.

FLOWER: Hawthorn blossom.

TREE: Flowering dogwood.

INSECT: Honeybee.

ROCK: Mozarkite (chert, or flint rock).

FOSSIL: Crinoid.

MINERAL: Galena.

TIME: 6 AM CST = noon GMT.

1 LOCATION AND SIZE

Located in the western north-central US, Missouri ranks 19th in size among the 50 states. The total area of Missouri is 69,697 square miles (180,516 square kilometers). Missouri extends 284 miles (457 kilometers) east-west; its greatest north-south extension is 308 miles (496 kilometers). The total boundary length of Missouri is 1,438 miles (2,314 kilometers).

2 TOPOGRAPHY

Missouri is divided into four major land regions: the Dissected Till Plains, which comprise rolling hills, open fertile flatlands, and well-watered prairie; the Osage Plains, covering the western part of the state; the Mississippi Alluvial Plain, made up of fertile black lowlands; and the Ozark Plateau, which comprises most of southern Missouri and contains Taum

Sauk Mountain, the highest elevation in the state at 1,772 feet (540 meters).

Missouri has more than 1,000 miles (1,600 kilometers) of navigable waterways. The Mississippi and Missouri rivers, the two largest in the US, form the state's eastern border and part of its western border. The largest lake is the artificial Lake of the Ozarks, covering a total of 93 square miles (241 square kilometers).

3 CLIMATE

Missouri has a continental climate, but with considerable local and regional variation. The average annual temperature is 50°F (10°C) in the northwest, but is about 60°F (16°C) in the southeast. The coldest temperature ever recorded in Missouri was –40°F (–40°C) in 1905; the hottest, 118°F (48°C) in 1954. The average annual precipitation for the state is about 40 inches (100 centimeters). Springtime is the peak tornado season.

4 PLANTS AND ANIMALS

Representative trees of Missouri include the shortleaf pine, scarlet oak, peachleaf willow, and dogwood (the state tree). Various types of wild grasses proliferate in the northern plains region. Missouri's state flower is the hawthorn blossom. Other wildflowers include Queen Anne's lace, meadow rose, and white snakeroot. The American elm, common throughout the state, is considered endangered because of Dutch elm disease.

Native mammals include the common cottontail, muskrat, and white-tailed deer. The state bird is the bluebird. Other com-

Missouri Population Profile

Total population in 2000:	5,595,211
Population change, 1990–2000:	9.3%
Hispanic or Latino†:	2.1%
Population by race	
One race:	98.5%
White:	84.9%
Black or African American:	11.2%
American Indian/Alaska Native:	0.4%
Asian:	1.1%
Native Hawaiian/Pacific Islander:	0.1%
Some other race:	0.8%
Two or more races:	1.5%

Population by Age Group

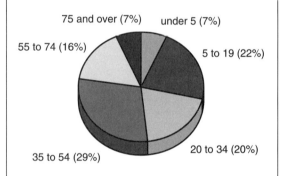

75 and over (7%)   under 5 (7%)
55 to 74 (16%)
5 to 19 (22%)
35 to 54 (29%)
20 to 34 (20%)

Top Cities by Population

City	Population	% change 1990–2000
Kansas City	441,545	1.5
St. Louis	348,189	–12.2
Springfield	151,580	7.9
Independence	113,288	0.9
Columbia	84,531	22.3
St. Joseph	73,990	3.0
Lee's Summit	70,700	52.3
St. Charles	60,321	10.6
St. Peters	51,381	12.2
Florissant	50,497	–1.4

Notes: †A person of Hispanic or Latino origin may be of any race. NA indicates that data are not available.
Sources: U.S. Census Bureau. Public Information Office. *Demographic Profiles.* [Online] Available http://www.census.gov/Press-Release/www/2001/demoprofile.html. Accessed June 1, 2001. U.S. Census Bureau. *Census 2000: Redistricting Data.* Press release issued by the Redistricting Data Office. Washington, D.C., March, 2001.

MISSOURI

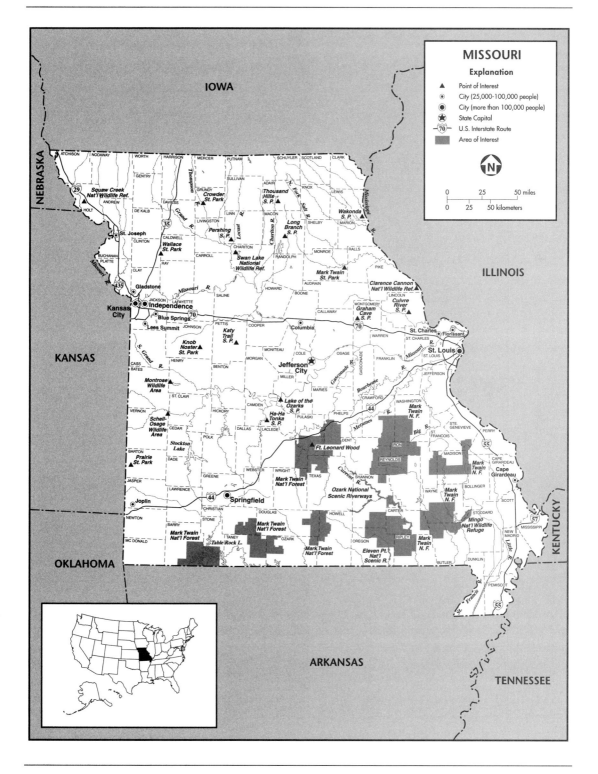

mon birds are the cardinal and solitary vireo. A characteristic amphibian is the plains leopard frog. Native snakes include garter, ribbon, and copperhead. Bass, carp, perch, jack salmon (walleye), and crayfish abound in Missouri's waters. The chigger, a minute insect, is a notorious pest. Listed as endangered in Missouri are the Ozark big-eared, gray, and Indiana bats; bald eagle; and whooping crane.

5 ENVIRONMENTAL PROTECTION

Missouri's principal environmental protection agencies are the Department of Conservation, which manages the state forests and fish hatcheries and maintains wildlife refuges, and the Department of Natural Resources, responsible for state parks, energy conservation, and environmental quality programs.

An important environmental problem is soil erosion. Rain washes away an average of 71 million tons of topsoil each year. St. Louis ranks high among US cities for the quantities of lead and suspended particles found in the atmosphere, but conditions improved between the mid-1970s and early 1980s. The state had 22 hazardous waste sites as of 1998.

6 POPULATION

Missouri ranked 17th among the 50 states at the 2000 census, falling behind Tennessee and Washington. It had a population of 5,595,211, with a density of 81.2 persons per square mile (31.4 persons per square kilometer), nearly identical to the national average. The population projection for 2005 is 5.7 million.

In 1990, 68.7% of all Missourians lived in urban areas and 31.3% in rural areas. The largest cities and their 2000 populations were Kansas City, 441,545; St. Louis, 348,189; Springfield, 151,580; and Independence, 113,288. Like Michigan, Indiana, and Illinois, 29% of Missouri's population is 19 years of age and younger.

7 ETHNIC GROUPS

Of those claiming descent from at least one specific ancestry group in 1990, over 1.84 million named German, 743,232 English, and 1.04 million Irish. Black Americans have represented a rising proportion of Missouri's population in recent decades, accounting for about 11.2% in 1997. According to the 1990 census, some 34% of Missouri's black population lived in St. Louis (which was more than 47% black). In 1997 Missouri also had an estimated 82,200 people of Hispanic origin, including many of Mexican ancestry. The Asian community in 1997 was estimated at 57,700, consisting primarily of Chinese, Filipinos, Koreans, Japanese, and Asian Indians. The 1997 federal estimate showed a Native American population of 20,500.

8 LANGUAGES

Four westward-flowing language streams met and partly merged in Missouri. Northern and North Midland speakers settled north of the Missouri River and in the western border counties, bringing their Northern *pail* and *sick to the stomach* and their North Midland *fishworm* (earthworm), *gunnysack* (burlap bag), and *sick at the stomach*. South of the Missouri River, and notably in the Ozark Highlands, South Midland domi-

Missouri Population by Race

Census 2000 was the first national census in which the instructions to respondents said, "Mark one or more races." This table shows the number of people who are of one, two, or three or more races. For those claiming two races, the number of people belonging to the various categories is listed. The U.S. government conducts a census of the population every ten years.

	Number	Percent
Total population	5,595,211	100.0
One race	5,513,150	98.5
Two races	77,339	1.4
White *and* Black or African American	15,566	0.3
White *and* American Indian/Alaska Native	27,998	0.5
White *and* Asian	9,387	0.2
White *and* Native Hawaiian/Pacific Islander	1,192	—
White *and* some other race	12,957	0.2
Black or African American *and* American Indian/Alaska Native	3,161	0.1
Black or African American *and* Asian	1,109	—
Black or African American *and* Native Hawaiian/Pacific Islander	243	—
Black or African American *and* some other race	2,678	—
American Indian/Alaska Native *and* Asian	271	—
American Indian/Alaska Native *and* Native Hawaiian/Pacific Islander	57	—
American Indian/Alaska Native *and* some other race	507	—
Asian *and* Native Hawaiian/Pacific Islander	920	—
Asian *and* some other race	1,166	—
Native Hawaiian/Pacific Islander *and* some other race	127	—
Three or more races	4,722	0.1

Source: U.S. Census Bureau. *Census 2000: Redistricting Data*. Press release issued by the Redistricting Data Office. Washington, D.C., March, 2001. A dash (—) indicates that the percent is less than 0.1.

nates, though with a few Southern forms, especially in the cotton-growing floodplain of the extreme southeast.

About 96% of state residents five years old or older spoke only English at home in 1990. Of those who claimed to speak another language at home, the leading languages and number of speakers were Spanish, 59,585; German, 32,286; and French, 20,135.

9 RELIGIONS

In 1990, Missouri had 802,083 Roman Catholics. The principal Protestant denominations in 1990 were the Southern Baptist Convention, with 789,183 members; United Methodist Church, 255,111; Lutheran Church—Missouri Synod, 145,741; and the Christian Church (Disciples of Christ), 101,756. In 1994, Missouri's estimated Jewish population was 62,000.

10 TRANSPORTATION

Centrally located, Missouri is a leading US transportation center. Both St. Louis and Kansas City are hubs of rail, truck, and airline transportation. In 1998, there were 4,802 rail miles (7,726 kilometers) of track in the state. In 1995/96, the total number of Missouri Amtrak riders was 729,192. In 1997 there were 122,766 miles (197,530 kilometers) of roadway. Motor vehicle registration for the state in

The St. Louis Arch and city skyline.

1997 was over 4.35 million, including 2.55 million passenger cars, 1.78 million trucks, and 12,745 buses.

The Mississippi and Missouri rivers have long been important transportation routes. The Mississippi still serves considerable barge traffic, making metropolitan St. Louis an active inland port area, with 31.7 million tons of cargo handled in 1998. Charles A. Lindbergh, having spent a few years in the St. Louis area, had the backing of business owners from that city when he flew his *Spirit of St. Louis* across the Atlantic in 1927. Today, Kansas City International Airport and Lambert-St. Louis Municipal Airport are among the busiest airports in the country. These two boarded 4.8 million and 13.5 million passengers, respectively, in 1996, when the state had 383 airports and 116 heliports.

11 HISTORY

When the first Europeans arrived in the late 17th century, most of the few thousand Native Americans living in Missouri belonged to two main linguistic groups: Algonkian-speakers, mainly the Sauk, Fox, and Iliniwek (Illinois) in the northeast; and a Siouan group, including the Osage, Missouri, Iowa, Kansas, and other tribes, to the south and west. The flood of white settlers into Missouri after 1803 forced the Native Americans to move into Kansas and into what became known as Indian Territory (present-day Oklahoma). During the 1820s, the US government negotiated treaties with the Osage, Sauk, Fox, and Iowa tribes whereby they surrendered all their lands in Missouri. By 1836, few Native Americans remained.

The first Europeans to pass through land that was eventually included within Missouri's boundaries were Jacques Marquette and Louis Jolliet, who in 1673 passed the mouth of the Missouri River on their journey down the Mississippi. Robert Cavelier, Sieur de la Salle, claimed the entire Mississippi Valley for France in 1682. Missouri passed into Spanish hands with the rest of the Louisiana Territory in 1762. In 1764, the French fur trader Pierre Laclède established a trading post on the present site of St. Louis.

Although the Spanish did not attempt to settle Missouri, they did allow Americans to migrate freely into the territory. Spanish authorities granted free land to the new settlers, relaxed their restrictions against Protestants, and welcomed slaveholding families from southern states. Spanish rule ended abruptly in 1800 when Napoleon forced Spain to return Louisiana to France. Included in the Louisiana Purchase, Missouri then became part of the US in 1803.

Statehood

Missouri was part of the Louisiana Territory until 1 October 1812, when the Missouri Territory (including present-day Arkansas) was established. A flood of set-

Photo credit: Convention & Visitors Bureau of Greater Kansas City.

Dedicated in 1921, the Liberty Memorial in Kansas City honors the soldiers of the First World War.

tlers between 1810 and 1820 more than tripled Missouri's population from 19,783 to 66,586, leading Missourians to petition the US Congress for statehood as early as 1818. But Congress, divided over the slavery issue, withheld permission for three years, finally approving statehood for Maine and Missouri under the terms of the Missouri Compromise (1820), which sanctioned slavery in the new state but banned it in the rest of the former Louisiana Territory north of Arkansas. Missouri became the 24th state on 10 August 1821.

Missouri Governors: 1820–2001

1820–1824	Alexander McNair	Dem-Rep		1901–1905	Alexander Monroe Dockery	Democrat
1824–1825	Frederick Bates	Democrat		1905–1909	Joseph Wingate Folk	Democrat
1825–1826	Abraham J. Williams	Dem-Rep		1909–1913	Herbert Spencer Hadley	Republican
1826–1832	John Miller	Jacksonian		1913–1917	Elliot Woolfolk Major	Democrat
1832–1836	Daniel Dunklin	Democrat		1917–1921	Frederich D. Gardner	Democrat
1836–1841	Lilburn W. Boggs	Democrat		1921–1925	Arthur Mastik Hyde	Republican
1841–1844	Thomas Reynolds	Democrat		1925–1929	Samuel Aaron Baker	Republican
1844–1845	Meredith Miles Marmaduke	Democrat		1929–1933	Henry Stewart Caulfield	Republican
1845–1848	John Cummins Edwards	Democrat		1933–1937	Guy Brasfield Park	Democrat
1848–1852	Austin Augustus King	Democrat		1937–1941	Lloyd Crow Stark	Democrat
1852–1856	Sterling Price	Democrat		1941–1945	Forrest C. Donnell	Republican
1856–1857	Trusten Polk	Democrat		1945–1949	Phil Matthew Donnelly	Democrat
1857	Hankock Lee Jackson	Democrat		1949–1953	Forrest Smith	Democrat
1857–1861	Robert Marcellus Stewart	Democrat		1953–1957	Philip Matthew Donnelly	Democrat
1861	Claiborne Fox Jackson	Democrat		1957–1961	James Thomas Blair, Jr.	Democrat
1861–1864	Hamilton Rowan Gamble	Unionist		1961–1965	John Montgomery Dalton	Democrat
1864	Willard Preble Hall	Unionist		1965–1973	Warren E. Hearnes	Democrat
1865–1869	Thomas Clement Fletcher	Union-Rep		1973–1977	Christopher S. Bond	Republican
1869–1871	Joseph Washington McClurg	Republican		1977–1981	Joseph P. Teasdale	Democrat
1871–1873	Benjamin Gratz Brown	Liberal-Rep		1981–1985	Christopher S. Bond	Republican
1873–1875	Silas Woodson	Democrat		1985–1993	John Ashcroft	Republican
1875–1877	Charles Henry Hardin	Democrat		1993–2000	Mel Eugene Carnahan	Democrat
1877–1881	John Smith Phelps	Democrat		2000-	Bob Holden	Democrat
1881–1885	Thomas Theodore Crittenden	Democrat				
1885–1887	John Sappington Marmaduke	Democrat				
1887–1889	Albert Pickett Morehouse	Democrat			Democratic Republican – Dem-Rep	
1889–1893	David Rowland Francis	Democrat			Liberal Republican – Liberal-Rep	
1893–1897	William Joel Stone	Democrat			Union Republican – Union-Rep	
1897–1901	Lon Vest Stephens	Democrat				

Aided by the advent of steamboat travel on the Mississippi and Missouri rivers, settlers continued to arrive in the new state, whose population surpassed one million by 1860. There was a great deal of proslavery sentiment in the state, and thousands of Missourians crossed into neighboring Kansas in the mid-1850s to help elect a proslavery government in that territory. During the Civil War, Missouri remained loyal to the Union, though not without difficulty, supplying some 110,000 soldiers to the Union and 40,000 to the Confederacy. At a constitutional convention held in January 1865, Missouri became the first slave state to free all blacks.

1870s–1990s

In addition to conflicts caused by the Republican Reconstruction government, the 1870s saw a period of lawlessness, typified by the exploits of Jesse and Frank James, that earned Missouri the epithet of the "robber state." Of more lasting importance were the closing of the frontier in Missouri, the decline of the fur trade and steamboat traffic, and the rise of the railroads. The state's economy increasingly shifted from agriculture to industry, and Missouri's rural population declined from about three-fourths of the total in 1880 to less than one-third by 1970. Although the overall importance of mining declined,

Missouri remained the world's top lead producer, and the state has emerged as second only to Michigan in US automobile manufacturing.

Postwar prosperity was threatened beginning in the 1960s by the deterioration of several cities, notably St. Louis, which lost 47% of its population between 1950 and 1980. Both St. Louis and Kansas City undertook urban renewal programs to cope with the serious problems of air pollution, traffic congestion, crime, and substandard housing. During the early 1980s, millions of dollars in federal, state, and private funds were used to rehabilitate abandoned and dilapidated apartment buildings and houses.

In the spring and summer of 1993, Missouri was hit by devastating floods. Over half of the state was declared a disaster area and 19,000 people were evacuated from their homes. Damage to the state was estimated at $3 billion.

12 STATE GOVERNMENT

The legislative branch, or general assembly, consists of a 34-member senate and a 163-seat house of representatives. Senators are elected to staggered four-year terms; representatives for two. The state's elected executives are the governor and lieutenant governor (who run separately), secretary of state, auditor, treasurer, and attorney general. All serve four-year terms.

A bill becomes law when signed by the governor within 15 days of legislative passage. A two-thirds vote by both houses is required to override a gubernatorial veto. Constitutional amendments require a majority vote of both houses of the legislature and ratification by the voters.

Missouri Presidential Vote by Political Parties, 1948–2000

YEAR	MISSOURI WINNER	DEMOCRAT	REPUBLICAN	PROGRESSIVE	SOCIALIST
1948	*Truman (D)	917,315	655,039	3,998	2,222
1952	*Eisenhower (R)	929,830	959,429	—	—
1956	Stevenson (D)	918,273	914,289	—	—
1960	*Kennedy (D)	972,201	962,218	—	—
1964	*Johnson (D)	1,164,344	653,535	—	—
				AMERICAN IND.	
1968	*Nixon (R)	791,444	811,932	206,126	—
1972	*Nixon (R)	698,531	1,154,058	—	—
1976	*Carter (D)	998,387	927,443	—	—
				LIBERTARIAN	SOC. WORKERS
1980	*Reagan (R)	931,182	1,074,181	14,422	1,515
1984	*Reagan (R)	848,583	1,274,188	—	—
					NEW ALLIANCE
1988	*Bush (R)	1,001,619	1,084,953	434	6,656
					IND. (Perot)
1992	*Clinton (D)	1,053,873	811,159	7,497	518,741
1996	*Clinton (D)	1,025,935	890,016	10,522	217,188
					REFORM
2000	*Bush (R)	1,111,138	1,189,924	38,515	9,818

*Won US presidential election.

Harry S Truman (1884–1972) has been the only native-born Missourian to serve as US president or vice-president. Truman was Franklin D. Roosevelt's vice-presidential running mate in 1944 and succeeded to the presidency upon Roosevelt's death on 12 April 1945. The "man from Independence" was elected to the presidency in his own right in 1948, defeating Republican Thomas E. Dewey in one of the most surprising upsets in US political history.

13 POLITICAL PARTIES

Except for the Civil War and Reconstruction periods, the Democratic Party held the governorship from the late 1820s to the early 1900s. The outstanding figures of 20th century Missouri politics were both Democrats: Thomas Pendergast, the Kansas City political boss; and Harry S Truman, who began his political career as a Jackson County judge in the Kansas City area and in 1945 became the 33d president of the US.

Between 1980 and 1988, the state voted consistently for Republican presidential candidates. However, in 1992 and 1996 Democrat Bill Clinton carried the state. In the 2000 elections, Missouri returned to favoring the Republican candidate. George W. Bush won 50% of the vote and Democrat Al Gore received 47%. That same year, Democrat Bob Holden won the governorship by a narrow margin. As of 2001, Missouri's US Senators were both Democrats. Five of the US Representatives are Republicans and four are Democrats. In the state senate in 2001, there were 16 Democrats and 18 Republicans. In the state house, there were 86 Democrats and 74 Republicans (and three vacancies).

14 LOCAL GOVERNMENT

As of 1997, Missouri had 114 counties, 944 municipalities, 325 townships, 537 school districts, and 1,495 special districts. Elected county officials generally include a public administrator, prosecuting attorney, sheriff, assessor, and treasurer. The city of St. Louis, which is administratively independent of any county, has an elected mayor, a comptroller, and a 29-member board of aldermen (including the president). Most other cities are governed by an elected mayor and council.

15 JUDICIAL SYSTEM

The supreme court, the state's highest court, consisted of seven judges and three commissioners. The court of appeals consists of 32 judges in three districts. The circuit court is the only trial court and has original jurisdiction over all cases and matters, civil and municipal. Many circuit courts have established municipal divisions, presided over by judges paid locally. The 1998 crime rate for the state was 4,826.4 per 100,000. As of June 1999, there were 25,359 inmates in Missouri federal and state prisons.

16 MIGRATION

In recent decades, Missouri has been losing population through migration—322,000 people were lost to net migration between 1940 and 1970, followed by a net gain of 22,000 during the 1970s and a net loss of nearly 100,000 during the 1980s. During 1990–98, there was a net gain of 94,000 from other states and 34,000 from international migration. The dominant intrastate migration pattern has been the concentration of blacks in the major cities, especially St. Louis and Kansas City, and the exodus of whites from those cities to the suburbs and, more recently, to small towns and rural areas. As of 1990, just under 70% of all state residents had been born in Missouri.

17 ECONOMY

Missouri's central location and access to the Mississippi River contributed to its growth as a commercial center. The state's economy is diversified, with manufacturing, farming, trade, tourism, services, government, and mining as prime sources of income. Today, automobile and aerospace manufacturing are the state's leading industries, while soybeans and meat and dairy products are the most important agricultural commodities. The state's historic past, varied physical terrain, and modern urban attractions—notably the Gateway Arch in St. Louis—have made tourism a growth industry in recent decades. In the mid-1990s, private goods-producing industries accounted for 28% of the state's economic output; private services-producing industries, 61%; and government, 11%.

18 INCOME

With an income per capita (per person) of $25,150 in 1998, Missouri ranked 31st among the 50 states. Median household income was $37,640 in 1998. About 10.4% of state residents lived below the federal poverty level in 1998.

19 INDUSTRY

The leading industry groups, by value of shipments, are transportation equipment (mainly automobiles, aircraft, and rockets and missiles); food and food products; chemicals; electric and electronic equipment; and fabricated metal products. Shipments by Missouri manufacturers during 1997 amounted to $96 billion. McDonnell Douglas, with headquarters in St. Louis, is a leading manufacturer of aerospace products, including all the Mercury and Gemini space capsules, DC-9 and DC-10 commercial jet aircraft, and Tomahawk cruise missiles.

20 LABOR

In 1998, Missouri's civilian labor force was about 2.85 million. The unemployment rate was 4.5%. Missouri is a strong union state. Some 13.7% of all workers in the state belonged to labor unions in 1998.

21 AGRICULTURE

Missouri had 110,000 farms (second in the US) covering 30.1 million acres (12.2 million hectares) in 1998. Missouri's agricultural income reached $4.3 billion in 1999, 17th among the 50 states. Of this total, about 22% came from soybeans.

In 1998, Missouri was fourth among the states in grain sorghum production and fifth in soybean and rice production. In 1999, cash receipts from all crops totaled $1.8 billion. Farmers harvested 170 million bushels of soybeans, 285 million bushels of corn, 57.5 million bushels of wheat, 26.6 million bushels of grain sorghum, 350,000 bales of cotton, and 7.7 million tons of hay. Tobacco, oats, rye, apples, peaches, grapes, watermelons, and various seed crops are also grown in commercial quantities.

22 DOMESTICATED ANIMALS

Missouri is a leading livestock-raising state. Hog-raising is concentrated north of the Missouri River, cattle-raising in the western counties, and dairy farming in the southwest. In 1999, Missouri farms and ranches had 4.4 million cattle and 3.3 million hogs.

During 1997, Missouri's poultry farms produced 562.8 million pounds (228.5 million kilograms) of turkey (third in the nation) and 1,075 million pounds (487.6 million kilograms) of broilers.

Photo credit: © Nathan Benn/Woodfin Camp.

Hogs ready to be butchered. Missouri is a leading livestock-raising state. Hog-raising is concentrated north of the Missouri River, cattle-raising in the western counties, and dairy farming in the southwest.

23 FISHING

Commercial fishing takes place mainly on the Mississippi, Missouri, and St. Francis rivers. Sport fishing is enjoyed throughout the state, but especially in the Ozarks, whose waters harbor walleye, rainbow trout, bluegill, and largemouth bass.

24 FORESTRY

Missouri has about 14 million acres (5.7 million hectares) of forestland (32% of the state). Of the commercial forests, approximately three-fourths are of the oak/hickory type. Shortleaf pine and oak/pine forests comprise about 5%, while the remainder consists of cedar and bottomland hardwoods. Missouri leads the US in the production of charcoal, cedar products, and nutmeats. Railroad ties, veneers, wine and bourbon casks, and other forest-related items are also produced. Lumber production in 1998 totaled 578 million board feet.

More than 580,000 acres (235,000 hectares) of conservation areas, managed by the Forestry Division, are used for timber production, wildlife and watershed protection, hunting, fishing, and other recreational purposes. A state-run nursery sells seedling trees and shrubs to Missouri landowners. The Mark Twain National Forest, in southern Missouri, covers 1.5 million acres (600,000 hectares).

25 MINING

Nonfuel mineral production in Missouri was estimated at over $1.36 billion in 1997. Missouri ranked third of 11 states producing lead in 1998. That same year, Missouri's crushed stone, lead, portland cement, and lime production comprised 88% of the total value. Crushed stone has typically been the state's most valuable mineral commodity since 1993.

26 ENERGY AND POWER

In 1998, electrical output totaled 74.9 billion kilowatt hours. Coal-fired plants accounted for 83% of all power production in 1998. The state has one operating nuclear plant. Fossil fuel resources are limited. Reserves of bituminous coal totaled six billion tons as of 1998, but only a small portion was considered recoverable. Small quantities of crude petroleum are also produced commercially. In 1999, such production totaled 92,000 barrels.

27 COMMERCE

Missouri has been one of the nation's leading trade centers ever since merchants in Independence began provisioning wagon trains for the Santa Fe Trail. The state's wholesale sales totaled $96 billion in 1997; retail sales were $52 billion. Foreign exports of Missouri products exceeded $5.7 billion in 1998.

28 PUBLIC FINANCE

The debt of Missouri state government in 1997 was $7.58 billion, or $1,403 per capita (per person). The revenues for 1997 were $16.6 billion; expenditures were $14.23 billion.

29 TAXATION

Missouri's total state tax revenues, traditionally low, totaled $7.8 billion in 1997. On a per capita (per person) basis, state taxes of $1,447 ranked 38th in the US in 1997. Missouri taxes personal and corporate income. The basic state sales tax in 1998 was 4.225%; cities and towns may add an additional tax. Other taxes levied by the state include charges on motor fuel, cigarettes, and alcoholic beverages along with motor vehicle and operator's license fees and taxes on inheritances. Property and sales taxes are the leading sources of local revenue. In 1995, Missouri contrib-

The Negro Leagues Baseball museum in Kansas City documents the history of black baseball. It is located a few blocks from where the Negro National League was founded by Andrew "Rube" Foster in 1920. The color line in organized baseball was broken in 1947 when Kansas City Monarchs shortstop Jackie Robinson signed with the Brooklyn Dodgers.

uted $30 billion in federal taxes and received $31 billion in federal funding.

30 HEALTH

The overall death rate of 1,012.6 per 100,000 population in 1998 was one of the highest in the US, reflecting the relatively high proportion of elderly Missourians in the population as a whole. Deaths from heart disease, cerebrovascular disease, and accidents—the major causes of death—were all above the national average. In 1998, Missouri had 122 community hospitals, with 20,685 beds. The average expense of hospitals for care in 1994 was $1,063 per inpatient day, or $6,296 for an average cost per stay. The state had 225 physicians per 100,000 in 1997. Registered full-time nurses numbered about 22,000. Almost 11% of state residents did not have health insurance in 1998.

31 HOUSING

In 1999, Missouri had an estimated nearly 2.4 million housing units. The median price of a single-family home in Missouri was $114,000 in 1998. The median costs for owners (including a mortgage) and renters in 1990 were $600 and $368, respectively, per month.

32 EDUCATION

In 1998, 82.9% of all Missourians 25 years of age or older were high school graduates. Missouri's 2,234 public elementary and secondary schools had an enrollment of 910,654 students in fall 1997. Expenditures for public elementary and secondary schools amounted to $4,629 per student in 1995/96 (41st among the states). Enrollment in private schools numbered 119,534 in the fall of 1997.

Missouri had 13 public and 57 private four-year institutions of higher education in 1996. Total full-time enrollment in the fall of 1997 was 302,896 students. The University of Missouri, the first state-supported university west of the Mississippi River, has four campuses. Its Columbia campus had an enrollment of 22,898 in fall 1999. There are five regional state universities and three state colleges. Two leading independent universities, Washington University and St. Louis University, are located in St. Louis.

33 ARTS

Theatrical performances are offered throughout the state, mostly during the summer. In Kansas City, productions of Broadway musicals and light opera are staged at the Starlight Theater. In St. Louis, the 12,000-seat Municipal Opera puts on outdoor theater, while the *Goldenrod,* built in 1909 and said to be the largest showboat ever constructed, is used today for vaudeville, melodrama, and ragtime shows.

Leading orchestras are the St. Louis Symphony and Kansas City Symphony. The Opera Theatre of St. Louis and the Lyric Opera of Kansas City are distinguished musical organizations. Springfield has a regional opera company.

During the 1920s and 1930s, Kansas City was the home of a thriving jazz community that included Charlie Parker and, later, Count Basie. Country music predominates in rural Missouri: the Ozark Opry at Osage Beach and the Baldknobbers Hillbilly Jamboree and Mountain Music Theater in Branson have seasons from May to October. In 1997, there were 350 arts associations and 51 local associations in Missouri.

34 LIBRARIES AND MUSEUMS

Missouri had 48 county and 14 regional library systems in 1998, when the combined book stock of all public libraries in the state was 22.5 million, and their combined circulation 27.4 million. The Missouri State Library, in Jefferson City, is the center of the state's interlibrary loan network. The University of Missouri-Columbia has the leading academic library, with 2.7 million volumes in 1997. The federally-administered Harry S Truman Library and Museum is at Independence.

Missouri has over 162 museums and historic sites. The William Rockhill Nelson Gallery/Atkins Museum of Fine Arts in Kansas City and the St. Louis Art Museum both house distinguished general collections. The Mark Twain Home and

Museum in Hannibal has a collection of manuscripts and other memorabilia.

[35] COMMUNICATIONS

As of 1999, about 95.6% of all state households had telephone service. As of 2000 there were 116 commercial AM stations and 219 FM stations in service. Missouri had 38 television stations. In 1996, the state had nine major cable systems in service. A total of 84,512 Internet domain names had been registered in Missouri in 2000.

[36] PRESS

Many Missouri journalists have achieved national recognition. The best known is Samuel Clemens (later Mark Twain). Hungarian-born Joseph Pulitzer created the *St. Louis Post–Dispatch* in 1878 and established the Pulitzer Prizes, which annually honor journalistic and artistic achievement. As of 1998, Missouri had 13 morning newspapers, 30 evening dailies, and 23 Sunday papers. The leading dailies with their 1998 daily circulations are the *St. Louis Post-Dispatch* (329,582) and the *Kansas City Star* (281,596). Periodicals include the St. Louis-based *Sporting News,* the bimonthly "bible" of baseball fans.

[37] TOURISM, TRAVEL, AND RECREATION

The principal attraction in St. Louis is the Gateway Arch; at 630 feet (192 meters) it is the tallest man-made national monument in the US. Designed by Eero Saarinen in 1948 but not constructed until 1964, three years after his death, the arch and the Museum of Westward Expansion form part of the Jefferson National Expansion Memorial on the western shore of the Mississippi River. In the Kansas City area are the modern Crown Center hotels and shopping plaza, the Truman Sports Complex, Jesse James's birthplace near Excelsior Springs, and Harry Truman's hometown of Independence. Branson is considered the "Live Music Show Capital of the World."

Memorabilia of Mark Twain are housed in and around Hannibal. The birthplace and childhood home of George Washington Carver is in Diamond. The Lake of the Ozarks, with 1,375 miles (2,213 kilometers) of shoreline, is one of the most popular vacation spots in mid-America. Other attractions are the Pony Express Stables and Museum at St. Joseph and the "Big Springs Country" of the Ozarks, in the southeast.

Missouri has 27 state parks. Lake of the Ozarks State Park is the largest, covering 16,872 acres (6,828 hectares). There were also 27 historic sites in 1998, when state parks and historic sites covered 105,000 acres (43,050 hectares). They attract nearly 15 million visitors annually. Hunting and fishing are popular recreational activities.

[38] SPORTS

There are six major league professional sports teams in Missouri: the Kansas City Royals and the St. Louis Cardinals of Major League Baseball; the Kansas City Chiefs and St. Louis Rams of the National Football League; the St. Louis Blues of the National Hockey League; and the Kansas City Wizards of Major League Soccer. In collegiate sports, the University of Missouri competes in the Big 12 Conference. Other annual sporting events include the National Intercollegiate Basketball Tournament, held in Kansas City in March. Thoroughbred-racing can be seen during a summer and fall season at Cahokia Downs, outside St. Louis.

39 FAMOUS MISSOURIANS

Missouri's best-known senator was Thomas Hart Benton (b.North Carolina, 1782–1858), who championed the interests of Missouri and the West for 30 years.

Meriwether Lewis (b.Virginia, 1774–1809) and William Clark (b.Virginia, 1770–1838) explored Missouri and the West during 1804–06. Lewis later served as governor of Louisiana Territory, with headquarters at St. Louis, and Clark was governor of Missouri Territory from 1813 to 1821.

Distinguished scientists include agricultural chemist George Washington Carver (1864–1943) and astronomer Edwin P. Hubble (1889–1953). Charles A. Lindbergh (b.Michigan 1902–74) was a pilot and aviation instructor in the St. Louis area during the 1920s before winning worldwide acclaim for his solo New York-Paris flight.

Prominent Missouri businessmen include Joseph Pulitzer (b.Hungary, 1847–1911), who established the *St. Louis Post-Dispatch* (1878) and later endowed the journalism and literary prizes that bear his name; and James Cash Penney (1875–1971), founder of the J. C. Penney Company.

Photo credit: EPD Photos

Missouri's most popular author is Mark Twain (Samuel Langhorne Clemens, 1835–1910), whose Adventures of Tom Sawyer *(1876) and* Adventures of Huckleberry Finn *(1884) evoke his boyhood in Hannibal.*

Distinguished painters who lived in Missouri include James Carroll Beckwith (1852–1917). Among the state's important musicians are ragtime pianist-composer Scott Joplin (b.Texas, 1868–1917); composer-critic Virgil Thompson (1896–1989); and jazzman Coleman Hawkins (1907–69).

40 BIBLIOGRAPHY

Bennett, Michelle. *Missouri*. New York: Benchmark Books, 2001.

Crawford, Mark. *Confederate Courage on Other Fields: Four Lesser-known Accounts of the War Between the States.* Jefferson, N.C.: McFarland, 2000.

Gaskell, Richard. *The Missouri State Fair: Images of a Midwestern Tradition.* Columbia: University of Missouri Press, 2000.

Greene, Lorenzo J., et al. *Missouri's Black Heritage.* St. Louis: Forum, 1980.

McAuliffe, Emily. *Missouri Facts and Symbols.* Mankato, Minn.: Hilltop Books, 2000.

Thompson, Kathleen. *Missouri.* Austin, Tex.: Raintree Steck-Vaughn, 1996.

Wilkerson, J. L. *From Slave to World-class Horseman: Tom Bass.* Kansas City: Acorn Books, 1999.

Web sites

Governor of Missouri. State of Missouri KIDS Home Page. [Online] Available http://www.gov.state.mo.us/kids Accessed May 16, 2001.

State of Missouri. Missouri State Government Home Page. [Online] Available http://www.state.mo.us/ Accessed May 16, 2001.

MONTANA

State of Montana

ORIGIN OF STATE NAME: Derived from the Latin word meaning "mountainous."

NICKNAME: The Treasure State. (Also: Big Sky Country.)

CAPITAL: Helena.

ENTERED UNION: 8 November 1889 (41st).

SONG: "Montana."

MOTTO: *Oro y Plata* (Gold and silver).

FLAG: A blue field, fringed in gold on the top and bottom borders, surround the state coat of arms, with "Montana" in gold letters above the coat of arms.

OFFICIAL SEAL: In the lower center are a plow and a miner's pick and shovel; mountains appear above them on the left, the Great Falls of the Missouri River on the right, and the state motto on a banner below. The words "The Great Seal of the State of Montana" surround the whole.

ANIMAL: Grizzly bear.

BIRD: Western meadowlark.

FISH: Black-spotted (cutthroat) trout.

FLOWER: Bitterroot.

TREE: Ponderosa pine.

GEMS: Yogo sapphire; Montana agate.

GRASS: Bluebunch wheatgrass.

TIME: 5 AM MST = noon GMT.

1 LOCATION AND SIZE

Located in the northwestern US, Montana is the largest of the eight Rocky Mountain states and ranks fourth in size among the 50 states. The total area of Montana is 147,046 square miles (380,849 square kilometers). The state's maximum east-west extension is 570 miles (917 kilometers); its extreme north-south distance is 315 miles (507 kilometers). Its total boundary length is 1,947 miles (3,133 kilometers).

2 TOPOGRAPHY

Montana has an approximate mean elevation of 3,400 feet (1,000 meters). The Rocky Mountains cover the western two-fifths of the state, with the Bitterroot Range along the Idaho border. The high, gently rolling Great Plains occupy most of central and eastern Montana. The highest point in the state is Granite Peak, at an elevation of 12,799 feet (3,901 meters). The Continental Divide passes through the western part of the state. Ft. Peck Reservoir is Montana's largest body of inland water; Flathead Lake is the largest natural lake. The state's most important rivers are the Missouri and the Yellowstone.

3 CLIMATE

The Continental Divide separates the state into two distinct climatic regions: the west generally has a milder climate than the east, where winters can be especially harsh. Montana's maximum daytime temperature averages 27°F (–2°C) in January and 85°F (29°C) in July. The all-time low temperature in the state, –70°F (–57°C) in 1954, is the lowest ever recorded in the continental US. The all-time high, 117°F (47°C), was set in 1937. Great Falls receives an average annual precipitation of 15 inches (38 centimeters), but much of north-central Montana is arid.

4 PLANTS AND ANIMALS

The subalpine region, in the northern Rocky Mountains, is rich in wildflowers during a short midsummer growing season. The plants of the montane zone consists largely of coniferous forests, principally alpine fir, and a variety of shrubs. The plains are characterized by an abundance of grasses, cacti, and sagebrush species. Game animals of the state include elk, moose, and mountain goat. Rattlesnakes and other reptiles occur in most of the state. The black-footed ferret, Eskimo curlew, and greenback cutthroat trout are on the endangered list.

5 ENVIRONMENTAL PROTECTION

Montana's major environmental concerns are management of mineral and water

Montana Population Profile

Total population in 2000:	902,195
Population change, 1990–2000:	12.9%
Hispanic or Latino†:	2.0%
Population by race	
One race:	98.3%
White:	90.6%
Black or African American:	0.3%
American Indian/Alaska Native:	6.2%
Asian:	0.5%
Native Hawaiian/Pacific Islander:	0.1%
Some other race:	0.6%
Two or more races:	1.7%

Population by Age Group

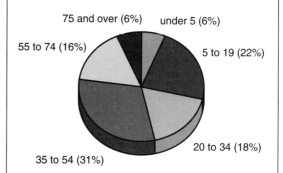

75 and over (6%)   under 5 (6%)
55 to 74 (16%)
5 to 19 (22%)
20 to 34 (18%)
35 to 54 (31%)

Top Cities by Population

City	Population	% change 1990–2000
Billings	89,847	10.7
Missoula	57,053	32.9
Great Falls	56,690	2.9
Butte-Silver Bow	34,606	2.0
Bozeman	27,509	21.4
Helena	25,780	4.9
Kalispell	14,223	19.4
Havre	9,621	–5.7
Anaconda-Deer Lodge	9,417	–8.4
Miles City	8,487	0.3

Notes: †A person of Hispanic or Latino origin may be of any race. NA indicates that data are not available.
Sources: U.S. Census Bureau. Public Information Office. *Demographic Profiles.* [Online] Available http://www.census.gov/Press-Release/www/2001/demoprofile.html. Accessed June 1, 2001. U.S. Census Bureau. *Census 2000: Redistricting Data.* Press release issued by the Redistricting Data Office. Washington, D.C., March, 2001.

MONTANA

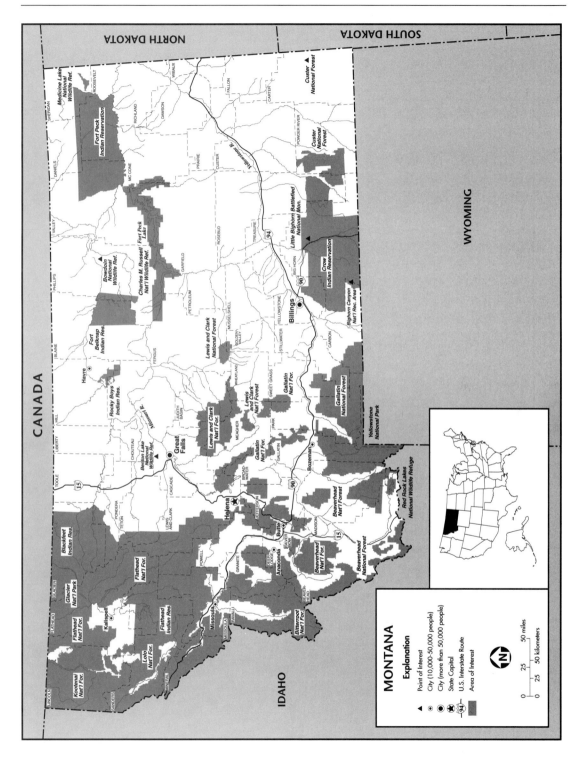

Photo credit: Travel Montana/R. Valentine Atkinson.

Glacier National Park, Glacier County.

resources and reclamation of strip-mined land. The Montana Environmental Policy Act, the Major Facilities Siting Act, and the Montana Resource Indemnity Trust Act (the latter imposes a tax on coal sales) reflect the determination of Montanans to protect the beauty of the Big Sky Country while maintaining economic momentum. The state had nine hazardous waste sites as of 1998.

6 POPULATION

According to the 2000 census, Montana ranked 44th among the 50 states, with a population of 902,195 (just less than the 2000 city population of Detroit, Michigan). Montana's density of only 6.2 persons per square mile (2.4 persons per square kilometer) is one of the lowest in the country. The projection for 2005 is just over 1 million. Approximately 28% of the population is 19 years of age and younger. Over one-fifth is 55 years and older.

7 ETHNIC GROUPS

According to the 1997 federal estimate, there were approximately 54,700 Native Americans in Montana (6.2%, the fifth highest ratio among the states). Blackfeet and Crow are the most numerous. The black and Asian populations are very small comprising 0.4% and 0.6%, respectively. About 1.7% of all residents had Hispanic origins in 1997.

Montana Population by Race

Census 2000 was the first national census in which the instructions to respondents said, "Mark one or more races." This table shows the number of people who are of one, two, or three or more races. For those claiming two races, the number of people belonging to the various categories is listed. The U.S. government conducts a census of the population every ten years.

	Number	Percent
Total population	902,195	100.0
One race	886,465	98.3
Two races	15,003	1.7
White *and* Black or African American	1,016	0.1
White *and* American Indian/Alaska Native	9,116	1.0
White *and* Asian	1,710	0.2
White *and* Native Hawaiian/Pacific Islander	268	—
White *and* some other race	1,945	0.2
Black or African American *and* American Indian/Alaska Native	300	—
Black or African American *and* Asian	40	—
Black or African American *and* Native Hawaiian/Pacific Islander	7	—
Black or African American *and* some other race	50	—
American Indian/Alaska Native *and* Asian	117	—
American Indian/Alaska Native *and* Native Hawaiian/Pacific Islander	34	—
American Indian/Alaska Native *and* some other race	196	—
Asian *and* Native Hawaiian/Pacific Islander	91	—
Asian *and* some other race	95	—
Native Hawaiian/Pacific Islander *and* some other race	18	—
Three or more races	727	0.1

Source: U.S. Census Bureau. *Census 2000: Redistricting Data*. Press release issued by the Redistricting Data Office. Washington, D.C., March, 2001. A dash (—) indicates that the percent is less than 0.1.

8 LANGUAGES

English in Montana fuses Northern and Midland features, the Northern influence declining from east to west. In 1990, 703,198 Montanans spoke only English at home. Other languages spoken at home, and number of speakers, included German, 9,644; various Native American languages, 8,207; and Spanish, 8,083.

9 RELIGIONS

As of 1990, Protestant groups had 467,345 known members in Montana. Leading denominations included American Lutheran Church Association, 16,172; United Methodist, 19,461; and Latter-day Saints (Mormons), 28,620. Montana had 125,799 Roman Catholics in 1990 and an estimated 1,000 Jews in 1994.

10 TRANSPORTATION

Montana is served by three major railroads, operating on about 3,293 rail miles (5,298 kilometers) of track. Amtrak operated one long-distance route (Chicago–Seattle/Portland) through the state, which served 12 stations. The total number of Montana riders in 1995/96 was 97,855.

Because of its large size, small population, and difficult terrain, Montana was slow to develop a highway system. As of 1997, the state had 69,672 miles (112,102 kilometers) of public roads, streets, and highways. There were 979,700 registered motor vehicles. Late in 1995, Montana became the first state to abolish speed limits on certain highways. Montana had 122 public-use airports, with the leading ones at Great Falls and Billings.

11 HISTORY

Montana's first European explorers were probably French traders and trappers from Canada who arrived during the 17th and 18th centuries. However, it was not until 1803 that the written history of Montana began. In that year, the Louisiana Purchase gave the United States most of Montana, and the Lewis and Clark expedition, dispatched by President Thomas Jefferson in 1804, added the rest. Soon afterwards, the first American trappers, traders, and settlers entered Montana.

The fur trade dominated Montana's economy until 1858, when gold was discovered east of the present-day community of Drummond, bringing with it a temporary gold boom. In 1863, the eastern and western sectors of Montana were joined as part of Idaho Territory. On 26 May 1864, President Abraham Lincoln signed the Organic Act, which created Montana Territory.

The territorial period was one of rapid and profound change. By the time Montana became a state on 8 November 1889, the remnants of Montana's Native American culture had been largely confined to federal reservations, following the surrender of the Nez Percé tribe to federal forces. As the Indian threat subsided, cattle

Photo credit: Travel Montana/P. Fugleberg.

A statue at Fort Benton commemorating the explorers Lewis and Clark.

ranchers wasted little time in putting the seemingly limitless open range to use. However, the "hard winter" of 1886/87, when perhaps as many as 362,000 head of cattle starved, marked the end of a cattle frontier based on the "free grass" of the open range and taught the stockmen the value of a secure winter feed supply.

1880s–1990s

Construction of Montana's railroad system between 1880 and 1909 breathed new life into mining as well as the livestock industry. By 1890, the Butte copper pits were producing more than 40% of the nation's copper requirements. The struggle to gain financial control of the enormous mineral wealth of Butte Hill led to the "War of the Copper Kings," whose victor, Anaconda Copper Mining, practically controlled the press, politics, and governmental processes of Montana until the 1940s and 1950s.

The railroads also brought an invasion of agricultural homesteaders. Montana's population doubled between 1900 and 1920, while the number of farms and ranches increased form 13,000 to 57,000. Drought and a sharp drop in wheat prices after World War I brought an end to the homestead boom. Conditions worsened with the drought and depression of the early 1930s. Then the New Deal—enormously popular in Montana—helped revive farming and silver mining and financed irrigation and other public works projects.

The decades since the end of World War II have seen moderate growth in Montana's population, economy, and social services. Although manufacturing developed slowly, the state's fossil fuels industry grew rapidly during the national energy crisis of the 1970s. However, production of coal, crude oil, and natural gas leveled off after the crisis and even declined in the early 1980s.

12 STATE GOVERNMENT

The state legislature consists of 50 senators, elected to four-year terms, and 100 representatives, who serve for two years. Elected officers of the executive branch include the governor and lieutenant gover-nor (who run jointly), secretary of state, and attorney general. Each serves a four-year term. To become law, a bill must pass both houses by a simple majority and be signed by the governor, or remain unsigned for five days, or be passed over the governor's veto by a two-thirds vote of both houses.

Montana Governors: 1889–2001

1889–1893	Joseph Kemp Toole	Democrat
1893–1897	John Ezra Rickards	Republican
1897–1901	Robert Burns Smith	Populist, Democrat
1901–1908	Joseph Kemp Toole	Democrat
1908–1913	Edwin Lee Norris	Democrat
1913–1921	Sam Vernon Stewart	Democrat
1921–1925	Joseph Moore Dixon	Republican
1925–1933	John Edward Erickson	Democrat
1933–1935	Frank Henry Cooney	Democrat
1935–1937	William Elmer Holt	Democrat
1937–1941	Roy Elmer Ayers	Democrat
1941–1949	Samuel Clarence Ford	Republican
1949–1953	John Woodrow Bonner	Democrat
1953–1961	John Hugo Aronson	Republican
1961–1965	Donald Grant Nutter	Republican
1965–1969	Tim M. Babcock	Republican
1969–1973	Forest Howard Anderson	Democrat
1973–1981	Thomas Lee Judge	Democrat
1981–1989	Ted Schwinden	Democrat
1989–1993	Stan Stephens	Republican
1993–2000	Marc Francis Racicot	Republican
2000-	Judy Martz	Republican

13 POLITICAL PARTIES

Since statehood, Democrats have generally dominated in contests for the US House and Senate, while Republicans led in elections for state and local offices and in national presidential campaigns (except during the New Deal years). In 2000, Montanans gave Republican George W. Bush 58% and Democrat Al Gore 33%.

The governor of Montana as of 2001, Republican Judy Martz, was elected in 2000. Republican Conrad Burns was reelected to the Senate in 2000, and Democrat Max Baucus won re-election in 1996. The representatives for the house consist of one democrat and one republican.

The Republicans have gained control of the state senate. As of 2001, there were 31 Republicans and 19 Democrats. The Republicans also continue to control the state house with 57 seats to the Democrats' 43.

Montana Presidential Vote by Major Political Parties, 1948–2000

YEAR	MONTANA WINNER	DEMOCRAT	REPUBLICAN
1948	*Truman (D)	119,071	96,770
1952	*Eisenhower (R)	106,213	157,394
1956	*Eisenhower (R)	116,238	154,933
1960	Nixon (R)	134,891	141,841
1964	*Johnson (D)	164,246	113,032
1968	*Nixon (R)	114,117	138,835
1972	*Nixon (R)	120,197	183,976
1976	Ford (R)	149,259	173,703
1980	*Reagan (R)	118,032	206,814
1984	*Reagan (R)	146,742	232,450
1988	*Bush (R)	168,936	190,412
1992**	*Clinton (D)	154,507	144,207
1996**	Dole (R)	167,922	179,652
2000	*Bush (R)	137,126	240,178

*Won US presidential election.
** Independent candidate Ross Perot received 107,225 votes in 1992 and 55,229 votes in 1996.

14 LOCAL GOVERNMENT

As of 1997, Montana had 54 counties, 128 municipalities, 535 special districts, and 365 school districts. Typically elected county officials are three county commissioners, an attorney, a sheriff, a clerk, and a recorder.

15 JUDICIAL SYSTEM

Montana's highest court, the supreme court, consists of a chief justice and six associate justices. District courts are the courts of general jurisdiction. There are 37 district court judges. Justice of the peace courts are essentially county courts whose jurisdiction is limited to minor civil cases, misdemeanors, and traffic violations. Montana's crime rate in 1998 was 4,070.7 per 100,000.

16 MIGRATION

After a net gain of 16,000 from migration between 1970 and 1980, Montana had a net loss of 43,000 residents from migration during the 1980s. During 1990–98, the net gain from interstate migration was about 48,000. In 1990, 58.9% of all Montanans had been born in the state.

17 ECONOMY

Resource industries—agriculture, mining, lumbering—dominate Montana's economy, although tourism is of increasing importance. A lawsuit with the federal government, over the federal lands which have supplied much of the state's timber, has placed the timber industry's future in question. Residential construction grew in 1993 with a rise in population growth. In the mid-1990s, private goods-producing industries accounted for 23% of Montana's total economic output; private services-producing industries, 61%; and government, 16%.

A Montana cowboy.

18 INCOME

With a per capita (per person) income of $21,229 in 1998, Montana ranked 47th among the 50 states. Median household income was $30,348 in 1998. Some 16.4% of the state's population lived below the federal poverty level in 1998.

19 INDUSTRY

Montana's major manufacturing industries process raw materials from mines, forests, and farms. The total value of shipments by manufacturers in 1997 amounted to $5.2 billion. Major industries include lumber and wood products; food products; and printing and publishing.

20 LABOR

Montana's labor force varies sharply with the season, swelling in the summer and shrinking in the winter. As of 1998, the civilian labor force totaled 468,000 persons. The unemployment rate averaged 5.6% in 1998. Some 15.3% of all workers in the state were union members in 1998.

21 AGRICULTURE

Montana's farms numbered 27,500 in 1998. Farm income totaled $1.7 billion in 1999. In that year, Montana was the nation's fourth-leading wheat producer, with an output of 166.8 million bushels, valued at $594.3 million. Other major crops were barley (second in the US), 57.6 million bushels; sugarbeets (sixth), 1.4 million bushels; and hay (12th), 5 million tons. Oats, potatoes, flax, and dry beans are also grown.

22 DOMESTICATED ANIMALS

Livestock production accounts for about half of Montana's farm income. In 1999, the state had 2.6 million cattle. Hogs numbered 190,000 in 1998. Sales of cattle products account for about 40% of agricultural receipts.

23 FISHING

Montana's designated fishing streams offer some 10,000 miles (16,000 kilometers) of good-to-excellent freshwater fishing. Federal hatcheries distributed 2.2 million cold-water species fish and 10 million fish eggs (mostly trout) in 1996.

24 FORESTRY

Montana has about 23.2 million acres (9.4 million hectares) of forestland in 1997. There are ten national forests, comprising roughly 16.9 million acres (6.8 million hectares). The lumbering industry produces about one billion board feet per year.

25 MINING

The estimated value of nonfuel mineral production for Montana in 1998 was $500 million. Metallic minerals—copper, gold, iron ore, lead, molybdenum, platinum group metals, silver, and zinc—accounted for 73% of the state's total nonfuel mineral production.

26 ENERGY AND POWER

In 1998, Montana produced 27.6 billion kilowatt hours of electricity, 40% from hydropower and 60% by coal-burning. The state has no nuclear power plants. Oil and natural gas supply about 60% of Montana's energy requirements. In 1995, the state produced 16.5 million barrels of crude oil. Natural gas production totaled 57.6 billion cubic feet (1.6 billion cubic meters). As of 1998, coal reserves were estimated at 119.7 billion tons—first in the US and over 24% of the US total.

27 COMMERCE

Montana's wholesale sales totaled $8.2 billion in 1997; retail sales were $8 billion. Montana's foreign exports in 1998 totaled $421 million. Wheat accounted for 65% of the state's foreign exports that year.

28 PUBLIC FINANCE

The estimated revenues for 1997 were $3.52 billion; estimated expenditures were $3.2 billion. The state's debt as of 1997 totaled $2.06 billion, or $2,339 per capita (per person).

29 TAXATION

Montana taxes personal and corporate income and levies a property tax but no sales or use tax. In 1997, the state tax burden was $1.26 billion, or $1,433 per person (40th among the states). State residents paid $2 billion in federal taxes in 1995 and received $4.8 billion in federal funding.

30 HEALTH

Of the major causes of death in 1998, only the heart disease rate was below the national norm. There were 53 community hospitals in 1998, with 4,413 beds. The average expense of a hospital providing service in 1998 was $519.70 per inpatient day and $5,863.60 per hospital admission. There were 188 physicians per 100,000 in 1997. Licensed full-time nurses numbered about 2,500 in 1998. Some 19.6% of state residents did not have health insurance in 1998.

31 HOUSING

In 1999, Montana had an estimated 346,000 housing units. The state authorized 2,600 new housing units valued at $217 million in 1998. In 1990, the median home value was $56,600. The median monthly cost for the owner (including a mortgage) was $575 that year. Renters had a median monthly cost of $311 in 1990.

32 EDUCATION

As of 1998, 89.1% of Montanans 25 years and older had completed high school, and 23.9% were college graduates. Public school enrollments in fall 1997 were 111,951 for grades preschool–8 and 50,384 in grades 9–12. Expenditures for public elementary and secondary schools

amounted to $5,202 per student in 1995/96 (30th among the states). As of fall 1997, 44,141 students attended institutions of higher education. Of these, the University of Montana (Missoula) enrolled 11,886, and Montana State University (Bozeman) had 11,562.

33 ARTS

The C. M. Russell Museum in Great Falls honors the work of Charles Russell. Other fine art museums include the Museum of the Rockies in Bozeman, Yellowstone Art Center at Billings, the Montana Historical Society Museum and Archives in Helena, and the Missoula Museum of the Arts.

34 LIBRARIES AND MUSEUMS

Montana had 79 public libraries, 28 public library branches, 6 institutional libraries, and 573 school libraries serving 56 counties. The combined book stock of all Montana public libraries was 2.64 million and their combined circulation was 4.97 million.

Distinguished collections include those of the University of Montana (Missoula) and Montana State University (Bozeman). Among the state's 74 museums are the Montana Historical Society Museum, Helena; World Museum of Mining, Butte; and Museum of the Plains Indian, Browning. National historic sites include the Little Big Horn battlefield.

35 COMMUNICATIONS

In 1999, 95.3% of the state's households had telephone service. There were 126 commercial radio stations in 2000, and 23 television stations.

36 PRESS

As of 1998, Montana had seven morning dailies, four evening dailies, and seven Sunday newspapers. The leading papers and their circulations were the *Billings Gazette* (51,773 mornings, 56,474 Sundays) and the *Great Falls Tribune* (34,257 mornings, 40,175 Sundays).

37 TOURISM, TRAVEL, AND RECREATION

Many tourists seek out the former gold rush camps, ghost towns, and dude ranches. Scenic wonders include Glacier National Park in the northwest, and Yellowstone National Park, which also extends into Idaho and Wyoming. Bighorn Canyon National Recreation Area is another popular destination.

38 SPORTS

There are no major league professional sports teams in Montana. The University of Montana Grizzlies and Montana State University Bobcats both compete in the Big Sky Conference. Skiing is a very popular participation sport. Rodeos are held across the state.

39 FAMOUS MONTANANS

Prominent national officeholders from Montana include US Senator Thomas Walsh (b.Wisconsin, 1859–1933), who directed the investigation that uncovered the Teapot Dome scandal; Jeannette Rankin (1880–1973), the first woman member of Congress and the only US representative to vote against American participation in both world wars. Crazy Horse (1849?–77) led a Sioux-Cheyenne army in battle at Little Big Horn.

Creative artists from Montana include Alfred Bertram Guthrie, Jr. (b.Indiana, 1901–91), author of *The Big Sky* and the Pulitzer Prize-winning *The Way West*; and Charles Russell (b.Missouri, 1864–1926), Montana's foremost painter and sculptor. Hollywood stars Gary Cooper (Frank James Cooper, 1901–61) and Myrna Loy (1905–93) were also from Montana.

40 BIBLIOGRAPHY

Aylesworth, Thomas G. *The Great Plains: Montana, Nebraska, North Dakota, South Dakota, Wyoming.* New York: Chelsea House, 1996.

George, Charles. *Montana.* New York: Children's Press, 2000.

Graetz, Rick. *Montana: East of the Mountains.* Helena, Mont.: Northern Rockies, 1998.

Sateren, Shelley Swanson. *Montana Facts and Symbols.* Mankato, Minn.: Hilltop Books, 2000.

Sullivan, Gordon. *Beautiful America's Montana.* Woodburn, Ore.: Beautiful America, 2000.

Web sites

Discovering Montana. [Online] Available http://www.discoveringmontana.com/css/default.asp/ Accessed May 16, 2001.

Travel Montana and The Information Technology Resource Center. Montana Is for Kids: Welcome to Montana Kids! [Online] Available http://kids.state.mt.us/ Accessed May 16, 2001.

NEBRASKA

State of Nebraska

ORIGIN OF STATE NAME: Derived from the Oto Indian word *nebrathka*, meaning "flat water" (for the Platte River).

NICKNAME: The Cornhusker State.

CAPITAL: Lincoln.

ENTERED UNION: 1 March 1867 (37th).

SONG: "Beautiful Nebraska."

MOTTO: Equality Before the Law.

FLAG: The great seal appears in the center in gold and silver, on a field of blue.

OFFICIAL SEAL: Agriculture is represented by a farmer's cabin, sheaves of wheat, and growing corn; the mechanic arts, by a blacksmith. Above is the state motto; in the background, a steamboat plies the Missouri River and a train heads toward the Rockies. The scene is surrounded by the words "Great Seal of the State of Nebraska, March 1st 1867."

ANIMAL: White-tailed deer.

BIRD: Western meadowlark.

FLOWER: Goldenrod.

TREE: Western cottonwood.

GEM: Blue agate.

ROCK: Prairie agate.

GRASS: Little bluestem.

INSECT: Honeybee.

FOSSIL: Mammoth.

TIME: 6 AM CST = noon GMT; 5 AM MST = noon GMT.

1 LOCATION AND SIZE

Located in the western north-central US, Nebraska ranks 15th in size among the 50 states. The total area of the state is 77,355 square miles (200,349 square kilometers). Nebraska extends about 415 miles (668 kilometers) east-west and 205 miles (330 kilometers) north-south. The boundary length of Nebraska totals 1,332 miles (2,143 kilometers).

2 TOPOGRAPHY

Most of Nebraska is prairie; more than two-thirds of the state lies within the Great Plains. The elevation slopes upward gradually from east to west, from a low of 840 feet (256 meters) to 5,426 feet (1,654 meters). The main lakes in the state are mostly artificial. The Missouri, Platte, Niobrara, and Republican rivers flow through Nebraska.

3 CLIMATE

Nebraska has a continental climate, with highly variable temperatures. The central region has a normal monthly maximum of 76°F (24°C) in July and a minimum of 22°F (–6°C) in January. The record low for the state was –47°F (–44°C) in 1899; the record high of 118°F (48°C) was recorded in 1936. Normal yearly precipitation ranges from 17 inches (43 centimeters) in the west to 30 inches (76 centimeters) in the southeast.

4 PLANTS AND ANIMALS

Nebraska's deciduous forests are generally oak and hickory. Conifer forests are dominated by western yellow (ponderosa) pine. Slough grasses, needlegrasses, western wheatgrass, and buffalo grass are found in the prairies. Common Nebraska wildflowers include wild rose, columbine, and sunflower.

Common mammals native to the state are the pronghorn sheep, white-tailed and mule deer, and coyote. There are more than 400 kinds of birds, the mourning dove and western meadowlark (the state bird) among them. Carp, catfish, and trout are fished for sport. The bald eagle, Arctic peregrine falcon, and black-footed ferret are among the state's endangered species.

5 ENVIRONMENTAL PROTECTION

The Department of Environmental Quality protects the quality of Nebraska's water, air, and land resources. There were ten hazardous waste sites as of 1998.

Nebraska Population Profile

Total population in 2000:	1,711,263
Population change, 1990–2000:	8.4%
Hispanic or Latino†:	5.5%
Population by race	
One race:	98.6%
White:	89.6%
Black or African American:	4.0%
American Indian/Alaska Native:	0.9%
Asian:	1.3%
Native Hawaiian/Pacific Islander:	—
Some other race:	2.8%
Two or more races:	1.4%

Population by Age Group

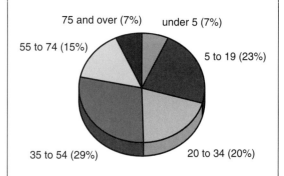

75 and over (7%)   under 5 (7%)
55 to 74 (15%)
5 to 19 (23%)
35 to 54 (29%)
20 to 34 (20%)

Top Cities by Population

City	Population	% change 1990–2000
Omaha	390,007	16.1
Lincoln	225,581	17.5
Bellevue	44,382	43.3
Grand Island	42,940	9.0
Kearney	27,431	12.4
Fremont	25,174	6.3
Hastings	24,064	5.4
North Platte	23,878	5.6
Norfolk	23,516	9.5
Columbus	20,971	7.7

Notes: †A person of Hispanic or Latino origin may be of any race. NA indicates that data are not available.
Sources: U.S. Census Bureau. Public Information Office. *Demographic Profiles.* [Online] Available http://www.census.gov/Press-Release/www/2001/demoprofile.html. Accessed June 1, 2001. U.S. Census Bureau. *Census 2000: Redistricting Data.* Press release issued by the Redistricting Data Office. Washington, D.C., March, 2001.

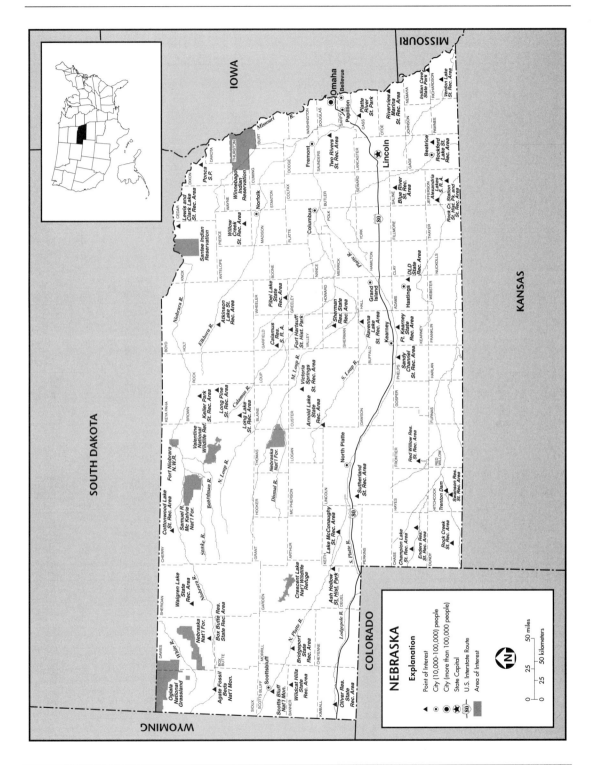

6 POPULATION

Nebraska dropped behind West Virginia and New Mexico, ranking 38th in the US in 2000. Its census population that year was nearly 1,711,263. A population of 1.76 million is projected for 2005. The largest cities are Omaha, with a 2000 population of 390,007; Lincoln, with 225,581; and Bellevue, 44,382. Nebraska's median age of 35.3 was identical to the national average in 2000. Approximately 30% of the population is 19 years of age and younger.

7 ETHNIC GROUPS

In 1990, 794,911 Nebraskans identified their ancestry as German; 208,616, English; 272,185, Irish; 90,043, Czech; and 99,263, Swedish. Nebraska's proportion of white population in 1997 was the tenth highest, at 93.8%. The 1997 population estimate also included 66,200 blacks; 21,000 Asians and Pacific Islanders; and some 14,800 Native Americans.

8 LANGUAGES

Nebraska English is almost pure North Midland, except for slight South Midland and Northern influences. In 1990, 1,389,032 Nebraskans spoke only English at home. The number of residents who spoke other languages at home included Spanish, 24,555; and German, 13,927. In 1990, about 1,700 Nebraskans spoke Native American languages at home.

9 RELIGIONS

In 1990, the state's Catholic population numbered 335,372. Lutherans constituted the largest Protestant group with 114,944 members of the Missouri Synod and 129,239 of the Evangelical Lutheran Church in America. A total of 145,248 were United Methodists, and 48,591 were Presbyterians. The Jewish population was estimated at 7,000 in 1994.

10 TRANSPORTATION

In 1998, Nebraska had 13 rail lines with 3,696 rail miles (5,947 kilometers) of track. Nebraska carried 388.7 million tons of freight by rail. Amtrak had a total of 38,173 Nebraska riders in 1996. The state's road system was estimated at 92,813 miles (149,336 kilometers) in 1997. A total of 1.5 million motor vehicles were registered in 1997, of which 811,678 were automobiles and 689,821 were trucks. Eppley Airfield, Omaha's airport, is by far the busiest in the state, handling 25,131 aircraft departures with 1.67 million passengers in 1996.

11 HISTORY

By 1800, the Pawnee, Ponca, Omaha, and Oto tribes, along with several others, were living in present-day Nebraska. The area was claimed by both Spain and France and was French territory at the time of the Louisiana Purchase in 1803, when it came under US jurisdiction. During the first half of the 19th century, the area was explored by Lewis and Clark, Zebulon Pike, and others.

Military forts were established in the 1840s to protect travelers from attack by Native Americans. The Kansas-Nebraska Act of 1854 established Nebraska Territory, which assumed its present shape in 1861. Still sparsely populated, Nebraska

Nebraska Population by Race

Census 2000 was the first national census in which the instructions to respondents said, "Mark one or more races." This table shows the number of people who are of one, two, or three or more races. For those claiming two races, the number of people belonging to the various categories is listed. The U.S. government conducts a census of the population every ten years.

	Number	Percent
Total population	1,711,263	100.0
One race	1,687,310	98.6
Two races	22,591	1.3
White *and* Black or African American	4,651	0.3
White *and* American Indian/Alaska Native	5,285	0.3
White *and* Asian	3,344	0.2
White *and* Native Hawaiian/Pacific Islander	310	—
White *and* some other race	6,057	0.4
Black or African American *and* American Indian/Alaska Native	704	—
Black or African American *and* Asian	302	—
Black or African American *and* Native Hawaiian/Pacific Islander	50	—
Black or African American *and* some other race	669	—
American Indian/Alaska Native *and* Asian	113	—
American Indian/Alaska Native *and* Native Hawaiian/Pacific Islander	15	—
American Indian/Alaska Native *and* some other race	356	—
Asian *and* Native Hawaiian/Pacific Islander	181	—
Asian *and* some other race	461	—
Native Hawaiian/Pacific Islander *and* some other race	93	—
Three or more races	1,362	0.1

Source: U.S. Census Bureau. *Census 2000: Redistricting Data.* Press release issued by the Redistricting Data Office. Washington, D.C., March, 2001. A dash (—) indicates that the percent is less than 0.1.

escaped the violence over the slavery issue that afflicted Kansas. However, from 1860 to the late 1870s, western Nebraska was a battleground for US soldiers and Native Americans, who moved onto reservations in Nebraska, South Dakota, and Oklahoma by 1890.

Statehood

Settlement of Nebraska Territory was rapid, escalated by the Homestead Act of 1862, under which the US government provided 160 acres (65 hectares) to a settler for a small fee. On 1 March 1867, Nebraska became the 37th state to join the Union. Farming and ranching devel-

oped as the state's two main enterprises. However, by 1890, depressed farm prices, high railroad shipping charges, and rising interest rates were hurting the state's farmers, and a drought in the 1890s worsened their plight.

When the dust storms of the 1930s began, thousands of people fled Nebraska for the West Coast. However, the onset of World War II brought prosperity in other areas. Military airfields and war industries were placed in the state because of its safe inland location, bringing industrial growth that extended into the postwar years. Much of the new industry developed since that time is agriculture-related, including

Chimney Rock on the Oregon Trail.

the manufacture of farm machinery and irrigation equipment.

Farm output and income increased dramatically into the 1970s. Many farmers took. on large debt burdens to finance expanded output, with their credit supported by strong farm-product prices and exports. When prices began to fall in the early 1980s, many found themselves in trouble. A 1982 state constitutional amendment prohibits the sale of land used for farming or ranching to anyone other than a Nebraska family farm corporation.

12 STATE GOVERNMENT

Nebraska's legislature is unique among the states. It is a single-chamber body of 49 members not elected by political party. Elected executives are the governor, lieutenant governor, secretary of state, auditor, treasurer, and attorney general. A bill becomes law when passed by a majority of the legislature and signed by the governor. If the governor does not approve, the bill is returned with objections, and a three-fifths vote of the legislature is required to override the veto. A bill automatically becomes law if the governor does not take action within five days after receiving it.

13 POLITICAL PARTIES

In 1994 there were 464,955 registered Republicans, or 49% of the total number of registered voters; 389,102 registered

Democrats, or 41%; and 97,897 independents, or 10%. In the 2000 elections, Republican challenger George W. Bush secured 62% of the vote while Democrat Al Gore received 33% of the votes. In the November 1994 elections, Democrat Bob Kerrey was reelected to the US Senate and another Democrat, Ben Nelson, won the election for governor. In 2000, Nelson won the Senate race against Republican Don Stenberg, 51% to 49%. Republican Chuck Hagel won election to the US Senate in 1996. As of 2001, all three US House Seats were held by Republicans.

14 LOCAL GOVERNMENT

In 1997, Nebraska had 93 counties, 461 townships, 535 municipalities, and 681 school districts. Municipalities are governed by mayors.

Nebraska Governors: 1867–2001

1867–1871	David C. Butler	Republican
1871–1873	William Hartford James	Republican
1873–1875	Robert Wilkinson Furnas	Republican
1875–1879	Silas Garber	Republican
1879–1883	Albinus Nance	Republican
1883–1887	James William Dawes	Republican
1887–1891	John Milton Thayer	Republican
1891	James E. Boyd	Democrat
1891–1892	John Milton Thayer	Republican
1892–1893	James E. Boyd	Democrat
1893–1895	Lorenzo Crounse	Republican
1895–1899	Silas Alexander Halcomb	Populist
1899–1901	William Amos Poynter	Fusion
1901	Charles Henry Dietrich	Republican
1901–1903	Ezra Perin Savage	Republican
1903–1907	John Hopwood Mickey	Republican
1907–1909	George Lawson Sheldon	Republican
1909–1911	Ashton Cockayne Shallenberger	Democrat
1911–1913	Chester Hardy Aldrich	Republican
1913–1917	John Henry Morehead	Democrat
1917–1919	M. Kieth Neville	Democrat
1919–1923	Samuel Roy McKelvie	Republican
1923–1925	Charles Wayland Bryan	Democrat
1925–1929	Adma McMullen	Republican
1929–1931	Arthur J. Weaver	Republican
1931–1935	Charles Wayland Bryan	Democrat
1935–1941	Robert LeRoy Cochran	Democrat
1941–1947	Dwight Palmer Griswold	Republican
1947–1953	Val Frederick Demar Peterson	Republican
1953–1955	Robert Berkey Crosby	Republican
1955–1959	Victor Emanuel Anderson	Republican
1959–1960	Ralph Gilmour Brooks	Democrat
1960–1961	Dwight Willard Burney	Republican
1961–1967	Frank Brenner Morrison	Democrat
1967–1971	Norbert Theodore Tiemann	Republican
1971–1979	John James Exon	Democrat
1979–1983	Charles Thone	Republican
1983–1987	Robert Kerrey	Democrat
1987–1991	Kay A. Orr	Republican
1991–1999	Earl Benjamin Nelson	Democrat
1999–	Michael Johanns	Republican

15 JUDICIAL SYSTEM

The state's highest court is the supreme court, consisting of a chief justice and six other justices. Below the supreme court are the district courts, trial courts of general jurisdiction. County courts handle criminal misdemeanors and civil cases involving less than $5,000. Nebraska's crime rate is well below the national average—in 1998 it was 4,405.2 per 100,000. In June 1999, prison inmates in state and federal prisons numbered 3,663.

Nebraska Presidential Vote by Major Political Parties, 1948–2000

YEAR	NEBRASKA WINNER	DEMOCRAT	REPUBLICAN
1948	Dewey (R)	224,165	264,774
1952	*Eisenhower (R)	188,057	421,603
1956	*Eisenhower (R)	199,029	378,108
1960	Nixon (R)	232,542	380,553
1964	*Johnson (D)	307,307	276,847
1968	*Nixon (R)	170,784	321,163
1972	*Nixon (R)	169,991	406,298
1976	Ford (R)	233,692	359,705
1980	*Reagan (R)	166,424	419,214
1984	*Reagan (R)	187,866	460,054
1988	*Bush (R)	259,235	397,956
1992**	Bush (R)	217,344	344,346
1996**	Dole (R)	236,761	363,467
2000	*Bush (R)	231,780	433,862

* Won US presidential election.

** Independent candidate Ross Perot received 174,687 votes in 1992 and 71,278 votes in 1996.

16 MIGRATION

From 1930 to 1960, the state suffered a net loss of nearly 500,000 people, with more than one-third of the total leaving during the dust-bowl decade, 1930–40. This trend continues, with Nebraska experiencing a net out-migration of 27,400 for the period 1985–90. During 1990–98, the net gain of migration from other states was just 2,000, but the net gain from international migration was 14,000.

17 ECONOMY

Agriculture is the backbone of Nebraska's economy. Cattle, corn, hogs, and soybeans lead the state's list of farm products. However, Nebraska is attempting to diversify and has been successful in attracting new business, in large part because of its location near western coal and oil deposits.

18 INCOME

Nebraska's per capita (per person) income was $25,924 in 1998, giving the state a rank of 24th in the nation. Median household income that year was $35,661. Some 10.8% of the state's population was living below the federal poverty level in 1998.

19 INDUSTRY

Nebraska has a small but growing industrial sector. In 1997, processing of food products was the leading industry, accounting for 50% of the total value of shipments, which was $28 billion. Value of shipments by manufacturers in other industries included industrial machinery, $1.7 billion; electronic equipment, $1.3 billion; and transportation equipment, $1.2 billion.

20 LABOR

Nebraska's labor force totaled 916,000 in 1998, of whom 2.7% were unemployed. There were approximately 40 labor unions operating in the state in 1998. Membership in unions totaled 10.3% of total employment that same year.

21 AGRICULTURE

With total farm marketings valued at over $8.5 billion in 1999, Nebraska ranked fourth among the 50 states. Farms in Nebraska are major businesses, requiring large landholdings to justify investments. The average Nebraska farm in 1998 covered 844 acres (340 hectares) and had a value of over $581,090. However, Nebraska farms still tend to be owned by single persons or families, rather than by large corporations.

In 1998, Nebraska ranked third among the states in production of corn and sorghum for grain. Crop production in 1998 (in bushels) included corn, 1.24 billion; soybeans, 165 million; sorghum grain, 56.4 million; wheat, 82.8 million; oats, 5.3 million; and rye, 288,000.

22 DOMESTICATED ANIMALS

In 1998, Nebraska ranked second behind Texas in the US in number of cattle (6.6 million head). The state also ranked second (after Texas) in the quantity of cattle produced (3.9 million pounds/1.8 million kilograms) in 1995. Nebraska's hog-raising business is the nation's fourth largest. The state had about 3.4 million hogs in 1998.

Photo credit: Greater Omaha Convention & Visitors Bureau.

The Omaha skyline.

Cattle marketings account for about 50% of agricultural receipts; hog marketings, 9%.

23 FISHING

Commercial fishing is not significant in Nebraska. The North Platte and Valentine State Fish Hatcheries provide fish for anglers; federal hatcheries distributed over 36,100 fish and 362,750 fish eggs within the state in 1996.

24 FORESTRY

Arbor Day, now observed throughout the US, originated in Nebraska in 1872 as a way of encouraging tree-planting in the sparsely forested state. Forestland occu-pies 947,000 acres (383,000 hectares), or 2% of all Nebraska. Ash, box elder, oak, walnut, elm, and willow trees are common to eastern and central Nebraska, while pine and cedar prevail in the west. The state's two national forests—Nebraska and Samuel R. McKelvie—are actually primarily grassland and are managed for livestock grazing. The two national forests cover 46,000 acres (18,600 hectares), including 16,000 acres (6,500 hectares) of planted forest.

25 MINING

The value of nonfuel mineral production in Nebraska in 1998 was approximately $174 million. All nonfuel minerals produced in Nebraska, with the exception of gem stones, were basic construction materials. In 1998, mineral production included 14.4 million metric tons of sand and gravel, 7 million metric tons of crushed stone, and 193 metric tons of clay.

26 ENERGY AND POWER

Total energy consumed in Nebraska in 1997 was an all-time record of 617.1 trillion Btu (155 trillion kcal). Nebraska is the only state with an electric power system totally owned by the public, through cooperatives and municipal plants. In 1998, electrical output totaled a record 28.7 billion kilowatt hours. As of 1999, crude petroleum production in Nebraska was 2.66 million barrels. Natural gas production totaled 1.7 billion cubic feet (48 million cubic meters) in 1998. The state has two nuclear power plants.

27 COMMERCE

Nebraska's wholesale sales totaled $40 billion for 1997; retail sales were $16.4 billion. Nebraska's exports of goods totaled $2.3 billion in 1999.

28 PUBLIC FINANCE

Nebraska's constitution prohibits the state from incurring debt in excess of $100,000. A separate legal entity that is blended into the financial activity of the state issues bonds. The two state-authorized financing authorities are not subject to the constitutional ban on incurring debt.

Total revenues for fiscal year 1997 were $5.54 billion; total expenditures were $4.8 billion.

29 TAXATION

A constitutional amendment in 1967 prohibited the use of property tax revenues for state government. This forced the passage of both a sales/use tax and an income tax, which had long been resisted. In 1997, the state tax burden was $2.54 billion, or $1,538 per person (28th among the states). Nebraska's federal income tax burden in 1996 was $7.4 billion, and the state received $7.6 billion in federal funding.

30 HEALTH

Nebraska had 86 community hospitals in and 8,133 beds in 1998. There were 213 physicians per 100,000 in 1997. Licensed full-time nurses numbered over 6,000 in 1998. About 9% of state residents did not have health insurance in 1998, the lowest percentage of any state. Major causes of death in 1998 were heart disease, cerebrovascular diseases, pneumonia and influenza, accidents, and suicide.

31 HOUSING

In 1999, there were some 711,000 housing units in Nebraska. Median value for owner-occupied homes was $50,400 in 1990, when owners with a mortgage had a median monthly cost of $610. Renters had a median cost of $348 per month. In 1998, 9,600 new privately owned housing units that were authorized by the state had a total value of $787 million.

32 EDUCATION

In 1997, there were 1,333 public schools in Nebraska: 964 were elementary schools, 349 were secondary schools, and 20 were special education schools. Public school

Photo credit: Greater Omaha Convention & Visitors Bureau.

The Great Plains Black Museum, the largest Black American historical and cultural center west of the Mississippi River.

enrollments for fall 1997 were elementary, 201,684; and secondary, 90,997. There was a total public school enrollment of 292,681 (preschool through 12th grade). Non-public schools enrolled 40,943 students. Expenditures for public elementary and secondary schools amounted to $5,166 per student in 1995/96 (32nd among the states).

The University of Nebraska is the state's largest postsecondary institution, with campuses in Kearney, Lincoln, and Omaha. In 1997, there were also 3 state colleges, 17 independent colleges and universities, and 6 community colleges. In fall 1996, 23,887 students were enrolled the University of Nebraska–Lincoln and 14,974 at the University of Nebraska–Omaha, 19,651 at independent institutions of higher learning, and 41,761 at community colleges.

33 ARTS

The Orpheum Theater in Omaha provides performance space for opera, symphony concerts, ballet, plays, and popular music. Opera/Omaha, Inc., presents three operas there each year, drawing an annual audi-

Photo credit: Greater Omaha Convention & Visitors Bureau.

(Father) Flanagan's Boys Town in Omaha.

ence of 28,000. The 15-member Nebraska Arts Council is appointed by the governor to administer state programs in all the arts.

34 LIBRARIES AND MUSEUMS

In 1998, the state had 12 county libraries and 270 public libraries. A total of 6.6 million volumes were in the public library system in 1995. Total circulation was 11 million. The Joslyn Art Museum in Omaha is the state's leading museum. Other important museums include the Nebraska State Museum of History and the University of Nebraska State Museum.

35 COMMUNICATIONS

About 95.9% of the state's occupied housing units had telephones in 1999. In 2000, 96FM stations and 51 AM stations were operating. There were also 28 TV stations. In 1996, there were three large cable television systems. A total of 23,752 Internet domain names registered in the state in 2000.

36 PRESS

In 1998, Nebraska had 6 morning dailies, 12 evening dailies, and 6 Sunday newspapers. The leading newspaper in 1998 was the *Omaha World–Herald,* with a daily circulation of 219,891 and a Sunday circulation of 273,982. The *Lincoln Journal–Star* had a daily circulation of 74,841 and a Sunday circulation of 82,091.

37 TOURISM, TRAVEL, AND RECREATION

The 8 state parks, 9 state historical parks, 12 federal areas, and 55 recreational areas are main tourist attractions; fishing, swimming, picnicking, and sightseeing are the principal activities. Pawnee State Recreation Area and Fremont State Recreation Area are the most popular attractions.

38 SPORTS

There are no major league professional sports teams in Nebraska. The most popular spectator sport is college football. Horse-related activities, including racing and rodeos, are popular. Major annual sporting events are the NCAA College Baseball World Series and the World's Championship Rodeo, both held in

Omaha. The University of Nebraska Cornhuskers compete in the Big 12 football conference. The Cornhuskers went on to win the Fiesta Bowl in 2000.

39 FAMOUS NEBRASKANS

Nebraska was the birthplace of only one US president, Gerald R. Ford (Leslie King, Jr., b.1913). William Jennings Bryan (b.Illinois, 1860–1925), a US representative from Nebraska, served as secretary of state and was three times the unsuccessful Democratic candidate for president.

Native American leaders important in Nebraska history include Oglala Sioux chiefs Red Cloud (1822–1909) and Crazy Horse (1849?–77), and Ponca chief Standing Bear (1829–1908). Father Edward Joseph Flanagan (b.Ireland, 1886–1948) was the founder of Boys Town, a home for underprivileged youth. Two native Nebraskans became Nobel laureates in 1980: Lawrence R. Klein (b.1920) in economics and Val L. Fitch (b.1923) in physics.

Writers associated with Nebraska include Willa Cather (b.Virginia, 1873–1947), who used the Nebraska frontier setting of her childhood in many of her writings and won a Pulitzer Prize in 1922; Mari Sandoz (1896–1966), who wrote of her native Great Plains; and author Tillie Olsen (b.1912). Composer-conductor Howard Hanson (1896–1982), born in Wahoo, won a Pulitzer Prize in 1944.

Nebraskans important in entertainment include actor-dancer Fred Astaire (Fred Austerlitz, 1899–1984); actors Henry Fonda (1905–82), and Marlon Brando

Photo credit: EPD Photos/National Archives.

Chief Red Cloud (1822–1908) led the Sioux people in opposition to U.S. expansion. Red Cloud, born in present day Garden County, Nebraska, was inducted into the Nebraska Hall of Fame in 2001

(b.1924); and television star Johnny Carson (b.Iowa, 1925).

40 BIBLIOGRAPHY

Aylesworth, Thomas G. *The Great Plains: Montana, Nebraska, North Dakota, South Dakota, Wyoming.* New York: Chelsea House, 1996.

Conrad, Pam. *Prairie Visions: the Life and Times of Solomon Butcher.* New York: HarperCollins, 1991.

McAuliffe, Emily. *Nebraska Facts and Symbols.* Mankato, Minn.: Hilltop Books, 1999.

McNair, Sylvia. *Nebraska.* New York: Children's Press, 1999.

Nichols, John. *Big Red: the Nebraska Cornhuskers Story.* Mankato, Minn.: Creative Education, 1999.

Thompson, Kathleen. *Nebraska.* Austin, Tex.: Steck-Vaughn, 1996.

Wills, Charles. *A Historical Album of Nebraska.* Brookfield, Conn.: Millbrook Press, 1994.

Web sites

State of Nebraska. Official Website. [Online] Available http://www.state.ne.us/ Accessed May 16, 2001.

Visit Nebraska. Homework: Quick Guide to Nebraska's Past. [Online] Available http://visitnebraska.org/ Accessed May 16, 2001.

Glossary

ALPINE: generally refers to the Alps or other mountains; can also refer to a mountainous zone above the timberline.

ANCESTRY: based on how people refer to themselves, and refers to a person's ethnic origin, descent, heritage, or place of birth of the person or the person's parents or ancestors before their arrival in the United States. The Census Bureau accepted "American" as a unique ethnicity if it was given alone, with an unclear response (such as "mixed" or "adopted"), or with names of particular states.

ANTEBELLUM: before the US Civil War.

AQUEDUCT: a large pipe or channel that carries water over a distance, or a raised structure that supports such a channel or pipe.

AQUIFER: an underground layer of porous rock, sand, or gravel that holds water.

BLUE LAWS: laws forbidding certain practices (e.g., conducting business, gaming, drinking liquor), especially on Sundays.

BROILERS: a bird (especially a young chicken) that can be cooked by broiling.

BTU: The amount of heat required to raise one pound of water one degree Fahrenheit.

CAPITAL BUDGET: a financial plan for acquiring and improving buildings or land, paid for by the sale of bonds.

CAPITAL PUNISHMENT: punishment by death.

CIVILIAN LABOR FORCE: all persons 16 years of age or older who are not in the armed forces and who are now holding a job, have been temporarily laid off, are waiting to be reassigned to a new position, or are unemployed but actively looking for work.

CLASS I RAILROAD: a railroad having gross annual revenues of $83.5 million or more in 1983.

COMMERCIAL BANK: a bank that offers to businesses and individuals a variety of banking services, including the right of withdrawal by check.

COMPACT: a formal agreement, covenant, or understanding between two or more parties.

CONSOLIDATED BUDGET: a financial plan that includes the general budget, federal funds, and all special funds.

CONSTANT DOLLARS: money values calculated so as to eliminate the effect of inflation on prices and income.

CONTERMINOUS US: refers to the "lower 48" states of the continental US that are enclosed within a common boundary.

CONTINENTAL CLIMATE: the climate typical of the US interior, having distinct seasons, a wide range of daily and annual temperatures, and dry, sunny summers.

COUNCIL-MANAGER SYSTEM: a system of local government under which a professional administrator is hired by an elected council to carry out its laws and policies.

CREDIT UNION: a cooperative body that raises funds from its members by the sale of shares and makes loans to its members at relatively low interest rates.

CURRENT DOLLARS: money values that reflect prevailing prices, without excluding the effects of inflation.

DEMAND DEPOSIT: a bank deposit that can be withdrawn by the depositor with no advance notice to the bank.

ELECTORAL VOTES: the votes that a state may cast for president, equal to the combined total of its US senators and representatives and nearly always cast entirely on behalf of the candidate who won the most votes in that state on Election Day.

ENDANGERED SPECIES: a type of plant or animal threatened with extinction in all or part of its natural range.

FEDERAL POVERTY LEVEL: a level of money income below which a person or family qualifies for US government aid.

FISCAL YEAR: a 12-month period for accounting purposes.

FOOD STAMPS: coupons issued by the government to low-income persons for food purchases at local stores.

GENERAL BUDGET: a financial plan based on a government's normal revenues and operating expenses, excluding special funds.

GENERAL COASTLINE: a measurement of the general outline of the US seacoast. See also TIDAL SHORELINE.

GREAT AWAKENING: during the mid–18th century, a Protestant religious revival in North America, especially New England.

GROSS STATE PRODUCT: the total value of goods and services produced in the state.

GROWING SEASON: the period between the last 32°F (0°C) temperature in spring and the first

32°F (0°C) temperature in autumn.

HISPANIC: a person who originates from Spain or from Spanish-speaking countries of South and Central America, Mexico, Puerto Rico, and Cuba.

HOME-RULE CHARTER: a document stating how and in what respects a city, town, or county may govern itself.

HUNDREDWEIGHT: a unit of weight that equals 100 pounds in the US and 112 pounds in Britain.

INPATIENT: a patient who is housed and fed—in addition to being treated—in a hospital.

INSTALLED CAPACITY: the maximum possible output of electric power at any given time.

MASSIF: a central mountain mass or the dominant part of a range of mountains.

MAYOR-COUNCIL SYSTEM: a system of local government under which an elected council serves as a legislature and an elected mayor is the chief administrator.

MEDICAID: a federal-state program that helps defray the hospital and medical costs of needy persons.

MEDICARE: a program of hospital and medical insurance for the elderly, administered by the federal government.

METRIC TON: a unit of weight that equals 1,000 kilograms (2,204.62 pounds).

METROPOLITAN AREA: in most cases, a city and its surrounding suburbs.

MONTANE: refers to a zone in mountainous areas in which large coniferous trees, in a cool moist setting, are the main features.

NO-FAULT INSURANCE: an automobile insurance plan that allows an accident victim to receive payment from an insurance company without having to prove who was responsible for the accident.

NONFEDERAL PHYSICIAN: a medical doctor who is not employed by the federal US government.

NORTHERN, NORTH MIDLAND: major US dialect regions.

OMBUDSMAN: a public official empowered to hear and investigate complaints by private citizens about government agencies.

PER CAPITA: per person.

PERSONAL INCOME: refers to the income an individual receives from employment, or to the total incomes that all individuals receive from their employment in a sector of business (such as personal incomes in the retail trade).

PIEDMONT: refers to the base of mountains.

POCKET VETO: a method by which a state governor (or the US president) may kill a bill by taking no action on it before the legislature adjourns.

PROVED RESERVES: the quantity of a recoverable mineral resource (such as oil or natural gas) that is still in the ground.

PUBLIC DEBT: the amount owed by a government.

RELIGIOUS ADHERENTS: the followers of a religious group, including (but not confined to) the full, confirmed, or communicant members of that group.

RETAIL TRADE: the sale of goods directly to the consumer.

REVENUE SHARING: the distribution of federal tax receipts to state and local governments.

RIGHT-TO-WORK LAW: a measure outlawing any attempt to require union membership as a condition of employment.

SAVINGS AND LOAN ASSOCIATION: a bank that invests the savings of depositors primarily in home mortgage loans.

SECESSION: the act of withdrawal, such as a state that withdrew from the Union in the US Civil War.

SERVICE INDUSTRIES: industries that provide services (e.g., health, legal, automotive repair) for individuals, businesses, and others.

SHORT TON: a unit of weight that equals 2,000 pounds.

SOCIAL SECURITY: as commonly understood, the federal system of old age, survivors, and disability insurance.

SOUTHERN, SOUTH MIDLAND: major US dialect regions.

SUBALPINE: generally refers to high mountainous areas just beneath the timberline; can also more specifically refer to the lower slopes of the Alps mountains.

SUNBELT: the southernmost states of the US, extending from Florida to California.

SUPPLEMENTAL SECURITY INCOME: a federally administered program of aid to the aged, blind, and disabled.

TIDAL SHORELINE: a detailed measurement of the US seacoast that includes sounds, bays, other outlets, and offshore islands.

TIME DEPOSIT: a bank deposit that may be withdrawn only at the end of a specified time period or upon advance notice to the bank.

VALUE ADDED BY MANUFACTURE: the difference, measured in dollars, between the value of finished goods and the cost of the materials needed to produce them.

WHOLESALE TRADE: the sale of goods, usually in large quantities, for ultimate resale to consumers.

Abbreviations & Acronyms

AD—Anno Domini
AFDC—aid to families with dependent children
AFL–CIO—American Federation of Labor–Congress of Industrial Organizations
AI—American Independent
AM—before noon
AM—amplitude modulation
American Ind.—American Independent Party
Amtrak—National Railroad Passenger Corp.
b.—born
BC—Before Christ
Btu—British thermal unit(s)
bu—bushel(s)
c.—circa (about)
C—Celsius (Centigrade)
CIA—Central Intelligence Agency
cm—centimeter(s)
Co.—company
comp.—compiler
Conrail—Consolidated Rail Corp.
Corp.—corporation
CST—Central Standard Time
cu—cubic
cwt—hundredweight(s)
d.—died
D—Democrat
e—evening
E—east
ed.—edition, editor
e.g.—exempli gratia (for example)
EPA—Environmental Protection Agency
est.—estimated
EST—Eastern Standard Time
et al.—et alii (and others)
etc.—et cetera (and so on)
F—Fahrenheit
FBI—Federal Bureau of Investigation
FCC—Federal Communications Commission
FM—frequency modulation
Ft.—fort
ft—foot, feet
GDP—gross domestic products
gm—gram
GMT—Greenwich Mean Time
GNP—gross national product
GRT—gross registered tons
Hist.—Historic
I—interstate (highway)

i.e.—id est (that is)
in—inch(es)
Inc.—incorporated
Jct.—junction
K—kindergarten
kg—kilogram(s)
km—kilometer(s)
km/hr—kilometers per hour
kw—kilowatt(s)
kwh—kilowatt-hour(s)
lb—pound(s)
m—meter(s); morning
m^3—cubic meter(s)
mi—mile(s)
Mon.—monument
mph—miles per hour
MST—Mountain Standard Time
Mt.—mount
Mtn.—mountain
mw—megawatt(s)
N—north
NA—not available
Natl.—National
NATO—North Atlantic Treaty Organization
NCAA—National Collegiate Athletic Association
n.d.—no date
NEA—National Education Association or National Endowment for the Arts
N.F.—National Forest
N.W.R.—National Wildlife Refuge
oz—ounce(s)
PM—after noon
PST—Pacific Standard Time
r.—reigned
R—Republican
Ra.—range
Res.—reservoir, reservation
rev. ed.—revised edition
s—south
S—Sunday
Soc.—Socialist
sq—square
St.—saint
SRD—States' Rights Democrat
UN—United Nations
US—United States
USIA—United States Information Agency
w—west

NAMES OF STATES AND OTHER SELECTED AREAS

	Standard Abbreviation(s)	Postal Abbreviation
Alabama	Ala.	AL
Alaska	*	AK
Arizona	Ariz.	AZ
Arkansas	Ark.	AR
California	Calif.	CA
Colorado	Colo.	CO
Connecticut	Conn.	CN
Delaware	Del.	DE
District of Columbia	D.C.	DC
Florida	Fla.	FL
Georgia	Ga.	GA
Hawaii	*	HI
Idaho	*	ID
Illinois	Ill.	IL
Indiana	Ind.	IN
Iowa	*	IA
Kansas	Kans. (Kan.)	KS
Kentucky	Ky.	KY
Louisiana	La.	LA
Maine	Me.	ME
Maryland	Md.	MD
Massachusetts	Mass.	MA
Michigan	Mich.	MI
Minnesota	Minn.	MN
Mississippi	Miss.	MS
Missouri	Mo.	MO
Montana	Mont.	MT
Nebraska	Nebr. (Neb.)	NE
Nevada	Nev.	NV
New Hampshire	N.H.	NH
New Jersey	N.J.	NJ
New Mexico	N.Mex.(N.M.)	NM
New York	N.Y.	NY
North Carolina	N.C.	NC
North Dakota	N.Dak. (N.D.)	ND
Ohio	*	OH
Oklahoma	Okla.	OK
Oregon	Oreg. (Ore.)	OR
Pennsylvania	Pa.	PA
Puerto Rico	P.R.	PR
Rhode Island	R.I.	RI
South Carolina	S.C.	SC
South Dakota	S.Dak. (S.D.)	SD
Tennessee	Tenn.	TN
Texas	Tex.	TX
Utah	*	UT
Vermont	Vt.	VT
Virginia	Va.	VA
Virgin Islands	V.I.	VI
Washington	Wash.	WA
West Virginia	W.Va.	WV
Wisconsin	Wis.	WI
Wyoming	Wyo.	WY

*No standard abbreviation